Putting the Poor First
How Base-of-the-Pyramid Ventures Can Learn from Development Approaches

 **Piera Waibel** has been researching about and working with Sustainability Management for over ten years. She has worked on an 'Affordable Housing' project in Latin America; as Senior Consultant for an international group of consultancy firms specialising in Sustainability Management; and as Sustainability Analyst for a Zurich-based asset management company. In her current work, she focuses on inclusive solutions for agricultural and rural development.

Piera holds a PhD and Master's degree in Business Administration from the University of Zurich, and is an Associated Expert of Endeva—Enterprise Solutions for Development. This book is based on her PhD thesis, which involved her spending one and a half years at the Tropical Agricultural Research and Higher Education Centre (CATIE) in Turrialba, Costa Rica.

Piera is Swiss, and based in Zurich, but—as she will tell you—half her heart belongs to Latin America. She is passionate about the natural environment, especially forest and marine environments.

PUTTING THE THE POOR FIRST

HOW BASE-OF-THE-PYRAMID VENTURES CAN LEARN FROM DEVELOPMENT APPROACHES

PIERA WAIBEL

Greenleaf
PUBLISHING

© 2012 Greenleaf Publishing Limited

Published by Greenleaf Publishing Limited
Aizlewood's Mill
Nursery Street
Sheffield S3 8GG
UK
www.greenleaf-publishing.com

Cover by LaliAbril.com
Cover photo credits:
row 2 photo 2: foryouinf / Shutterstock.com
row 3 photo 2: Pierre-Jean Durieu / Shutterstock.com
row 3 photo 3: Juriah Mosin / Shutterstock.com
row 4 photo 1: PavelSvoboda / Shutterstock.com
row 4 photo 2: Jacek Kadaj / Shutterstock.com

Printed in the UK on environmentally friendly, acid-free paper
from managed forests by CPI Group (UK) Ltd, Croydon

MIX
Paper from
responsible sources
FSC
www.fsc.org   FSC® C013604

British Library Cataloguing in Publication Data:
  A catalogue record for this book is available from the British Library.

ISBN-13: 978-1-906093-74-7 [hardback]

Para Chirripó

Contents

Part IV: Framing the bottom-up development perspective in the innovation process of BoP ventures 175

Part V: Final conclusions and reflections on further research 191

Foreword

Miguel Angel Gardetti

Center for Study of Corporate Sustainability, Argentina

Sustainable solutions to global poverty will only result from a new development practice: one that allows for an agenda of change, jointly defined in association (Simanis, Hart and Duke 2008).

We have made great strides since 2002 when, together with Professor Stuart L. Hart, currently at Cornell University, we began to conceptualise the Learning Lab at the Base of the Pyramid in Argentina, the first one in South America. Against the background of the country's social and economic complexity at the time, the idea took shape a year later, in 2003, when the subject matter was raised in the Annual Sustainability and Business Programme delivered by the Center for Study of Corporate Sustainability and aimed at an audience of business executives. The Lab has been active ever since, and its purposes have remained unchanged. They are, namely, to develop theoretical and practical knowledge to encourage the private sector to eradicate poverty as a proactive partner, relying on the potential of local actors, and to participate in inclusive business projects which, on the one hand, add value to the company and, on the other, offer development opportunities to people living in poverty.

In 2005, the Learning Lab at the Base of the Pyramid in Argentina was accepted as an active member of the BoP Learning Lab Global Network, which was established by Professor Hart. It has provided inputs at many levels. For example, the multi-sector meetings—attended by companies, NGOs (and social entrepreneurs), members of government and academia, business associations and development agencies—are catalysts for cross-functional and applied analysis and research, reaching every sector involved. In addition, its 'itinerant' nature makes the Lab unique: activities are developed in numerous different universities, which enables the promotion of dissertations and research papers on the subject in those various academic institutions that host the Lab. The Lab's work has been published in collections (Gardetti and Lassaga 2008; Gardetti 2011) and in the UK journal *Greener Management International* (Issues 51 and 56). Also noteworthy is the book *Textos sobre La Base de la Pirámide: Hacia la Co-creación de Valor y Desarrollo* (*Texts on the Base of the Pyramid: Towards the Co-creation of Value and Development*) (Gardetti 2009), which has made an important regional impact.

Academics that have made significant contributions to the subject have also participated in the Lab: note, in this regard, the presence of Stuart L. Hart, Mónica Touesnard and Mark Milstein from Cornell University, Erik Simanis of Cornell University, and Ted London of the University of Michigan. Other specialists have also participated: for example, Gustavo Pedraza, who was then working for the Dutch Cooperation Service (2008); Sabha Sobani from the Growing Inclusive Markets programme of the United Nations (2009); and Luiz Ros from 'Oportunidades para la Mayoría' ('Opportunities for the Majority'), a programme of the Inter-American Development Bank (2009).

We define 'poverty' as powerlessness, exclusion and/or a position of marginality within a society that does not hear people's voices. Alleviating poverty has more to do with correcting these social relationships than it does with addressing the material needs of marginalised people or groups, which latter approach sometimes results in the unwanted outcome of actually reinforcing poverty.[1] The 'New Commons' philosophy considers development and poverty alleviation as an ongoing and creative dialogue between individuals and organisations, regardless of power, status, and gender or education differences. Thus, individuals regain their autonomy and take part in conversations about development. From the business point of view, this school is not simply concerned about new product development. It also questions whether the executive in charge of a certain product has ever shared a meal with the poor, and if the resulting business idea and model arose from mutual learning that derives from dialogue and co-creation (Simanis, Hart and Duke 2008). Dr Waibel makes these concepts clear in her work. This is a process not a production issue, based on a personal approach towards the community. Such joint undertakings will bring together the capacities and knowledge of companies with those of communities. This approach represents an interesting alternative for BoP 2.0 strategy development, a concept also discussed here.

Our first contact with Piera Waibel was in August 2009, while we were involved in a special issue of the journal *Greener Management International* on the BoP in Latin America (Issue 56). From that moment on, we have developed a relationship based on mutual respect and the commonalities between our Lab in Argentina and her PhD thesis, which may be encapsulated by Simanis *et al.*'s definition of the meaning of a corporate strategy for the base of the pyramid: 'it is a profound learning process, the consequence of which is the co-generation of ideas and opportunities, strengthening local capabilities and socio-economic systems to create stakeholder value' (Simanis *et al.* 2005, 2008). It becomes clear through the research conducted

---

1 Conversation with Erik Simanis (Cornell University) in 2010.

by Dr Waibel that it is far from easy to put the co-creation process into practice. However, the benefits are significant: it entails an opportunity to promote human development among the poor of our region. From a corporate perspective, both flexibility and the capacity to learn quickly from the members of the BoP should form part of a company's core competences in order to successfully develop strategies at the base of the pyramid. They are among the skills managers need to possess. In one of our Lab's multi-sector meetings, where we had invited a number of speakers representing people and organisations from the base of the pyramid, Mr José Testa, then CEO of DuPont Argentina, stated that the Lab should pay more attention to those voices 'since we need to learn from them'.

It is very interesting to see the connection Dr Waibel makes in her work with the Millennium Development Goals. I believe our region should be more committed to them. And, along this line, we should note the Principles of Responsible Management Education, a UN initiative within the framework of the Global Compact,[2] which gathers, among others, the world's foremost business schools and universities in order to create a reference framework to lay the foundations of common and comprehensive education within an increasingly globalised society which needs new values for a more sustainable development of the world.[3] Within this initiative, we are working with various colleagues from around the world in the 'Poverty as a Challenge to Management Education' working group, the vision of which is to be an advocate for the integration of poverty-related discussions into all levels of management education worldwide.[4]

The bottom-up approach, very well described in Dr Waibel's work, calls for companies to shift the paradigm that says that people in conditions of poverty are victims, and instead to embrace the knowledge and wisdom they can offer. This shift has an effect both on people from marginal sectors and also on the company itself, it being a starting point for eradicating such marginality, on the one hand, and achieving valuable corporate learning, on the other. Thus, the collective imagination is energised, which is truly 'generative' and leads to value propositions and business models that exceed what either the company or the community could conceive of or entertain alone. It is of particular interest when Dr Waibel analyses the drivers for applying this mechanism to BoP ventures and when to use them. I

---

2 The Global Compact is a joint initiative of the United Nations Development Programme (UNDP), the Economic Commission for Latin America and the Caribbean (ECLAC) and the World Labour Organisation (WLO), aimed at enabling corporate social responsibility development, fostering human rights, labour standards, environmental protection and anti-corruption. The main goal of the Global Compact is to help align corporate policies and practices to universally agreed and internationally applicable ethical goals. For more information, visit www.unglobalcompact.org.

3 For more information visit www.unprme.org.

4 For more information on this working group, please contact: Milenko Gudic (Milenko. Gudic@iedc.si), Al Rosemblom (right2al@comcast.net) and Miguel Angel Gardetti (mag@ sustentabilidad.org.ar).

believe Dr Waibel's research provides a valuable resource for the private sector in proactively promoting development among the poor by listening to their voices.

Miguel Angel Gardetti,
Buenos Aires, Argentina, May 2012

Bibliography

Gardetti, M.A. (2007) 'A Base-of-the-Pyramid Approach in Argentina: Preliminary Findings from a BOP Learning Lab', *Greener Management International Journal* 51 (June 2007): 65-77.

—— (2009) *Textos sobre La Base de la Pirámide: Hacia la Co-creación de Valor y Desarrollo* (Buenos Aires: IESC).

—— (ed.) (2010) 'The Base of the Pyramid in Latin America', *Greener Management International Journal* 56 (special issue).

—— (2011) 'Power Distribution in Argentina: Are the strategies for the base of the pyramid actually BoP strategies?', in P. Marquez and C. Rufín (eds.), *Private Utilities and Poverty Alleviation: Market Initiatives at the Base of the Pyramid* (Cheltenham, UK: Edward Elgar).

—— and G. D'Andrea (2010) 'Masisa and the Evolution of its Strategy at the Base of the Pyramid: An Alternative to the BoP Protocol Process?', *Greener Management International* 56: 75-91.

—— and G. Lassaga (2008) 'Edenor SA: Energy and Development for the Base of the Pyramid', in P. Kandachar and M. Halme (eds.), *Sustainability Challenges and Solutions at the Base of the Pyramid: Business, Technology and the Poor* (Sheffield, UK: Greenleaf Publishing).

Simanis, E., S.L. Hart, G. Enk, D. Duke, M. Gordon and A. Lippert (2005) *Strategic Initiatives at the Base of the Pyramid: Base of the Pyramid Protocol (First Version)* (Racine, WI: Base of the Pyramid Protocol Group).

——, S.L. Hart, J. DeKoszmovszky, P. Donohue, D. Duke, G. Enk, M. Gordon and T. Thieme (2008) *The Base of the Pyramid Protocol: Toward Next Generation BoP Strategy (Second Version)* (Ithaca, NY: Cornell University).

——, S.L. Hart and D. Duke (2008) 'The Base of the Pyramid Protocol', *Innovations* 3.1: 57-84.

Acknowledgements

First of all, I want to thank my supervisor Prof. Andreas G. Scherer for his continuous support and the faith he had in me. I also want to thank my co-supervisor Prof. Sybille Sachs for her continuous interest in my topic. Valuable input and support came also from various other professors—Ingo Pies, Claus-Heinrich Daub, Stuart L. Hart, Ted London, Miguel Angel Gardetti and Christian Seelos.

Special thanks go to Glenn Golloway (Dean) who enabled my stay at the Tropical Agricultural Research and Higher Education Centre (CATIE) in Turrialba, Costa Rica. My local adviser Dietmar Stoian accompanied my learning processes and provided valuable feedback and inputs. I was also very fortunate to receive financial support from the Swiss National Science Foundation (SNSF) for my 18 months' stay abroad.

Several academics and practitioners helped me with the search for the case studies and kept me in the loop of current developments. I especially want to thank Aline Krämer, Christina Gradl, Claudia Knobloch and Martin Herrndorf (Endeva), María Fernanda Pérez Fernández (AED Costa Rica), Oswaldo Segura and Elfid Torres (FUNDES), Filippo Veglio (WBCSD), Daniel González (Avina), Martín López Jaimes (CESPEDES), Juliana Mutis Marin (BoP Lab Spain), Francisco Noguera (nextbillion), Paula Carrión (negociosinclusivos.org), Alonso Buenrostro (BoP Lab Mexico) and Víctor Manuel Velázquez Cortés (Fondo de Capitalización e Inversión del Sector Rural).

Without the invaluable insight into the practice of the companies participating in the case study research, their openness, and their willingness to contribute to my thesis, it would not have been possible to do this research. At Sucromiles, I especially want to thank the management and team of 'mercadeo social'. Special thanks goes to Eliana Villota and Sandra Lasso who not only gave me a deep understanding of their project, but also taught me a lot about their country and became my friends. Thanks also to the *TriCaldamas* Astrid Villalobos Camacho, Maria Fernanda Rodriguez, Diana del Pilar Lopez, Gloria Macuace and Patricia Cruz who showed me their work and allowed me to learn more about their lives. At Nestlé, I would like to thank Hans Jöhr who opened the doors at Nestlé Brazil for me, Alexandre Costa and Sylvain Darnil who organised my stay in São Paulo and introduced me to their project. The whole team of 'Regionalização & BoP', as well as the 'selling ladies', supervisors and micro-distributors whose input vastly enriched my research. In the case of BAC | Credomatic I am mainly thankful to Laura Porras Alfaro (BAC COM), María Marta Padilla (FINCA), and the people working for FINCA and Edesa for sharing their extensive experience with me. I would also like to thank the people involved at the Communal Credit Enterprises whom I visited in Suretka, Shiroles, Amubri, Las Nubes, Sacrin and La Fuente, especially Bahid Seguro, Chase Adam, Nidietth Cortes Quesada, Jenny Maria Prado Mora and Mayela Romero Mendez, who introduced me to the respective communities and let me stay in their homes.

I also owe a debt to those who responded to the questionnaire and the information provided by their companies. Thanks to Alfonso Barquero (Tecnosol), Guillermo Jaime Calderón (Grupo MIA), Javier Contreras (Siconterra), Soledad Garcia (Avon), Wilson A. Jacomé (TIA/IDE Business School), Stefanie Koch (Holcim), Gabriel Lanfranchi (Fundación Pro Vivienda Social), César Augusto Roldán Jaramillo and Beatriz Castaño Otalvaro (EPM), Henning Alts Schoutz (Cemex), and Octavio Sotomayor (Qualitas Agroconsultores).

To the many others who crossed my path in Latin America and in Europe, thank you. You criticised constructively, opened my eyes and enabled me to develop and learn new things, as well as providing motivation, appreciation, tolerance and inspiration. A special thanks to you all!

Piera Waibel

List of abbreviations

ABCD	asset-based community development
CBD	community-based development
CBO	community-based organisation
CCE	Communal Credit Enterprise
CDD	community-driven development
EIP	educational investment programme
FDI	foreign direct investment
GDP	gross domestic product
GNI	gross national income
GNP	gross national product
HDI	human development index
HDR	human development report
IDB	Inter-American Development Bank
IFC	International Finance Corporation
IFAD	International Fund for Agricultural Development
ILO	International Labour Organisation
IMF	International Monetary Fund
LAC	Latin America and the Caribbean
LDM	leader-disciplining mechanism
MDG	Millennium Development Goal
MNC	multinational corporation
MNE	multinational enterprise
NGO	non-governmental organisation
ODA	official development assistance
OECD	Organisation for Economic Cooperation and Development
PRA	participatory rural appraisal
PRSP	poverty reduction strategy paper
PPP	purchasing power parity
ROCE	return on capital employed
RNFE	rural non-farm economy
TNC	transnational corporation
UN	United Nations

UNDP	United Nations Development Programme
WBCSD	World Business Council for Sustainable Development
WHO	World Health Organisation

The 'Estrella' in Siloé, a slum in Cali, Colombia, was built to draw attention to the slum-dwellers.

Spring onion production in Sacrin, Costa Rica: financed with micro-credit

Sewing company, financed with micro-credit, in Sacrin, Costa Rica

Selling mobile minutes in Cali, Colombia

Proud owners of a chicken farm, financed with micro-credit, in Suretka, Costa Rica

In Siloé, a slum in Cali, Colombia

Board meeting of the community credit enterprise in Las Nubes, Costa Rica

Part I
Introduction

Part I of this book gives an introduction to the research project and its problem focus, global poverty.

1

About the research project

After explaining the research context, the problem statement, research questions and objectives as well as methods applied are elaborated.

1.1 Research context: business and development

Since the turn of the millennium it has become strikingly evident that development aid, charity or 'global business-as-usual' will not deliver solutions to poverty as expected (Kandachar and Halme 2005). More and more companies try to link their business activities with a contribution to solving big global issues such as poverty or climate change. Economic development—from a long-term perspective—can go hand in hand with social and ecological development (Banerjee 2003).

> We believe that the fundamental purpose of business is to provide continually improving goods and services for increasing numbers of people at prices that they can afford. [. . .] We see shareholder value as a measure of how successfully we deliver value to society, rather than as an end in itself (WBCSD 2006: 4).

This approach to the role of corporations is not new, but with globalised activities the value that can be delivered to society is based on different needs. These needs are often the barriers to worldwide sustainable development (Bansal 2002).

One huge need is poverty alleviation, as for example demonstrated and addressed by the Millennium Development Goals (MDGs) of the United Nations (UN). The eight goals related to poverty reduction were agreed upon by all member states.[1]

---

1 For more details on the goals see Section 2.4.

Figure 1.1 **Context**

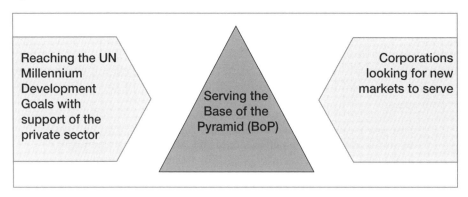

They are the only common ground for development goals at a global level (Kuhn and Rieckmann 2006; Unmüssig 2006). Five years away from the deadline of achieving the goals, the UN MDG Report 2010 and the summit on the MDG held in New York in September 2010[2] concluded that far greater effort is required to reach the goals by 2015. Some countries have made progress in some areas. First and foremost East Asia and South-East Asia have made the most progress in poverty reduction over the last few years. In contrast, in Sub-Saharan Africa and Latin America absolute poverty is stagnating or even increasing. Especially remote rural areas are struggling to reach the development goals (UN 2010a).

Thus far it has been chiefly the responsibility of governments and civil society organisations to contribute to the achievement of the goals. Companies, however, also have an important role (e.g. Gradl 2010a; Engel and Veglio 2010; Nelson and Prescott 2003; Poole 2005). Corporations consider themselves important partners in reaching the goals for the following reasons:

- Business has global reach, scale and power

- Business has a lot to contribute (e.g. know-how)

- Western markets are often saturated. Therefore, new markets need to be developed (Neath 2006)

When, at the launch on 25 July 2003 of the Commission on Private Sector and Development within the UN Development Programme (UNDP), former UN Secretary-General Kofi Annan announced that '. . . we cannot reach these goals without support from the private sector',[3] he was pointing out the pivotal role of local entrepreneurs in developing countries. At the summit of the MDG 2010 in New York, the

---

2 www.un.org/en/mdg/summit2010, accessed 3 October 2002.
3 www.un.org/apps/news/story.asp?NewsID=7834&Cr=millennium&Cr1=goals, accessed 3 October 2002.0

private sector forum attracted many prominent representatives of corporations and business organisations. In his welcome note, UN Secretary-General Ban Ki-moon issued a strong call to global businesses to support the MDG, acknowledging that '. . . business is a primary driver of innovation, investment and job creation. There is no longer any doubt that business plays an integral role in delivering economic and social progress'.[4] Through global market activities in developing and emerging countries, companies have a substantial influence on private sector development in poor areas.

> Business, as an engine of growth and development, has a critical role to play in accelerating progress towards the MDGs through increasing investment, creating jobs, increasing skills, and developing goods, technologies and innovations which can make people's lives better (Engel and Veglio 2010).

So, business is seen as a major driver for poverty alleviation.

On the other hand, corporations based in developed economies face stagnating, shrinking or saturated markets. To grow further, they need to penetrate new markets. Many companies are already engaged with developing and emerging economies through sourcing activities and production facilities or by selling their products and services to the rich buyer segment of those countries. However, the poor[5] are often not yet considered as an important market. Developing and emerging economies are low-income, rapid-growth, and companies need to develop unique strategies to cope with the broad scope and rapidity of economic and political change in those countries (Hoskisson *et al.* 2000). Western-style patterns of economic development may not occur in these local business environments (London and Hart 2004: 350).

The need for corporations to find and develop new markets on the one hand, and the important role that business plays in reaching the MDGs on the other, have led to a growing set of new concepts: 'inclusive business' (World Business Council for Sustainable Development [WBCSD], SNV); 'growing inclusive markets' (UNDP); 'opportunities for the majority' (Inter-American Development Bank [IDB]); 'business for development' (Organisation for Economic Cooperation and Development [OECD]), 'pro-poor business' or serving the 'base of the pyramid' (BoP)[6] (Prahalad and Hart 2002) are only some of the concepts and buzzwords that have emerged over the last ten years. The different concepts frequently overlap but they are all

---

4 www.un.org/apps/news/infocus/sgspeeches/statments_full.asp?statID=951, accessed 3 October 2002.
5 Acknowledging that the term 'poor' has a negative tonality, this book uses it nonetheless—instead of 'low-income population' for example—as the underlying concept used in this book has a broader understanding than income poverty alone (see Chapter 2.1).
6 In the literature, the expressions 'bottom of the pyramid' and 'base of the pyramid' are used synonymously. This book follows Hart and London's suggestion to use 'base of the pyramid' to avoid any implication that those on the lower end of the income scale are in any way inferior to those at the high end (Hart 2007: 137).

aimed at making the economy more inclusive for the poor, be it as suppliers, employees or customers. This research corresponds to the BoP concept as it has emerged with a focus on the poor as consumers. The poor may not, however, be seen solely as customers. In very recent BoP literature (e.g. London and Hart 2010) the role of the poor as producers is emphasised as well. Furthermore, a BoP venture can include the poor as producers only, meaning that they move in a similar direction to inclusive business concepts. Nevertheless, the majority of researchers in the BoP field consider the poor as customers.

1.2 **Problem statement**

The main development problem addressed is poverty, with a focus on the issue in Latin America and the Caribbean (LAC). Poverty goes hand in hand with malnutrition, health problems, child mortality, delinquency, low education and so on. Even though the region has the highest income per capita among developing regions, it lags behind in achieving the poverty goal detailed in the MDGs, mainly due to the existence in this area of the world's largest income inequalities.

As we have seen, companies can support poverty alleviation in several ways. The concept of serving the BoP seeks to see the poor as a market whereby companies develop services, products and business models that are appropriate for the poor's resources and needs. One important factor for succeeding in finding new strategies to develop suitable services, products and business models for the BoP is engaging the target group itself in the innovation process. Local know-how of the poor has to be integrated and can then deliver new capacities for creating new competencies. This means that the poor are not only seen as (potential) customers, but play a more important role in the whole business model. So-called BoP 2.0 strategies bring the companies and the target group closer together. 'Proceeding with a bottom-up approach' (Hart 2005; Hart 2007), 'listening to fringe stakeholders' (Hart and Sharma 2004), 'becoming indigenous and developing native capability' (Hart 2007; Simanis and Hart 2008), 'engaging the BoP and gaining access to knowledge' (Prahalad 2006) or 'co-creation' (Gardetti 2009; London 2007) are some of the expressions used in literature to describe this paradigm shift which emphasises the role of the target group as partners in the process.

Development researchers made this paradigm shift around 30 years ago (Oakley *et al.* 1991; Simon 1997). The terms 'development cooperation' or 'development partnerships' are used instead of 'development aid'. Also here, the poor are seen as vital partners in the development process instead of the target in poverty reduction efforts. There are different approaches that can be summarised under the term 'bottom-up development' figure in this research area, such as, for example: 'participation'; 'community-driven development'; 'asset-based community development'; or 'local knowledge'. More responsibility is given to local partners in the developing/

emerging countries and institutions/organisations in the developed world figure more frequently ('only') as enablers and facilitators (e.g. Deza 2004; Obrovsky and Six 2005; Roselli 2006; Tembo 2003). Many BoP studies also claim that a bottom-up approach must be taken in order to tackle the new market at the BoP. Some aspects of the bottom-up development literature have even been considered by some BoP researchers (e.g. Simanis and Hart 2008); their application, however, has not been verified. At this exact point lies a research gap—the consideration of bottom-up development research in BoP literature seems random, and a comprehensive study that examines BoP ventures under the perspective of bottom-up development approaches is not available. There is a need for more cross-fertilisation between BoP literature and development studies literature in general, as was also pointed out at the 2009 BoP conference in Delft, the Netherlands.[7] It is assumed that integrating bottom-up development knowledge into the BoP concept leads to a greater development impact of those ventures. But companies can also benefit by learning more about how to act in these unfamiliar terrains. Which of the vast knowledge of bottom-up development can be applied and how it can be integrated in BoP 2.0 ventures is, for the first time, comprehensively unveiled in this book.

1.3 **Objectives and research questions**

The fundamental assumption is that a bottom-up perspective in BoP ventures leads to better results for development and corporate goals, as the poor are an important link in the process. They are not only viewed as consumers but rather gain value during the entire innovation process. Hence, learning from bottom-up development approaches can help companies to engage with new partners at the BoP.

This book focuses on the following research questions:

- What are the *drivers* in choosing a bottom-up development perspective in BoP ventures?
  - Companies can choose a bottom-up development perspective in their BoP ventures for various reasons. Is the application of this perspective driven by development goals or corporate goals? Are the reasons of companies the same as those of development organisations? What are the motives of companies? Why are they choosing such strategies?

- Which *circumstances* help or hinder the application of a bottom-up development perspective in BoP ventures?
  - Depending on company characteristics and the environment that surrounds companies, it is easier or more difficult to apply a bottom-up development perspective in BoP ventures. Which internal (corporate) factors help or hinder the application of a bottom-up development

perspective? Which external (environment) factors help or hinder the application? Under which conditions is a bottom-up development perspective favourable, and under which conditions is it less favourable?

- What are the *success*[8] *factors* when choosing a bottom-up development perspective in BoP ventures?
  - Depending on strategies, processes and activities implemented by companies, BoP ventures can perform better or worse when a bottom-up development perspective is applied. Which strategies work out well with a bottom-up development perspective, and which fail? How are they reaching scale? How do companies have to proceed in order to achieve well-functioning ventures when choosing a bottom-up development perspective?

By answering the questions of *why*, *when* and *how* to apply a bottom-up development perspective in BoP ventures, the following objectives are pursued:

- To elaborate theoretical assumptions detected in the different elements of bottom-up development approaches, which relate to the BoP concept
- To find out which propositions companies in LAC apply in the practice of BoP ventures
- To provide guidance for companies deciding to apply a bottom-up development perspective in BoP ventures

The overall objective of this research is therefore to determine which knowledge provided by bottom-up development approaches can be applied in the innovation process of BoP ventures. This research gives a comprehensive overview of the various issues that arise when applying a bottom-up development perspective within BoP ventures.

1.4 **Methods applied and structure**

Distinct methods (inductive and deductive) are used throughout this book; in the theoretical part, for the case studies and for the final findings. First, a systematic literature review of the BoP concept and bottom-up development approaches is conducted. The two research areas are theoretically combined by elaborating assumptions that form a priori constructs for the second phase: the case study research. In a qualitative research method, three in-depth case studies and answers from eight companies on a questionnaire help shape the propositions towards

---

8 Success does not necessarily have to mean profit in this case. Often, companies build up BoP ventures for other reasons (e.g. in order to grow or to 'prepare future markets').

their application in practice.[9] The result is a framework, which systemises and summarises the bottom-up development perspective in the innovation process of BoP ventures. It is grounded in the experience of BoP ventures in LAC, and guided by theoretical findings.

The book is structured into five parts: Part I explains the research project and gives a deeper insight into the subject matter of the book—poverty. Part II lays the theoretical foundation for the case study research. The reader becomes acquainted with the concepts surrounding business and development from different theoretical backgrounds before we focus on serving the BoP with suitable products and services, and the innovation process that lies behind that goal. By focusing on different approaches to innovations at the BoP, the paradigm shift, which emphasises a co-creation approach together with the poor (BoP 2.0), becomes clear. The other side of the theoretical coin is bottom-up development literature. After a foray into the historical background of these recently emerged approaches, the different approaches are described. Common elements are systematically gathered and linked to the BoP literature, which forms the base for the case study research. In Part III, the case study research and its results are illustrated. Detailed information on the methodology applied, background information about LAC, as well as a presentation of the companies participating in the in-depth case study research and the ensuing survey is given before the results are presented. Part IV discusses the differences and similarities between theories, the results from the case studies, and concludes by framing 26 resulting propositions of a bottom-up development perspective in BoP ventures. The closing Part V completes the book with final conclusions and reflections on further research.

---

9 More on the methodology for the case study research is given in Chapter 7.

2
Poverty

This chapter gives an insight into the complex and multi-dimensional issues of poverty and poverty alleviation in specific terms. Firstly, the concept of poverty, and how the poor live, earn and spend their money, is explained. Then the chapter, digs deeper into the specific circumstances of rural and urban poverty. As poverty alleviation is closely linked to economic growth, the third section is dedicated to this issue. Finally, the goals of poverty alleviation—manifested in the UN MDGs—are explained.

2.1 The meaning of poverty

Poverty is a dynamic and multi-dimensional issue. It is not only a state of existence, but also a process with many dimensions and complexities (Khan 2000: 26), characterised by deprivation, vulnerability and powerlessness (Lipton and Ravallion 1995; Sen 1999).

Aggregated to country level, the development of a country is mostly measured with national income accounts and gross domestic product (GDP). However, there is no broadly accepted definition of what a developing, emerging or developed country is. The International Monetary Fund (IMF) uses a flexible classification system that considers per capita income level, export diversification, and the degree of integration into the global financial system.[1] The World Bank classifies four income groups:[2]

- Low-income countries with a gross national income (GNI) per capita of US$975 or less

- Lower–middle-income countries with a GNI per capita of US$976–3,855

- Upper–middle-income countries with a GNI per capita between US$3,856 and 11,905

- High-income countries with a GNI above US$11,906

In the UN system, there is no established convention for the designation of 'developed' and 'developing' countries or areas. However, in common practice, Japan in Asia, Canada and the US, Australia and New Zealand in Oceania, and Europe are considered 'developed' regions or areas. In international trade statistics, the Southern African Customs Union is also treated as a developed region and Israel as a developed country. Countries emerging from the former Yugoslavia are treated as developing countries, and countries of Eastern Europe and of the Commonwealth of Independent States in Europe are not included under either developed or developing regions.[3]

Because aggregated incomes or GDPs at country level do not show distribution, subsistence activities, informal sector and household production, they are widely criticised as a measure of poverty (Hart 2007: 174; Martinussen 1997: 309). Therefore, household measures are seen as a better way by which to measure poverty. In the early 20th century Rowntree (1901) was the first to develop a poverty standard for individual families. In the 1960s, the measurement of the poverty line focused primarily on income levels (Philip and Rayhan 2004: 2).

A person is considered poor if his or her consumption or income level falls below a certain level necessary to meet basic needs. This level is usually called the 'poverty line'. Poverty lines vary in time and place, and each country uses lines that are appropriate to its level of development (World Bank,[4] Philip and Rayhan 2004: 15f.). Historically, the poverty line was defined as the budget needed to buy a certain amount of calories, plus some other indispensable purchases. A poor person

---

1 See www.imf.org/external/pubs/ft/weo/faq.htm#q4b for the classification and en.wikipedia.org/wiki/Developing_country for a list of all developing and emerging countries, both accessed 27 November 2009.

2 For more information and a downloadable list see web.worldbank.org/WBSITE/EXTERNAL/DATASTATISTICS/0,,contentMDK:20420458~menuPK:64133156~pagePK:64133150~piPK:64133175~theSitePK:239419,00.html, accessed 27 November 2009.

3 For more information and a list go to unstats.un.org/unsd/methods/m49/m49regin.htm#ftnc, accessed 27 November 2009.

4 See web.worldbank.org/WBSITE/EXTERNAL/TOPICS/EXTPOVERTY/EXTPA/0,,contentMDK:20153855~menuPK:435040~pagePK:148956~piPK:216618~theSitePK:430367,00.html, accessed 27 November 2009.

was therefore, by definition, someone without enough to eat (Banerjee and Duflo 2006: 4). Today, the poverty line is defined as the level of income beneath which a person cannot meet daily nutritional requirements and other basic needs. The extreme/absolute poverty line is defined in terms of income insufficient to meet the minimum daily nutritional requirements (Echeverría 1998). The World Bank uses reference lines set at US$1.25 (extreme/absolute poverty) and US$2 (poverty) per day, measured in 2005 purchasing power parity (PPP) items.[5] By now, most development experts and policy makers use these reference lines (Karnani 2009: 43). However, Banerjee and Duflo (2006) conducted an extensive study into the economic lives of the poor and noted that there is little difference in outcomes for those trying to live on between US$1.25 and US$2 a day.

This research is consistent with the broader definitions of poverty that were articulated in the 1980s (Philip and Rayhan 2004: 2). Prominent economists such as Amartya Sen stated that an increased income should be regarded as a means to improve human welfare rather than an end in itself (Sen 1999). Thus, the concept of poverty was broadened to include not only income level but also other factors such as lack of access to resources and income opportunities (Philip and Rayhan 2004: 1). According to Sen, development can be seen as a process of expanding the real freedoms that people enjoy. Growth of GNP or of individual incomes can be very important as a means of expanding the freedoms enjoyed by members of society. However, freedoms also depend on other determinants, for example social and economic arrangements as well as political and civil rights (Sen 1999: 3).

Sen's perspective is also represented in the human development index (HDI) reported in the human development reports (HDRs), a series issued annually since 1990 by the UNDP. The HDI arose, in part, as a result of growing criticism of the leading development approach of the 1980s, which presumed a close link between national economic growth and the expansion of individual human choices. In 1990, the first HDR introduced a new way of measuring development by combining indicators of life expectancy, educational attainment and income into a composite index, the HDI.[6] According to Mahubul Haq, founder of the HDR:

> The basic purpose of development is to enlarge people's choices. In principle, these choices can be infinite and can change over time. People often value achievements that do not show up at all, or not immediately, in income or growth figures: greater access to knowledge, better nutrition and health services, more secure livelihoods, security against crime and physical violence, satisfying leisure hours, political and cultural freedoms and sense of participation in community activities. The objective of development is to create an enabling environment for people to enjoy long, healthy and creative lives.[7]

5 See web.worldbank.org/WBSITE/EXTERNAL/TOPICS/EXTPOVERTY/EXTPA/0,,conten tMDK:20153855~menuPK:435040~pagePK:148956~piPK:216618~theSitePK:430367,00. html, accessed 27 November 2009.

6 For details and a country list see hdr.undp.org/en, accessed 27 November 2009.

7 hdr.undp.org/en/humandev, accessed 18 November 2009.

Poverty has many dimensions and manifestations. As a multi-dimensional phenomenon, poverty can be defined and measured in a multitude of ways:[8]

- Absolute/relative poverty

- Objective/subjective poverty

- Physiological and sociological poverty

Poor people themselves define their poverty in terms of lack of opportunity, empowerment and security. Opportunity is defined by material opportunity to private and public goods as well as access to market opportunities. Empowerment should make political systems more inclusive and participatory (Lustig and Stern 2000).

Just as the meaning of poverty is complex and multifaceted, so too are the causes. Khan[9] identifies the major causes of poverty in the political environment, systemic discrimination, ill-defined property rights, high concentration of land ownership, corruption, bureaucracy, large family size (high dependency ratios), national economic and social policy biases (Minh 2004: 501). Other causes mentioned by Philip and Rayhan (2004) are: war; agricultural cycles and natural disasters; illiteracy; and disease.

People can be defined as temporary or permanent poor (Philip and Rayhan 2004: 11f.). This has a lot to do with the so-called 'vicious cycles of economic and political poverty' (see Fig. 2.1)

Figure 2.1 **The vicious cycle of economic and political poverty**
Source: Martinussen 1997: 299

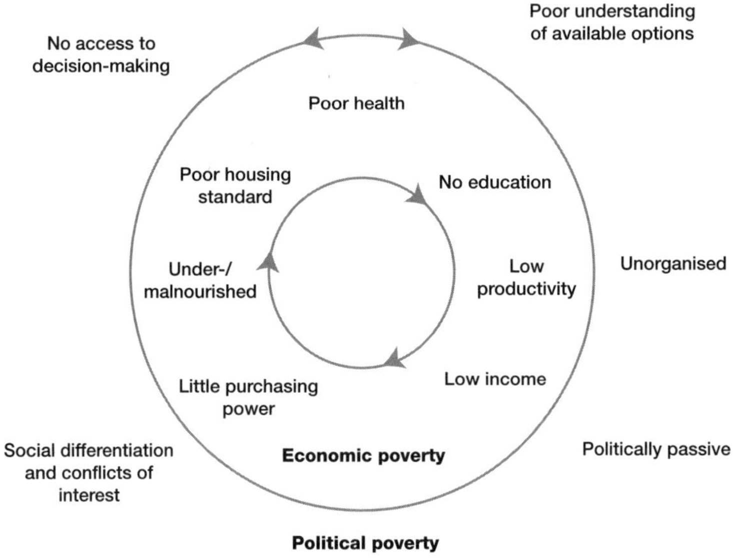

---

8 For details see Philip and Rayhan 2004: 7f.
9 Minh summarised the work of Khan (1986, 2000, 2001).

Once trapped in the cycle, it is hard to get out of it. The many people who are trapped in the poverty cycle are the last to benefit from economic growth, and they seldom experience real improvements as a result of aggregate economic growth. They are also the first to be hit during periods of decline and economic recession (Martinussen 1997: 300). Community decision-making processes and political issues determine their vulnerability (Philip and Rayhan 2004: 1).

2.1.1 The lives of the poor

Everyday I am afraid of the next (Russia)

For a poor person everything is terrible—illness, humiliation, shame. We are cripples; we are afraid of everything; we depend on everyone. No one needs us. We are like garbage that everyone wants to get rid of (Moldova)

Poverty is like living in jail, living under bondage, waiting to be free (Jamaica)

Poverty is lack of freedom, enslaved by crushing daily burden, by depression and fear of what the future will bring (Georgia)

If you want to do something and have no power to do it, it is *talauchi* [poverty] (Nigeria)

Lack of work worries me. My children were hungry and I told them the rice is cooking, until they fell asleep from hunger (Egypt)

Excerpts from Narayan *et al.* 2000

The outsider's view of the poor is often that they are inefficient, lazy, fatalistic, ignorant, stupid and responsible for their own poverty. Case studies, however, show the poor, usually, to be hard-working, ingenious and resilient. However, due to various disadvantages that trap them, they are not able to fully deploy their strengths (Chambers 1983: 103). The poor often have more assets than they know. Table 2.1 gives an overview of the possible assets available.

Land, for example, is an asset for many poor in rural areas (Banerjee and Duflo 2006: 7). Hence, incentives to invest the assets or work the land more productively are lacking (Banerjee and Duflo 2006: 17), mostly due to an absence of property rights but also to high bureaucratic hurdles (De Soto 2000). Lack of formal insurance schemes leads to under-investment in risky but potentially profitable investments (Banerjee and Duflo 2006: 15f.).

The poor frequently live together over many generations. Family size is around 6–12 persons. Often, many children and young people with different parents live together in one household (Banerjee and Duflo 2006: 3f.). Most poor are preoccupied by the daily need for sufficient food, while the lack of durable goods (e.g. TV, radio, microwave, etc.) can be seen as a marker of poverty (Banerjee and Duflo 2006: 7). The poor are often malnourished and therefore suffer from health problems.

Table 2.1 **Assets of the poor**

Source: Khan 2000: 27

Institutional assets	*Physical assets	*Human assets	Infrastructural assets
• Rights and freedoms • Participation in decision-making	• Natural capital • Machines/tools • Domestic animals/food • Financial capital	• Labour pools	• Transport • Communications • Schools • Health centres • Storage • Potable water • Sanitation

* Regulated through formal and informal networks among individuals and communities.

However, most of them could spend more of their income on calories (Banerjee and Duflo 2006: 8).[10] In spite of being stressed because of hunger and health, the poor mostly do not save money for bad times. When experiencing economic stress, the poor eat less and/or take their children out of school (Banerjee and Duflo 2006: 9-16). Access to education and health services are improving. However, absence rates of teachers and other personnel are very high, which means that, even if there is access, the students do not necessarily learn as much as they could. Many people therefore opt for private schools and hospitals where absence rates are indeed lower, but the personnel are less qualified (Banerjee and Duflo 2006: 18f.).

2.1.2 How the poor earn their money

Many poor have several jobs and typically also manage their own small business (either agricultural or non-agricultural). But the businesses of the poor are mostly too small to be efficient (Banerjee and Duflo 2006: 13). Even though there has been a boost in micro-credit lending facilities, they are often still not available to invest in bigger businesses (Banerjee and Duflo 2006: 20). In rural areas, people usually have a higher number of jobs at one time than in urban areas (Banerjee and Duflo 2006: 10). Small-scale and subsistence-oriented[11] farms, for example, are poverty traps, as the poor involved are powerless to middlemen (Hammond *et al.* 2007: 5). A pluriactive path (for example, off-farm employment for rural poor) is a way out of poverty (Ellis and Biggs 2001: 445; De Janvry and Sadoulet 2000: 404). Employment opportunities within companies are therefore also very important and often lead to a higher income than being self-employed (Echeverría 1998: 11f.). Rural non-farm economy (RNFE) represents roughly 25% of full-time rural employment,

---

10 See more on this issue in Section 2.1.3.

11 Most research on rural poverty is focused on the export of goods and not crops for subsistence (Chambers 1983).

and 35–40% of rural incomes across the developing world,[12] but has mostly been overlooked by non-governmental organisations (NGOs) and governments. Income diversification can be by way of households or economies. The first represents multi-occupational households (Ellis and Biggs 2001: 437) or the previously mentioned pluriactive path. Diversification by economies requires a broader approach to long-term structural transformations (Start 2001: 492). The RNFE can be very diverse—from handcrafts to computer chips (Ashley and Maxwell 2001: 409). It is often assumed that RNFE can be an engine of growth for rural development. However, most rural non-farm activities depend directly or indirectly on agriculture and other natural resource sectors. The potential for rural industrialisation within other sectors is usually over-estimated (Binswanger 2004: 10).

Off-farm employment is enhanced by infrastructure investment, decentralisation of economic activity, neighbourhood effects, development of secondary towns and coordination in the location of economic activity (De Janvry and Sadoulet 2000: 407).[13] As people with capital and skills usually profit more from growth in the RNFE, one has to make sure that the poor can also participate (Ashley and Maxwell 2001: 409). Leveraging education is usually a good way to do this, particularly for non-agricultural employment, though less for agricultural (De Janvry and Sadoulet 2000: 402).

To earn more, many poor migrate to places where the work is better paid. However, they never stay long and usually go back to their families before having a chance to gain promotion to better paying positions. Their levels of specialisation are therefore also very low (Banerjee and Duflo 2006: 12).

Once earned, money is usually spent. Most of the poor do not have a savings account. A savings account would have to have low administration fees and be protected from inflation. Mostly, the poor borrow money from relatives, shopkeepers and moneylenders; rarely from banks. Only very few do not pay back their loans, although repayment is sometimes delayed (Banerjee and Duflo 2006: 14f.).

Higher earnings of the poor in developing countries usually lead to higher expenses. The 'marginal propensity to consume' is virtually one, which means that almost all additional income is spent (Warnholz 2007: 5).

2.1.3 How the poor spend their money

The poor spend most of their budget on food (Hammond *et al.* 2007: 89). According to Banerjee and Duflo (2006: 5), the rural poor spend 56–78% and the urban poor 56–74% of their income on food. Food in poor communities can cost up to 30% more than in richer areas since there is no access to bulk discount stores (Prahalad and Hammond 2002: 49). Many poor also spend—depending on the country—a fairly high proportion of their income on alcohol and tobacco. Interestingly,

---

12 In Latin America and sub-Saharan Africa, RNFE accounts for 40–45% of total household income, in South Asia for 30–40% (Ashley and Maxwell 2001).

13 For more detailed strategies that support RNFE, see Ashley and Maxwell 2001: 410.

a significant part is also spent on entertainment (festivals, TVs, weddings), usually around 10% (Banerjee and Duflo 2006: 5). The conclusion of Banerjee and Duflo's in-depth study is that the poor have a 'choice to consume'. If they had no choice, they would buy more calories instead of alcohol, tobacco and entertainment. Karnani (2009: 40f.) argues that the poor are short-term-oriented and therefore tend to make bad decisions (regarding their health) in their buying behaviour. Alcohol, tobacco, drugs and fatty food help overcome suffering in the short term, but do harm over the long term. When income rises by one currency unit, only two-thirds of it is spent on more calories. Of the increased income spent on food, half goes on cheap calories (e.g. rice, maize, corn) while the other half goes on expensive ones such as sugar (Banerjee and Duflo 2006: 6). Generally speaking, the poor spend a smaller proportion of their money on calories than they did a decade ago, but the reason for this could be that work is not as physically demanding now (Banerjee and Duflo 2006: 7). Education is usually not that costly because schools are mostly public but, as mentioned previously, high absence rates force people to go to private schools even though the quality of teaching is not high (Banerjee and Duflo 2006: 9f.). A lot of money and time is spent looking for, and buying, fuel (Banerjee and Duflo 2006: 11).

2.2 **Rural and urban poverty**

Almost 63% of the world's poverty is found in rural areas. The term 'rural' is ambiguous. There is no exact definition of the term, but rural areas are clearly recognisable. They constitute the space where humans and their infrastructure occupy only small parts of the landscape. Fields and pastures, woods and forests, water, mountains and desert dominate the majority of the landscape (Wiggins and Proctor 2001: 427f.). The International Fund for Agricultural Development (IFAD) estimates that 75% of the extremely poor live in rural areas (Ashley and Maxwell 2001: 395[14]). Rural poverty is dominant in Africa and Asia, whereas urban poverty dominates in Eastern Europe and Latin America (Hammond *et al.* 2007: 3f.). Around two-thirds of the extremely poor are either small farmers or low-paid farm workers[15] (Khan 2000: 27; Minh 2004: 500). Landless non-cultivators are the poorest of the rural poor (Khan 2000: 27).

The fate of most of the world's extremely poor people depends on their countries' and regions' performance in agricultural and rural development (Binswanger 2004: 1). If a country's GDP grows, inequality in rural areas usually does not improve (De Janvry and Sadoulet 2000: 394). However, whether or not agricultural or industrial development is more important to alleviate poverty is part of an ongoing discussion

---

14 Data from 2001 (IFAD 2001: 15).
15 Data from 2000.

(Martinussen 1997: 129). According to Hall (2006: 15), for example, the future of the rural sector will see the majority of people as landless workers in non-agricultural sectors, with farming being carried out commercially.

Conditions (in terms of personal consumption and access to education, health-care, potable water and sanitation, housing, transport and communications) faced by the rural poor are usually far worse than those faced by the urban poor (Khan 2000: 27). According to Nemes (2005: 12ff.), disadvantages can be access-type (physical, economic and political access) or resource-type (financial, human and institutional resources). The former is caused by underdevelopment of different infrastructures, resulting in limited products, money, information and communication. The latter is the limited ability and resources to produce goods and services that can be sold on the global market. Access-type disadvantages are usually visible and quantifiable outcomes of uneven development.

The rural poor depend largely on agriculture, fishing and forestry, as well as related small-scale industries and services. While agriculture has declined sharply in relative terms as employer and contributor to GDP, there has been rapid development in the RNFE (Ashley and Maxwell 2001: 398). The rural poor can be classified according to their access to agricultural land—cultivators have access to land as small landowners and tenants; non-cultivators are landless and/or unskilled workers (Khan 2000: 27).

The rural poor generally have four possible paths out of poverty—emigration to urban areas, local agricultural development, pluriactivity[16] or assistance (Poole 2004: 55). The rural population grows in absolute terms, but shrinks in relative terms. By 2020, it is estimated that urban populations will exceed rural populations in developing countries. This change is associated with a growth in mega-cities and a movement of population to areas of economic dynamism (Ashley and Maxwell 2001: 398; Wratten 1995: 11). The centripetal system is reinforcing, which leads to a brain drain from rural to urban regions (Chambers 1983: 5).

During the 1980s and 1990s poverty became increasingly concentrated in urban settlements due to economic and demographic reasons (Wratten 1995: 11). Historically, development literature has focused on inequalities between poor rural and better-off urban populations, and the linkages between urbanisation, the spread of capitalism and poverty. Far less attention has been paid to the urban–rural divide (Wratten 1995: 18). In the colonial period, it was widely assumed that poverty in the South could be solved through urbanisation and the transfer of labour from low-productivity subsistence agriculture to high-productivity modern industry (Lewis 1958). However, by now, over one-third of the poor in cities live in so called slums (Prahalad 2006: 7) and urban poverty has been pushed up the development agenda (Wratten 1995: 18).

Poor urban neighbourhoods contain a diversity of household types as they attract rural migrants and refugees with various ethnic, cultural and linguistic origins. The proportion of female-headed households is often higher than in surrounding rural

16 See Section.1.2.

areas and these households tend to have fewer income-earning opportunities. One of the results of this is the phenomenon of 'street children'. Social diversity is likely to create new tensions and, in the urban context, relationships may be more impersonal. Lifestyles, kinship and neighbourhood support networks are different from those in rural areas. Where the rich and poor live side by side, temptation and opportunities for crime may be greater (Wratten 1995: 23).

As there is no subsistence agriculture by urban poor, they require more money to buy basic items, such as food. They also have to pay for goods and services, which might not be available in rural areas but are normally consumed in the city (e.g. electricity and hospital fees). The pressure to earn money therefore increases. The main asset the urban poor can sell in order to gain income is their labour. The work options available to them are usually constrained by a lack of formal educational qualifications. Urban poor without savings or capital assets are extremely vulnerable to changes in the demand for labour and the price of basic goods (Wratten 1995: 22).

Research from Haddad *et al.* (1999) shows that, in the majority of countries surveyed, the absolute number of poor and undernourished individuals living in urban areas has increased as well as the share of poverty and undernourishment coming from urban areas. Also, the urban poor are often faced with environmental and health problems which are a result of the spatial juxtaposition of industrial and residential functions, high living densities and overcrowded housing in hazardous areas (Wratten 1995: 21).

In general, rural and urban poor have much in common but their lives differ in certain regards. However, it is difficult to separate the categories of urban and rural poverty completely, as the definition of the categories is arbitrary. There are, for example, no common criteria for deciding whether a settlement is a town or a rural village (Wratten 1995: 20).

2.3 **Economic growth and inequality**

It has long been suggested that economic growth alone can foster development and as a result, alleviates poverty (Martinussen 1997: 36). In fact, many studies have confirmed that economic growth is positively associated with poverty reduction (Lustig and Stern 2000). But there was no broad agreement regarding the exact meaning of economic growth, and increasing per capita income was often also due to a lack of more complicated statistical data in the developing world (Martinussen 1997: 36). Schumpeter, however, distinguished between growth and development, even though this was not generally accepted within mainstream development economics (Martinussen 1997: 35). According to Schumpeter (1934), growth means more capital and increasing production, whereas development means new technologies, new organisations, new products etc. Helmsing (2001: 3) defines local economic development as: '. . . a process in which partnerships between local governments, community-based groups and the private sector are established to manage existing resources, to create jobs and stimulate the economy of a well-defined territory'.

Recently, scholars have come to the consensus that economic growth—while a necessary condition—is not in itself sufficient to reduce poverty. The type of growth and strategies for maximising the benefits for the poor are key factors (Echeverría 1998: 8). On the other hand, if economic downturns occur, the poor are the first to be hit (Lustig and Arias 2000: 30). Economic development can then be defined as: '. . . a process whereby the real per capita income of a country increases over a long period of time while simultaneously poverty is reduced and the inequality in society is generally diminished' (Meier 1989: 6). There is substantial evidence, that a very unequal distribution of income[17] is not conducive to economic growth or poverty reduction. Absolute poverty can only be alleviated if economic growth occurs (mean incomes rise) and at the same time is neutral to, or reduces, income inequality (Khan 2000: 26). Or, to put it differently, a more equal income and asset distribution is good for growth and the impact of growth on poverty reduction. In countries with low income inequality, growth is more effective in reducing poverty than it is in countries with high inequality (Binswanger 2004: 3; Lustig and Stern 2000). Persistent poverty of a substantial portion of the population can even dampen the prospects for economic growth, as a study in India has shown (Ravallion and Datt 1999). Reducing inequality in people's assets, including land and education, can improve efficiency and growth (Lustig and Deutsch 1998: i; Lustig and Stern 2000).

Knowledge of these interrelations has led to a broadening of the poverty alleviation agenda since the 1990s, including ingrained inequalities, institutional failures, social barriers and personal vulnerabilities (Lustig and Stern 2000). This is also manifested in the UN MDGs as outlined in the following section.

2.4 **The UN Millennium Development Goals**

The eight UN MDGs were set up in the year 2000 under the leadership of Kofi Annan. They form a blueprint agreed to by all the world's countries and leading development institutions and are the only common ground for development goals at a global level (Kuhn and Rieckmann 2006; Unmüssig 2006).

The eight goals are:[18]

1. Eradicate extreme poverty and hunger

2. Achieve universal primary education

---

17 As mentioned earlier, per capita income does not reflect the distribution of income (Martinussen 1997).
18 See www.un.org/millenniumgoals.

3. Promote gender equality and empower women

4. Reduce child mortality

5. Improve maternal health

6. Combat HIV/AIDS, malaria and other diseases

7. Ensure environmental sustainability

8. Develop a global partnership for development

Each goal has various sub-targets which are measured yearly with over 60 indi-cators.[19] The MDGs are also based on a broader poverty definition than income poverty alone (goal 1). The latest MDG Report 2010 of the UN concludes that many countries are moving forward, including some of the poorest, with the following caveat:

> But unmet commitments, inadequate resources, lack of focus and accountability, and insufficient dedication to sustainable development have created shortfalls in many areas. Some of these shortfalls were aggra-vated by the global food and economic and financial crises (UN 2010a: 4).

Data and analysis show that in some areas, rapid progress has occurred. In other areas, the poorest groups, those without education or those living in more remote areas, have not been provided with the conditions to improve their lives. The over-all poverty rate is expected to fall to 15% by 2015. Advances have been made in chil-dren's education. Improvements can also be seen in malaria and HIV control. The rate of deforestation appears to have slowed. There is an increased use of improved water sources in rural areas, even though the safety of water supplies remains a challenge.

Without an acceleration of progress, many of the MDG targets are likely to be missed in most regions. The impacts of climate change and natural disasters, armed conflicts, or financial and economic crises threaten the positive develop-ments made. Around one in four children under the age of five are underweight. Gender equality, as well as the empowerment of women, remain major issues, and huge progress is still needed with regard to maternal health:

> The Millennium Development Goals are still attainable. The critical ques-tion today is how to transform the pace of change from what we have seen over the last decade into dramatically faster progress (UN 2010a: 4).

Even though the outcomes of the MDG summit in New York 2010 have been criti-cised because of the lack of concrete promises, the discussion definitely gained

---

19 For more information on monitoring and the indicators, go to unstats.un.org/unsd/ mdg/Default.aspx. A list of all indicators can be found at unstats.un.org/unsd/mdg/ Host.aspx?Content=Indicators/OfficialList.htm. For the online atlas with statistics see www.mdg.collinsindicate.com, accessed 18 September 2009.

momentum. Now, the talk has to be walked. Lately, surprisingly large interest has been shown towards the private sector's role in contributing to the MDGs, as previously mentioned in Chapter 1. Besides philanthropic activities, sourcing from the poor or employing them, companies can develop and sell suitable products and services to the typically ignored BoP as potential consumers. It is in the interest of companies to serve this huge untapped market and, at the same time, to build on a functioning enabling environment. The next chapter focuses on the role of business in poverty alleviation.

Part II
Theoretical foundation: serving the base of the pyramid and bottom-up development

3
Business and poverty alleviation

The first part of this chapter shows how different parties—international governmental organisations, NGOs, local governments and businesses—play their part in the common goal of poverty alleviation. The second part then focuses on businesses and their role.

3.1 Poverty alleviation as shared challenge

Poverty is one of the world's biggest problems, and poverty alleviation has long been seen as a task of governmental institutions and aid agencies (Prahalad 2006: 3; UN 2010a). It has, however, been strongly argued that the dominant conceptualisations of 'development' and 'modernisation' reflect a Western cultural bias and a preoccupation with simply raising GNP per capita (Escobar 1995). It is also argued that much development work has even had negative effects on poverty alleviation, with the poor becoming dependent on Western aid. Due to the assumption that developing countries lack resources, over the past 30 years the industrialised world has focused on paying development aid to governments in developing countries with the intention that this money be invested to improve healthcare and education systems (Prahalad 2006: 78). De Soto (2000), significantly, challenges the assumption that poor countries are poor. He points out that, overall, they are asset-rich as opposed to capital-rich, but that the assets could be turned into capital if property rights in developing countries were established and enforced.

Nobody doubts that enabling institutions are very important (Mansuri and Rao 2003: 2; Binswanger 2004: 2). But recent developments in international organisations show that business should also play an important part in solving the problem of poverty (Engel and Veglio 2010; Nelson and Prescott 2003; OECD 2007; UN 2010a; UNDP 2004). Also more and more business scholars point out that business should have a more important role (e.g. Hart 2007; Prahalad 2006: 78). As Prahalad states (2006: 5):

> Poverty alleviation will become a business development task shared among the large private sector firms and local BOP[1] entrepreneurs.

The problems that have to be solved are huge and complex. For most scholars and development experts it has therefore become clear that the public, private and civil sectors at different levels—international and national governmental organisations, NGOs and business—need to work together to fight poverty (Binswanger and Aryar 2003: 31; Prahalad 2006: 2). According to Hammond *et al.* (2007: 6) the market-based approach that companies apply should be used to engage the poor as consumers and producers, and the traditional approach (aid agencies and organisations as well as governments) should focus on the very poor, lifting them up the ladder so they are also able to participate in the market approach. Binswanger (2004: 4f.) points out that communities and civil society—the target group itself—must also play a more significant role (see Fig. 3.1).

Figure 3.1 **Actors in development**
Source: Binswanger 2004: 4

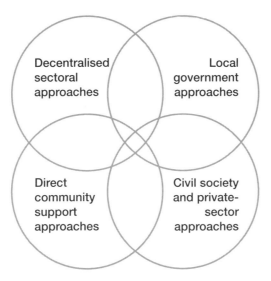

---

1 In this book, BoP is written with a small o, except where written otherwise in quotations, as here.

All groups involved need to take their comparative advantage into account. They have to think about how they can delegate functions to other co-producers, and how they have to reform themselves to be able to function under this paradigm (Binswanger 2004: 4). This book focuses on the stake of the private sector in poverty alleviation. Companies have—more than any other sector—an opportunistic interest in efficiency and effectiveness. In due course, this leads to solutions in which the poor themselves play the major role in their own development.

3.2 **The role of business in poverty alleviation**

So far, companies have been mostly excluded from development work and research. Except in the case of economic growth, no links between business and development have been made (Blowfield 2005: 516; WBCSD 2007: 6). But the view that business plays an important role in development—be it concerning environment, education and training, energy, enterprise development, health, mobility, trade or water—is increasingly accepted by the development community as was made clear at the 2010 MDG summit in New York.

The strengthening of a local economy depends on small, medium and large companies (Helmsing 2001: 7). While there is much information available about the promotion of small private enterprises in developing countries, information of the type needed by entrepreneurs when starting, operating and expanding an enterprise in developing countries is scarce (Haan 2005). Even though businesses of all sizes, both profit or non-profit, can play an important role in poverty alleviation; multinational corporations (MNCs) are likely to have the biggest impact. Over 60,000 MNCs with activities in more than one country exist; most of them with their headquarters in an industrialised country. They deliver 25% of the world's economic output. Foreign direct investment (FDI) far exceeds official development assistance (ODA) (Hart 2007: 219). Different features of MNCs ensure they are predestined to enter the market of the poor. In terms of size, function and wealth they have the managerial and technological resources needed, and they are well positioned to unite the range of actors required to reach the BoP. With their unique global knowledge base, they have an advantage that is not easily accessible to local entrepreneurs. They can leverage solutions from one market to another and can act as a bridging mechanism between different parties (Black 2006: 41). Innovations for the BoP can be adapted for use in the resource- and energy-intensive markets of the developed world (Hart 2007: 163). The latter opportunity is also one that Prahalad describes as an 'upstream' opportunity. Lessons learned can have an influence on current management practices of companies in their 'normal' markets (Prahalad 2006: 47f.). But, so far, few MNCs from Western countries have reached the point where they consider the poor market segment as an opportunity to be tackled with distinct strategies. Mendoza and Thelen (2008: 453) conclude that a growing number of for-profit business actors, which serve the poor by providing goods and services, come from companies that originate in developing and emerging countries.[2] Also, not-for-profit organisations and NGOs are turning to a variety of product and process innovations in order to attain greater financial viability.

Nevertheless, companies, especially MNCs, have been roundly criticised for causing damage in the developing world. Probably the greatest harm done has been to ignore the poor (Prahalad 2006: 5). At the 2010 MDG summit, World Bank president Robert Zoellick noted: 'The problem of the poor is not the dominance of markets, but its absence.'[3]

Markets and business should therefore be inclusive for the poor—this research area is called 'inclusive markets' or 'inclusive business' (UNDP 2008: 2):

> Inclusive business models include the poor on the demand side as clients and customers, and[4] on the supply side as employees, producers and business owners at various points in the value chain. They build bridges between business and the poor for mutual benefit.

According to Mendoza and Thelen (2008: 428), market inclusivity is only achieved when the poor are reached, when a positive development impact is generated, and when activities work towards the direction of achieving financial viability; which means that they at least break even. Advantages for the poor can be the ability to meet basic needs, be enabled to become more productive, increased incomes and empowerment (UNDP 2008: 22f.).

Not all projects that include the poor in market activities have to be profitable. Haugh (2007: 165) shows the different entrepreneurial ventures possible to help the poor participate in markets, and calls them 'social ventures'. Goals can be for-profit but do not have to be. The underlying assumption is that they use market-based solutions.[5]

Companies have been active in developing and emerging economies for a long time. The following sections elaborate on this issue from different points of view. The first gives an overview of research in the area of international business. A focus on the literature of responsible business explains another line of research leading

---

2 According to Pieter de Baan of SNV at the BoP Conference in Delft, 16–18 November 2009. 85% of the companies that are part of the inclusive business initiative of the WBCSD and SNV (www.inclusivebusiness.org) are domestic companies. This was not the intention, but as they are driving inclusive business in the Latin American region then work is done with them.

3 www.inclusivebusiness.org/2010/09/wbcsd-private-sector-forum-2010-on-the-millennium-development-goals.html, accessed 18 March 2011.

4 When looking at the case studies presented by the UNDP database of inclusive business (www.growinginclusivemarkets.org), only few models include the poor on the demand side as clients and customers, and on the supply side as employees, producers and business owners. In the large majority of cases it is either/or.

5 In practice, NGOs and state organisations increasingly use market-based approaches in their poverty alleviation projects.

to corporations doing business with the poor. The following section highlights the specific role of corporations in poverty alleviation and then unveils the challenges and the limits.

3.2.1 Companies in developing and emerging markets

Corporations need markets to do business. There are three types of markets: developed; emerging; and traditional markets (Hart 2007: 42). Although these different types can co-exist in one region or country, emerging markets tend to appear in developing and transition countries (e.g. the former Soviet states and China). Emerging market economies have a rapid pace of economic development fuelled by government policies that favour economic liberalisation and the adoption of a free-market system (Hoskisson *et al.* 2000: 249). Traditional markets are dominated by the poverty and isolation found in the rural villages of the developing world. The people there only participate slightly in the money or formal economy (Hart 2007: 50). In each developing or emerging economy, there is significant corporate organisational heterogeneity. Wright *et al.* (2005: 3) distinguish the variations as follows:

1. Incumbent firms, primarily business groups, state-owned enterprises and privatised firms

2. Entrepreneurial start-ups

3. Foreign entrants

Most research in international business is about MNCs entering emerging markets. Developing markets have only lately been attracting interest in the literature. The first wave of MNCs entering emerging and developing markets was in the 1980s when their focus was very much on the emerging middle class as a new market for their existing products. The assumption was that the big emerging markets were new markets for old products. Therefore, the focus was on countries with a wealthy elite (Pearce 2006: 45). Many investment decisions were made as a subjective response to moves made by leading rivals rather than on the basis of an independent objective evaluation of a country's location advantage in conjunction with the MNCs' ownership advantage (Pearce 2006: 46).

The aims of MNCs entering economies unknown to them are, according to Pearce (2006: 42f.):

- **Market seeking**: supplying its products and services to the markets of new countries

- **Efficiency seeking**: supplying an international market in a highly cost-competitive manner

- **Knowledge seeking**: involves the internationalisation of learning, technology generation and creative processes

MNCs can, at the same time, bring growth to one region but damage another (Martinussen 1997: 12). When entering an emerging or developing economy, MNCs have positive and negative spillovers on the host economy. Spillovers arise from non-market transactions when resources (e.g. knowledge) are spread without a contractual relationship—the so-called externalities. Yet the impact of MNCs on their host economy is not well understood. Scholars have predominantly focused on research looking into MNCs, rather than looking to the impact on the societies in which they operate (Meyer 2004: 260). Existing indicators show, however, that more negative impacts on the local economy appear in the short term but that, in the long run, positive effects dominate.[6] Meyer researched all the literature on spillovers and developed an organisational framework for FDI impact in emerging economies (see Fig. 3.2).

Figure 3.2 **FDI impact**

Source: Meyer 2004: 261

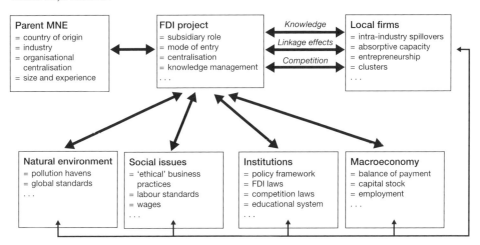

Strategy in emerging economies has been researched—but not extensively—under several perspectives: the institutional theory perspective; the transaction cost perspective; the principal–agent theory; and the resource-based perspective.[7] Of course, these perspectives are also linked in research.

Institutional theory emphasises the influences of the systems surrounding organisations (North 1990; Scott 1995). Perspectives derived to examine these institutional forces can have an economic orientation (Clague 1997; Coase 1998) and a sociological orientation (DiMaggio and Powell 1983; Scott 1995). New institutional economics has its focus on the interaction of institutions and firms that result from market imperfections (Harriss *et al.* 1995). Under this perspective, Peng and Health (1996) argued that the internal growth of companies in transition

6 For details see Meyer 2004: 263.
7 For an overview see, for example, Hoskisson *et al.* 2000 or Wright *et al.* 2005.

economies is limited by institutional constraints. They proposed a network-based growth strategy that was expected to be more viable in countries in transition. Even though transition economies differ from other developing or emerging economies, it can be assumed that the same applies in the latter mentioned economies. Oliver (1991) argued that institutions could also facilitate strategy, allowing enterprises to react to, and play a more active role in, an institutional environment and change it by developing strategic responses. However, companies need to have an adaptive ability that allows them to move beyond institutional constraints.

The transaction cost perspective[8] studies the firm–environment interface through a contractual or exchange-based approach (Williamson 1975). Emerging economies bear high transaction costs. Measurement (prices, resource allocation) and enforcement (law) are two critical transaction costs (Choi *et al.* 1999). High transaction costs suggest a preference for hierarchical governance structures over the private market, as opportunistic behaviour—normally reduced by contract law, trust or reputation—is also much more likely under such circumstances. Hybrid structures dominate both markets and hierarchies as the most efficient solution in emerging economies (Hoskisson *et al.* 2000: 254). The use of networks is suggested as a hybrid strategy. Pooling and coordinating resources can lead to economies of scale and scope, resulting in organisational learning. Network contacts and personal relations are used to reduce uncertainty (Peng and Heath 1996). Also, counter-trade and other forms of barter can be an efficient governance structure to discourage opportunistic behaviour in emerging economies because they create mutual commitments through hostage exchange (Choi *et al.* 1999).

The principal–agent theory (or just agent theory) suggests—like the transaction cost perspective—that a firm is a combination of contracts (Jensen and Meckling 1976). There is relatively little agent-based research concerning foreign entrants in developing and emerging economies (Wright *et al.* 2005: 5).

The resource-based perspective emphasises why firms differ and how they achieve and sustain competitive advantage via the influence of their resources and capabilities (Barney *et al.* 2001; Hoskisson *et al.* 2000: 256). Resources are based in a context. Companies therefore have to manage the social context of their resources and capabilities (Oliver 1997). In a similar way to most resources that create competitive advantage, those for emerging economies are often intangible and not necessarily product–market based. In emerging economies, competitive advantage is difficult to establish without good relations with home governments (Hoskisson *et al.* 2000: 256). One capability, therefore, can be relationship-based management that substitutes for the lack of institutional infrastructure. Examining dynamic capabilities such as the knowledge-based view of the firm (Conner and Prahalad 1996) has become more prominent in the study of emerging economies. Foreign entrants in emerging economies may also gain benefits for their own domestic markets (Bartlett and Ghoshal 1989).

---

8 In international business this perspective is also called internalisation theory (Wright *et al.* 2005).

When entering new markets, companies have to find new customers, new products and new services to sell, as well as new ways of promotion, production or distribution. In developing and emerging countries, they face markets that are very badly served or not served at all by the formal market economy (Hart 2007; Prahalad 2006; Weiser 2007). Table 3.1 shows the difference between tackling underserved markets and mainstream markets.[9]

Table 3.1 **Differences between underserved and mainstream markets**

Source: Weiser 2007: 33. © Emerald Group Publishing Limited all rights reserved.

What is different in underserved markets	What to do about it
• Local market information • Heterogeneous • Poorly documented • Different culture, assumptions	• New data sets • Information brokers • Learning labs
• Business model • Different trade-offs, preferences • Costs per unit high (esp. distribution) • Inadequate 'word of mouth'	• Reconfigure features, price, format • Distributors rooted in community • Build social networks to connect to potential customers, employees
• Incentives and assumptions • Structure and incentives aimed at mainstream • Inaccurate assumptions	• Build incentives into performance reviews • Create process to explicitly identify and test assumptions
• Partnerships and alliances • Market barriers: cost, information, complexity • Distrust of corporations	• Create partnerships to address barriers • Work with allies to improve community income and well-being
• Enabling environment • Inadequate infrastructure • Cumbersome regulations	• Invest in infrastructure • Advocate for change • Self-regulation

Most research in international business focuses on how to overcome the lack of a Western-style business environment (Peng 2001). In 2002, Prahalad and Hammond (2002: 54) insisted that '. . . the external barriers—poor infrastructure, inadequate connectivity, corrupt intermediaries, and the like—have to be removed'. While some are waiting for a more Western-style economy to develop, other management scholars explore the way in which managers can successfully implement strategies that help to overcome the lack of legal boundaries and difficulties in property rights protection (London and Hart 2004: 353). Companies do not have to wait until the business environment they are used to becomes available. A possible alternative is to '. . . work within the present environment and deploy market-based

---

9 Weiser's research focuses on underserved markets in general, not only in developing and emerging countries (Weiser 2007).

innovations—radical and incremental changes to products and processes—designed to help overcome some of the barriers hindering the poor from more actively participating in markets' (Mendoza and Thelen 2008: 428). Also, the UNDP (2008: 8) mentions investing to remove market constraints as a possible strategy for companies trying to enter emerging and developing markets, and suggests that companies work around them or remove them. Prahalad and Lieberthal (2003: 109) even state that MNCs need to move beyond the 'imperialist mindset' (that everyone must want to look and act like Westerners) in order to be successful away from the rich top of the pyramid in emerging and developing markets. Modifying (national responsiveness) and leveraging (global efficiency, or sharing worldwide learning) of existing products and services within firm boundaries may allow MNCs to overcome liabilities of foreignness when serving the wealthy top of the economic pyramid (Bartlett and Ghoshal 1989; Buckley and Casson 1991), but these capabilities are insufficient to reach the poor in developing and emerging markets. Companies need to acquire an additional capability—a native capability—that requires the expansion of the conception of the global economy to '. . . include the varied economic activities that occur outside of the formal, wage-based economy' (Hart 2007: 219).

To conclude, mainstream research on business in developing and emerging countries focuses on the wealthy top of the population—the population that most closely resembles the current customers in the home countries—and can only be applied up to a certain point. The BoP segment is characterised by specific circumstances that do not occur in developed markets (e.g. high proportion of informality, irregular income streams). Companies need to take these into account when developing a business at the BoP.

3.2.2 Responsible business in globalisation: from obligation to opportunity

Global corporations can be seen in different ways—or, more specifically, their role in helping to solve global problems can be seen in different ways. Over the last few years, different concepts have evolved that see the role of corporations to be broader, contributing to sustainable development.[10] Putting the role and management of business in context with sustainable development is an active yet still very young research field. There are different concepts and approaches that tackle the role and activities of companies linked to society and the ecological environment: business ethics; corporate citizenship; corporate (social) responsibility (C[S]R); corporate philanthropy; corporate sustainability; or stakeholder management (e.g. Crane *et al.* 2004; Hart and Milstein 2003; Herzig *et al.* 2005; Jonker and De

---

10 The official definition of sustainable development comes from the World Commission on Environment and Development (WCED 1987: 8): 'Sustainable development is development that meets the needs of the present without compromising the ability of future generations to meet their own needs.'

Witte 2006; Matten and Crane 2005; Münzing 2001; Palazzo and Scherer 2008; Post *et al.* 2002; Schaltegger and Wagner 2006; Scherer 2003). Differences between the approaches are theoretically not yet completely explained. What they have in common though is the consideration of social and ecological factors in business activities for long-term success, and the view that companies are part of an embedded society. Garriga and Melé (2004) propose a classification into four groups:

1. Instrumental theories in which the corporation is seen as only an instrument for wealth creation

2. Political theories that concern themselves with the power of corporations in society and a responsible use of this power

3. Integrative theories in which the corporation is focused on the satisfaction of social demands

4. Ethical theories based on ethical responsibilities of corporations to society. While companies are satisfying a social demand when serving the BoP with products and services, the prevailing theories that lie behind the issue, are of an instrumental nature

CSR, probably the most commonly used term, is often considered as philanthropy, not necessarily contributing directly to making profit (Waddock 2004: 10). For quite a long time it was believed that companies could only meet their societal obligations by sacrificing financial performance. Environmental and social regulation, as well as philanthropic and volunteering activities, were seen to be the solution to the problems caused by companies (Hart 2007: 6). The European Union (EU), for example, defines CSR as:

> A concept whereby companies integrate social and environmental concerns in their business operations and in their interaction with their stakeholders on a voluntary basis.[11]

CSR in these terms is mainly talked about to protect workers, communities and the environment from the undesired consequences of corporations' activities. However, other definitions of CSR do make a link to profit and describe it in a more positive way:

> The commitment of business to contribute to sustainable economic development, working with employees, their families, the local community and society at large to improve their quality of life, in ways that are both good for business and good for development (World Bank 2003: 1).

We can see a shift in thinking about CSR from being a 'way of combating the worst consequences of FDI' to also becoming a way of 'accelerating such investment', especially in the poorest countries (Blowfield 2005: 517). Prahalad (2006: xvi

---

11 See ec.europa.eu/enterprise/csr/index_en.htm.

Preface). distinguishes the BoP approach from CSR and corporate philanthropy as follows:

> These initiatives [CSR and philanthropy] can take the process of engagement between the poor and the large firm only so far. Great contributions can result from these initiatives, but these activities are unlikely to be fully integrated with the core activities of the firm.

The WBCSD goes in the same direction. As philanthropic activities are mostly sporadic and short-term, they are not sustainable and therefore not sufficient to combat the world's problems (WBCSD 2004). In the view of Hart (Hart 2007: 15), a sustainable global enterprise seeks to create corporate and competitive strategies by tackling the problems the world faces today, and acts as a positive force to support sustainable development. Social and environmental demands are seen as drivers for strategy and value creation of the firm rather than as obligations.

We can conclude that—depending on the issue, point of view and theoretical background—companies are either obliged to act responsibly or are motivated to see the business opportunities that lie behind sustainable development. To alleviate poverty, the necessity of regulation in certain areas (e.g. living wages, health and safety) cannot be neglected and the definition of CSR from the EU has its place. But even though obligation sometimes is the necessary way to go (especially when it concerns basic human rights and compliance with other internationally agreed conventions), and philanthropic activities can help to a certain degree, it is not the solution to all issues of poverty. In turn, the notion of opportunity, systemised by Hart and Milstein (2003), stimulates creativity to find new, market-based solutions for poverty alleviation on a corporate level.

The aim of this book corresponds to the notion of opportunity mentioned by Hart and Milstein (2003). By satisfying unmet needs—social demands—the BoP concept can be seen as an integrative theory. Hence, the unmet needs are tremendous and significantly more effort is required in order to achieve a world without poverty. The author is convinced that the necessary scale can only be reached if companies follow an opportunity-driven approach, and if BoP ventures make business sense. By considering the poor not only as consumers, but also as partners in the entire innovation process and, accordingly, taking a bottom-up development perspective, additional value can be generated for all parties involved.

3.2.3 Corporate activities as a driving force for poverty alleviation

Companies contribute to poverty alleviation in several ways. Philanthropic activities and volunteering are one possibility. Through sourcing activities, the poor are engaged as suppliers and producers, mostly of raw material. If a company installs local operations and production centres, the poor are part of the company as employees. Another way is seeing the poor as consumers and considering them as a buyer segment.[12] Ahlstrom (2010: 10) argues, that '. . . the main goal of business is to develop new and innovative products that generate growth and deliver important benefits to an increasingly wide range of the world's population'. Creating consumer surplus and generating income increases the earning power of the poor (Hart 2007: 148).

Nobody doubts that the poor should be integrated into economic activity, but if this should be as producers, employees or consumers is part of an ongoing discussion. When talking about concepts such as inclusive markets or inclusive business, the poor are normally seen either as producers/suppliers, employees or customers (Mendoza and Thelen 2008: 429; UNDP 2008). The BoP approach, which will be discussed in the next chapter in depth, mainly considers the poor as consumers (Prahalad 2006). Karnani insists that—more important than selling to the poor—creating opportunities for steady employment at reasonable wages is the best way to eradicate poverty. Leveraging the efficiency of the markets where the poor operate would raise their income (Karnani 2006: 108). Prahalad (2006: 1) describes the poor as 'resilient and creative entrepreneurs'. Karnani (2009: 43) disagrees on the grounds that most people do not have the skills, vision, creativity and persistence to be an entrepreneur. He points out that most micro-credit clients are not entrepreneurs by choice, as they would gladly take a job at a reasonable wage if one was available. However, neither one of these arguments is based on empirical proof. The solution might be a combination. The BoP approach can also be broadened, as in the eyes of Hart (2007: 156):

> Effectively serving the BoP means more than simply selling affordable products to the poor: it means partnering with the poor as producers, employees, and agents to create entirely new business ecosystems.

Producing in local communities to meet local needs is therefore crucial (Hart 2007: 194). This is also supported by Matsuyama's virtuous cycle of productivity gains and expending markets, where goods have to be produced locally to generate employment and incomes (Matsuyama 2002: 1035).

Let us have a closer look at the poor as consumers of companies. According to Prahalad and Hammond (2002: 48), companies can gain three advantages by serving the poor: new sources of revenue growth; greater efficiency; and access to innovation. But for most, the poor are not (yet) an important consumer segment. Several biases lead to this behaviour: the poor have no purchasing power; the distribution access is very difficult; the poor are not brand-conscious; the poor are not connected through networks; and the poor rarely accept new technologies (Prahalad 2006: 10ff.). They are also badly served by local vendors. Particularly in rural areas, actual service vacuums can be observed (Hart 2007: 149). And even when there are products and services available, the poor often pay a so-called 'poverty penalty'

---

12 This chapter focuses on the three latter mentioned ways, where the poor are integrated into the core business of companies. Philanthropic activities and volunteering—as an 'add-on'—are therefore not covered here.

(Hammond *et al.* 2007: 5; Mendoza 2008).[13] This is the result of local monopolies, inadequate access, poor distribution and strong traditional intermediaries (Prahalad 2006: 11). Therefore, providing consumer surplus through innovative new products and services is important to increase the poor's earning power. If they can save time and/or money, they can free up resources which can be used more productively for other purposes (Hart 2007: 149).

If the poor are converted into consumers, they receive—besides purchased products and services—the dignity of attention and choices from companies, which was previously reserved for the middle classes and the wealthy (Prahalad 2006: 20).

> When the poor at the BOP are treated as consumers, they can reap the benefits of respect, choice, and self-esteem and have an opportunity to climb out of the poverty trap (Prahalad 2006: 99).

But it is not as easy as it seems; the next section reviews the challenges and limits of a business-based approach to poverty alleviation.

3.2.4 Challenges and limits

In order to contribute to the achievement of development goals, through their ventures (be it for-profit or not-for-profit), managers have to overcome several constraints (Hart 2007: 145). The main barriers relate to the characteristics of different stakeholders and their environment, market failures and government failures (Mendoza and Thelen 2008: 432ff.). There are also barriers that prevent the poor from more actively participating in markets, be it as suppliers, producers, employees or consumers (Mendoza and Thelen 2008: 427). Their constraints can be seen as the concept of 'unfreedoms' mentioned by Sen (1999). Absence of property rights, ineffective regulatory environment, inadequate physical infrastructure and political instability are problems that are the responsibility of governments to address. In democracies they are also the responsibility of citizens. Limited market information, volatile exchange ranges, restricted access to financial products and services, gaps in knowledge and skills, lack of a solid technology base of trained scientists and world-class research universities, bribery and corruption complicate business in developing and emerging countries (Hoskisson *et al.* 2000: 252; Sull *et al.* 2003: 3; UNDP 2008: 29ff.).

MNCs, or business in general, cannot alleviate poverty alone. Too many factors for poverty alleviation depend on governments and are often out of the control of companies.[14] But, without doubt, business can play its part in alleviating poverty by treating the poor as consumers and partners for their business activities. As the environments they have to enter are hostile, the potential consumers have distinct

---

13 For en extensive overview see Mendoza 2008. For examples see also Prahalad and Hammond 2002.
14 See, for example, factors mentioned by Binswanger 2004: 2.

needs and companies therefore have to find unique ways to be successful in those markets. Or as Hart (2007: 144) puts it:

> [. . .] the biggest challenge for MNCs may have less to do with technology, intellectual property, or rule of law [. . .]. Instead, the fundamental challenge may be one of business model innovation—breaking free of the established mindsets, systems, and metrics that constrain the imagination of incumbent firms.

How this challenge can be tackled is the subject of the next chapter.

4

Innovation at the base of the pyramid

> Indeed, we believe the interconnected challenges of addressing poverty
> and human development and restoring global ecological systems present
> multinational corporations (MNCs) with a unique opportunity—a 'license
> to imagine', to re-conceptualise the corporation in a manner that can sus-
> tainably serve the diverse needs and values of people across the globe
> (Simanis and Hart 2008: 5).

Research on serving the BoP diverges roughly in two directions. The first years were
(and still are to a certain extent) concentrated on the issue of creating markets,
products and services *for* the poor solely as customers. With product and service
adaptations, the huge fortune at the BoP had to be tapped and profits were promised. In more recent BoP research, the BoP is indeed still seen as a potential customer base, but also as partner in the whole innovation process. Innovations *with*
the BoP or so called 'BoP 2.0' strategies place considerably more importance on
the role of the new target group with companies needing to apply a bottom-up
approach. Why do they do this? Which circumstances influence decisions? And
what are the success factors? Before we can answer these questions under a development research perspective, let us have a look at the concept of serving the BoP. In
this chapter, the concept and strategies are explained first. The following sections
then focus on innovations, primarily from a general perspective and, later, with a
focus on integrating the poor into innovation processes.

4.1 **Serving the base of the pyramid**

The first section explains more about the market at the BoP; the second, how the concept evolved. To dig deeper into the strategies that tackle the opportunities in those markets, literature in this area is discussed.

4.1.1 The market at the base of the pyramid

Generally, consumers can be divided into three groups. The top of the pyramid, a relatively small number of consumers, is responsive to international brands and have the income to afford them. Tier two is a much larger group of people who are less attracted to international brands. The base of the pyramid represents tier three—a massive group that is loyal to local customs, habits and, often, to local brands (Prahalad and Lieberthal 2003: 111).

Figure 4.1 **The income pyramid**

Source: Adapted and reprinted with permission from 'The Fortune at the Bottom of the Pyramid' by C.K. Prahalad and Stuart L. Hart from the First Quarter 2002 issue of *strategy+business* magazine, published by Booz & Company Inc. Copyright © 2002. All rights reserved. www.strategy-business.com.

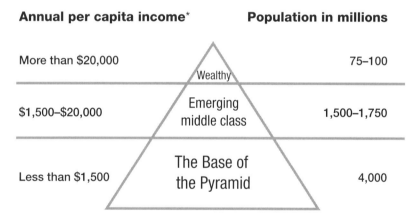

Annual per capita income* **Population in millions**

More than $20,000 — Wealthy — 75–100

$1,500–$20,000 — Emerging middle class — 1,500–1,750

Less than $1,500 — The Base of the Pyramid — 4,000

* Based on purchasing power parity in US$, Source: UN World Development Reports

BoP markets are often rural, very poorly served, dominated by the informal economy and, as a result, relatively inefficient and uncompetitive (Hammond *et al.* 2007: 2; Hart 2007: 116; Prahalad and Hart 2002: 4). Depending on the income line set and the calculation methods, the potential market at the BoP consists of around 4 to 5 billion people who represent around two-thirds of the world population. The overwhelming majority of this BoP market live in Africa, Asia, Eastern Europe and Latin America and the Caribbean (LAC).

Surprisingly, even in a revised version of their 1998 published article 'The End of Corporate Imperialism',[1] Prahalad and Lieberthal (2003) state that below the BoP[2] is another huge group made up of people who are 'unlikely to become active consumers anytime soon' (Prahalad and Lieberthal 2003: 111), even though this group was already considered and added to the BoP in 2002 (Prahalad and Hart 2002). There is also confusion about the actual number of people representing the BoP in literature. As we saw in Figure 4.1, Prahalad and Hart (2002: 4) draw the BoP line at US$1,500 purchasing power parity (PPP)[3] which results in 4 billion people at the BoP (numbers from UN World Development Reports, no indication of year). Prahalad and Hammond (2002: 5) state that there are 4 billion people earning less than US$2,000 per year (no additional information is given in terms of measurement). Prahalad (2006: 4) states that there are more than 4 billion people living below US$2 per day (no additional information is given in terms of measurement). The World Bank estimates that people living below US$2 PPP per day account for 2.7 billion of the world population (Karnani 2006: 100). For the purpose of this book, however, the exact total is not important. In any case, it is a market to consider.

In their report *The Next 4 Billion*, which for the first time shows a detailed economic portrait of the BoP, Hammond *et al.* (2007) deliver a more detailed segmentation of the BoP with the barrier at US$3,000 PPP (see Fig. 4.2).[4] This is important, as the different segments also have different needs and spending priorities (Karnani 2006: 100; Warnholz 2007: 6f.). The detailed research also shows differences across countries and in the composition of the BoP markets.

Figure 4.2 **The base of the pyramid**

Source: Hammond *et al.* 2007: 13

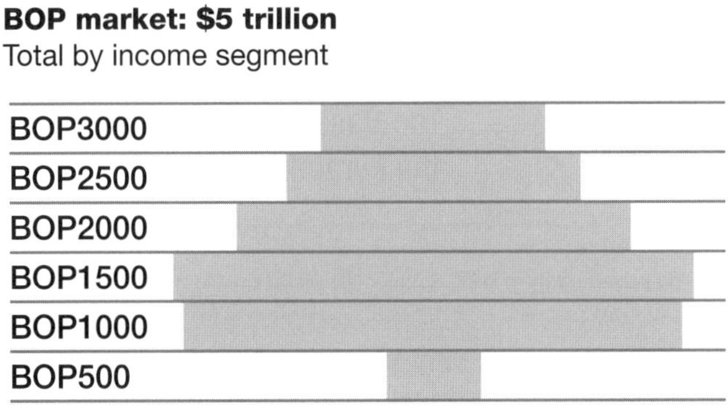

BOP market: $5 trillion
Total by income segment

BOP3000	
BOP2500	
BOP2000	
BOP1500	
BOP1000	
BOP500	

---

1 In *Harvard Business Review*.
2 They call it 'bottom of the pyramid'.
3 The level of the group below the BoP that is 'unlikely to become active consumers anytime soon' as defined by Prahalad and Lieberthal (1998: 71) was set at 'lower than US$5,000 PPP'!
4 The analysis draws on data from national household surveys in 110 countries and an additional standardised set of surveys from 36 countries (Hammond *et al.* 2007: 14).

Their segmentation contains a total of 72% of the world population (Hammond *et al.* 2007: 13). It is not only about the size of the potential market, but also about growth. The population of the more developed countries is predicted to stagnate, whereas the population of (currently) less developed countries is expected to grow enormously as shown in Figure 4.3.

Whereas the purchasing power of an individual at the BoP cannot be compared with that of a wealthy individual, by virtue of their sheer numbers the poor collectively represent a significant latent buying power (Prahalad 2006: 11). According to Hammond *et al.* (2007) the BoP constitutes a US$5 trillion PPP global consumer market. Prahalad (2006: 21) estimates the market at US$13 trillion PPP. As Karnani (2006: 101) states, from the perspective of a company from a developed country, profits are repatriated at the market exchange rates, not at PPP rates, and on this basis he criticises Prahalad's calculation. For 2001, Chen and Ravallion (2004: 34) estimate a mean income of poor people of US$1.25 PPP per day. Assuming 2.7 billion poor people, as per World Bank calculations, implies a BoP market size worth US$1.2 trillion PPP in 2002, far less than that estimated by Prahalad (2006) and Hammond *et al* (2007).

The discussion on the 'real' size of the BoP market (in terms of people and in terms of money) is part of an ongoing discussion, as we already saw in Chapter 2.1, about the 'real' number of the poor. But no matter what calculation is used, the BoP represents a huge part of the world population and is not properly served with products and services.

Hammond *et al.* (2007) further segment the BoP market by sector (see Fig. 4.4). The measured BoP markets expenditures are summarised in Table 4.1.

Of the four regions, Asia represents by far the biggest segment in all markets. Food dominates BoP household budgets, but as incomes rise the proportion of household income spent on food declines, while the share for housing remains relatively constant. The shares for transportation and telecommunications grow rapidly (Hammond *et al.* 2007: 4).

Who really is the target group of a company's BoP strategy? Karnani (2006: 101) observes that several of the business cases published so far (e.g. Hart 2007; Prahalad 2006) do not really target the <US$2 a day population which are considered to be poor. Warnholz (2007: 6f.) states that the <US$1 a day population (the extreme poor) is hardly ever targeted by the products and services described, but notes that it also represents a much smaller market (see also Fig. 4.2). Many companies target the BoP1,500 and BoP1,000.[5] On the other hand, Black (2006: 49) criticises the BoP paradigm of poverty as one homogenous state defined as being income-poor. London (2007: 11) also broadens the BoP definition:

> The base of the pyramid is a term that represents the poor at the base of the global socio-economic ladder, who primarily transact in an informal market economy.

5 Statement from different companies (e.g. Siemens, BASF) at a Theory–Practice–Dialogue in Wittenberg, July 2008.

Figure 4.3 **Estimated and projected population by major area, medium variant, 1950–2100 (billions)**

Source: UNFPA 2011

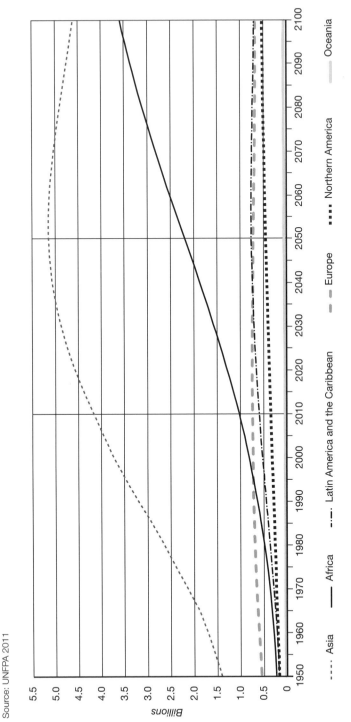

Figure 4.4 **The market at the BoP**

Source: Hammond *et al.* 2007: 29

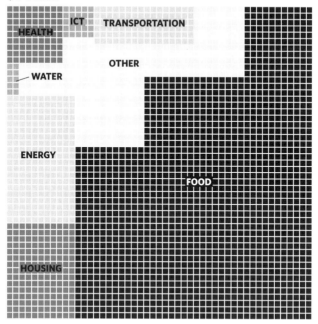

Estimated BOP market by sector
$5 trillion

Table 4.1 **BoP market expenditures**

Source: adapted from Hammond *et al.* 2007

Market	Expenditures (US$ PPP)	Number of countries included in measurement	Total estimated* market in Africa, Asia, Eastern Europe and LAC (US$ PPP)
Health	87.7 billion	Africa [12]; Asia [9]; Eastern Europe [5]; LAC [9]	158.4 billion
Information and communication (ICT)	30.5 billion	Africa [11]; Asia [9]; Eastern Europe [6]; LAC [9]	51.4 billion
Water	11.3 billion	Africa [11]; Asia [7]; Eastern Europe [5]; LAC [7]	20 billion
Transportation	105 billion	Africa [12]; Asia [9]; Eastern Europe [6]; LAC [9]	179 billion
Housing	187.5 billion	Africa [12]; Asia [9]; Eastern Europe [6]; LAC [9]	331.8 billion
Energy	228 billion	34 countries	433 billion
Food	1.53 trillion	Africa [12]; Asia [9]; Eastern Europe [6]; LAC [9]	2.89 trillion

* For calculation method see Hammond *et al.* 2007: 28.

If we follow the discussion about 'what is poverty?' in Chapter 2, one can suggest that it is not so much the matter of income and purchasing power, but of serving the complex needs of the poor, whatever they might be, in order that they are able to realise their opportunities. Hammond *et al.* (2007: 17) aptly sum it up:

> [. . .] the low income market includes far more people than the very poor—and the entire market must be analyzed and addressed for private sector strategies to be effective, even if there are segments of that market for which market-based solutions are not available or not sufficient.

It is not only about the target group, but also about the kind of products and services sold into the market. Prahalad and Hammond (2002: 49) disagree with the assumption made by many companies that people with low incomes have little to spend on goods and services other than basic needs such as food and shelter:

> It's also incorrect to assume that the poor are too concerned with fulfilling their basic needs to 'waste' money on non-essential goods. In fact, the poor often do buy 'luxury' items.

They refer to a study in the Mumbai shanty town of Dharavi, where 85% of households own a TV, 75% a pressure cooker and a mixer, 56% a gas stove and 21% have telephones (Prahalad and Hammond 2002: 49). In his detailed study, Warnholz (2007: 12) gives examples based on the percentage of monthly disposable income that would have to be spent on already existing and well-known brand products. We can conclude that the poor spend part of their income on other goods aside from satisfying basic needs and that there is money left for new, brand products from companies. How much the total market exactly accounts for is difficult to tell but also, from the point of view of a company, is non-essential information, as it is never the total market but a rather a part thereof in which a company is interested.

The market at the BoP so far is mostly informal. These markets are neither taxed nor monitored by governments, and are not calculated into the GNP. The International Labour Organisation (ILO) estimates that more than 70% of the workforce in developing countries operates in the informal economy (ILO 2002). The informal economy averages 30% of official GDP in Asia, 40% in Eastern Europe, and 43% in Africa as well as in LAC (Schneider 2005). Informality is a trap for the assets and the growth of micro and small businesses, and for those who work with them (Hammond *et al.* 2007: 16). Hammond *et al.* (2007: 17) conclude:

> Engaging the BOP in the formal economy must be a critical part of any wealth-generating and inclusive growth strategy.

The income and spending patterns of the BoP have, for too long, been hidden from business by lack of data on the informal economy (Hammond *et al.* 2007: 16). By providing land titles and lowering barriers to formal registration of small business, this 'dead capital' could be unlocked, substantially increasing the purchasing power of the BoP (De Soto 2000).

Maloney (2004), however, questions the widely held belief that informal arrangements are marginalised and seen as inferior. He argues that there might be a lack of penetration by goods and services of big business at the BoP, but that this does not imply that these markets are necessarily underserved. So, if big businesses successfully want to capture these markets, they will have to—in some cases—compete with and outperform current small-scale suppliers (Warnholz 2007: 6).[6] Hart (2007: 117) sees the solution in bridging the two markets:

> The challenge is to connect the informal and formal economies in a productive an mutually beneficial partnership.

How companies can capture this growth potential and define strategies in the markets at the BoP is part of this chapter, but first we will examine more of the concept itself.

4.1.2 The emergence of a new concept

The BoP approach refers to entrepreneurial activity that can help eradicate poverty in an economically viable way (Kandachar and Halme 2005: 1) so enabling mutual value creation (London *et al.* 2010: 583).[7] This very young research field was grounded by C.K. Prahalad and Stuart L. Hart[8] and is finding increasing acceptance in research and practice.[9] In the year 2000, the BoP Learning Laboratory was founded at the University of North Carolina's Kenan-Flagler Business School. It is a global consortium of corporations, NGOs and academics using business to address the needs of the poor.[10]

So far the majority of business experiments at the BoP have been initiated by NGOs or local firms in developing countries (Hart 2007: 81, 136), while 'Western' MNC activity has been limited essentially to the 'tip of the iceberg'—the upper-income people in developed countries and the small rich elite from the developing

---

6 Another discussion around this issue is that foreign entrants could banish the local and small-scale enterprises, which would lead to lower incomes for locals (Warnholz 2007: 6). But, as already mentioned earlier, studies show that in the long term, foreign entrants have positive effects on local markets (Meyer 2004: 263). The entry of additional firms into a market usually lowers the price and raises the quality, which leads to a higher consumer surplus and enhanced welfare of the poor (Warnholz 2007: 3).

7 In fact, the proposition of mutual value creation (relationship between business development and poverty alleviation) is considered important, but not yet well tested. First attempts can be found in London 2009 and London *et al.* 2010.

8 Development of the approach in literature: Hart (1997): 'Beyond Greening: Strategies for a Sustainable World', *Harvard Business Review*; Prahalad and Lieberthal (1998): 'The End of Corporate Imperialism', *Harvard Business Review*; Prahalad and Hart (2002): 'The Fortune at the Bottom of the Pyramid', *Strategy + Business*.

9 The main organisations that are active in the field are World Resources Institute, WBCSD, IFC, UNDP and IDB.

10 For more information see bopnetwork.ning.com, accessed 2 February 2010.

world (Hart 2007: 81, 114). The emerging middle classes in the developing world have been the focus of international business lately, as we saw in Section 3.2.1. Corporations are accustomed to serving the wealthy top of the pyramid in emerging and developing countries as they present less 'physical distance' than do the impoverished inhabitants of shanty towns and rural villages (Hart 2007: 115). So called 'corporate antibodies' seek to surround and kill any innovation that does not appear proximal and familiar (Hart 2007: 76). But this is not the only reason why MNCs and other companies are just starting to enter the market at the BoP. We have already talked about constraints in Section 3.2.4. The dominant logic in relation to the BoP as an important market has, so far, mostly been led by negative assumptions, as Table 4.2 shows.

Table 4.2 **Assumptions in BoP markets**

Source: PRAHALAD, C.K., FORTUNE AT THE BOTTOM OF THE PYRAMID, 1st Edition, © 2010. Reprinted by permission of Pearson Education, Inc., Upper Saddle River, NJ.

Assumption	Implication
The poor are not our target customers; they cannot afford our products and services	Our cost structure is a given; with our cost structure, we cannot serve the BoP market
The poor do not have use for products sold in developed countries	We are committed to form over functionality. The poor might need sanitation, but can't afford detergents in formats we offer. Therefore, there is no market in the BoP
Only developed countries appreciate and pay for technological innovations	The BoP does not need advanced technology solutions; they will not pay for them. Therefore, the BoP cannot be a source of innovations
The BoP market is not critical for long-term growth and vitality of MNCs	BoP markets are at best an attractive distraction
Intellectual excitement is in developed markets; it is very hard to recruit managers for BoP markets	We cannot assign our best people to work on market development in BoP markets

However, 'wealthy markets' are often saturated and launching new products and services is expensive. Corporations need to find new markets to reach the growth their investors require (Hart 2007: 111). The unmet needs of those at the BoP may present the best opportunity for companies to define a compelling trajectory for future growth:

> A more inclusive form of capitalism, characterised by collaboration with stakeholders previously overlooked or ignored by firms (such as [. . .] shanty town dwellers, or the rural poor in developing countries), can help open new pathways for growth in previously unserved markets (Hart 2007: 73f.).

Hart (2007: 112) calls the penetration of the market at the BoP the 'great leap downward'. Figure 4.5 shows how viewpoints have been changed.

Figure 4.5 **Changes in viewpoints**

Source: adapted from PRAHALAD, C.K., FORTUNE AT THE BOTTOM OF THE PYRAMID, 1st Edition, © 2010. Reprinted by permission of Pearson Education, Inc., Upper Saddle River, NJ.

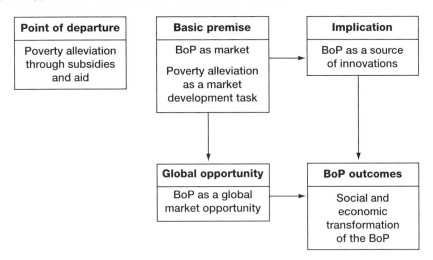

What are the differences between the BoP concept and other poverty alleviation approaches? London (2007) reviewed the existing literature on the BoP and put forth a set of principles that—when combined—distinguish the BoP perspective from other poverty alleviation approaches:

- The BoP perspective requires the entry of an exogenous, or external, venture or entrepreneur into the informal economy where the poor live and operate

- Those at the BoP are active participants in the conceptualisation of the business model and the design of any technological solutions

- The venture connects BoP products or consumers to non-local markets that they were previously not able to access

- The venture has a long-term orientation and the patience to scale only after the business model has demonstrated success

- For the BoP venture and its ecosystem partners, profits associated with competitive advantage are the primary source of long-term growth for the enterprise

Many examples taken from practice mentioned in BoP literature do not correspond to the principles mentioned above; as also pointed out in a study by Márquez *et al.* (2010: 6ff.) on socially inclusive business. Still, London's principles can be seen as a foundation. London also defines two kinds of BoP ventures—'BoP-as-consumer ventures' and 'BoP-as-producer ventures'. The first are 'scalable profit-oriented ventures operating in the informal economy, catalyzed by external participation and co-created with those at the BoP, that connect non-local goods and services to BoP markets'. The latter can be described as 'scalable profit-oriented ventures operating in the informal economy, catalyzed by external participation and co-created with those at the BoP, that connect BoP producers of goods and services to non-local markets' (London 2007: 26). The huge majority of BoP literature sees the poor mainly as customers (which does not mean that they cannot also be producers in a venture). The consumer–producer differentiation is made more often in the literature of inclusive business as we have seen before.[11] As many examples from practice also show, a venture does not necessarily or exclusively have to operate in the informal economy, nor does it have to be profit oriented.

We have seen that there is a large underserved market at the BoP. Companies can use their products and services as the driving force for human improvement, and can support people in climbing the economic ladder. However, to be successful, companies need to find new, innovative ways to tackle the challenges and opportunities at the BoP. Because of the distinct context the poor are in, attempts to use the same management approaches as with the top of the pyramid appear destined to fail (Hart 2007: 140; London and Hart 2004: 360ff.).

What companies have to adhere to is discussed in the content of the following sections.

4.1.3 Strategies for serving the base of the pyramid[12]

The main goal for corporations entering the BoP is, as mentioned before, corporate growth. Ansoff (1957) generally describes four strategies to affect growth: market penetration; market development; product development; and diversification.

Market penetration means that companies penetrate an existing market with their current products without departing from their original product–market strategy. This strategy has its limits, as the market becomes saturated. The market development strategy means that companies enter new markets (additional market segments or geographical regions) with their existing products. This strategy usually entails greater risk because the company is expanding into a new market. Developing new products for existing markets and customers is termed product development. This strategy is also more risky than simply attempting to increase market share in existing markets and with existing products. The diversification strategy is the fourth way to achieve growth—developing new products in new

---

11 New tendencies (London and Hart 2010: 9) show, however, that the BoP approach is moving in the direction of inclusive business, including both the BoP-as-consumer and BoP-as-producer approaches.

12 Strategy is not clearly differentiable from innovation as also 'strategic innovations' exist (Mendoza and Thelen 2008). This section describes the general strategies chosen while the following two sections focus more on the innovation process itself.

Figure 4.6 **Product/market growth strategies**

Souyrce: adapted from Ansoff 1957: 114

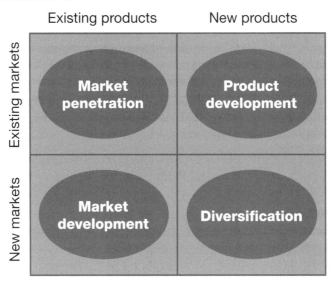

markets. These new areas may be related or unrelated to the existing business. Diversification is the strategy associated with the most risks. For most companies, the BoP is a new market.[13] Hence, they choose a market development or diversification strategy. When new products are developed for the BoP, which is predominantly the case, the diversification strategy is chosen.

As in the strategy literature in general, literature about BoP business strategies is also very diverse. However, according to Anderson and Markides (2007: 88), strategic innovation takes place at the BoP much the same as it does in developed markets: Companies find gaps in the industry positioning map, they go after them, and they exploit the opportunity. According to the research of Hammond *et al.* (2007: 10) successful enterprises operating in BoP markets use four broad strategies—alone or combined—that appear to be critical:

- Companies should focus on the BoP with unique products, unique services, or unique technologies that are appropriate to BoP needs and that require a complete re-imagining of the business, often through significant investment of money and management talent

---

13 In fact, functioning markets are not often found at the BoP (e.g. Simanis 2009, 2010). For most MNCs, it is not about competition but rather about value creation. The focus is on getting out of existing market boundaries by creating a leap in value for buyers and the company. These strategies are called 'blue ocean' (e.g. Chan Kim and Mauborgne 2005, 2007).

- Companies should localise value creation through franchising, through agent strategies that involve building local ecosystems of vendors or suppliers, or by treating the community as the customer, all of which usually involve substantial investment in capacity building and training

- Companies should enable access to goods or services. This can happen financially through single-use or other packaging strategies that lower purchase barriers, prepaid or other innovative business models that achieve the same result, or financing approaches. Another way the access can be enabled is physically through novel distribution strategies or deployment of low-cost technologies

- Companies should work together with unconventional partners such as local governments, NGOs or groups of multiple stakeholders to bring the necessary capabilities to the table

The business opportunities lie where the needs of the poor are under- or unserved. Hart delivers three ways in which needs and opportunities at the BoP can be identified (2007: 144ff.):

- Seek to identify and remove constraints that prevent the poor from taking control of their own futures

- Seek to increase the earning power of the poor through business models

- Consciously seek to create new economic and social potential at the BoP

The various constraints hindering the poor and companies were previously mentioned in Section 3.2.4. Managers should look beyond their served markets and learn to see these constraints from the point of view of the poor. This is the best way to identify new breakthrough business strategies (Hart 2007: 145). If managers gain a better understanding of the constraints that influence the behaviour of the poor, they can construct new business models designed to remove these constraints—and profit in the process (Hart 2007: 148). The earning power of the poor can be increased in two ways—by creating a consumer surplus and by generating income. A consumer surplus is created if products and services become cheaper and less time is needed to find and buy goods and services. The freed-up resources (money, time) then create the consumer surplus. Earning power is also increased by generating jobs. Companies can do this by engaging the poor as suppliers, producers or employees (Hart 2007: 148f.). Mendoza and Thelen (2008: 429) note that the poor are able to engage more fully in innovation processes if they are able to stabilise and increase their income streams through increased labour market participation. Based on their experiences with the wealthy top of the pyramid, companies strive for capital intensity and labour productivity. Yet time, for the poor, is an under-used resource. One-third of the world's population is unemployed or is only partially employed. Given the vast number of underemployed people at the BoP, the business model must provide jobs for many (Hart 2007: 235).

Within their case study research, the UNDP (2008) concluded on five strategies that are used in practice.[14] Together with the constraints they elaborated, a matrix was developed (see Fig. 4.7). The darker the shade of the squares, the more case studies were using those combinations.

Figure 4.7 **Strategies and constraints in BoP markets**

Source: UNDP 2008: 8

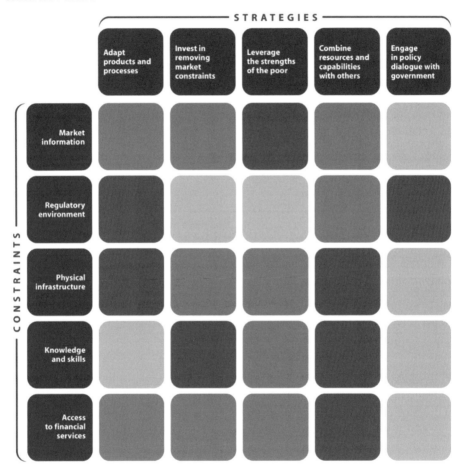

To fit into the market environment, products and services can be adapted. This is actually nothing new, but the market environments in which the poor are living and working (e.g. informal markets) differ from known markets. Companies can also invest in order to remove market constraints. This is especially interesting for businesses active in the infrastructure sector (e.g. energy, water, health) or in

14 The UNDP uses the term 'inclusive business' rather than BoP. Inclusive business strategies can also be used for BoP ventures, however.

terms of education, to prepare current and future employees. The third strategy, leveraging the strengths of the poor, seeks to engage the poor's assets into the business model. A company can increase access, trust and accountability by engaging the poor as intermediaries and building on their social networks. Combining resources and capabilities refers to collaboration with non-traditional partners, such as NGOs and public service providers. This expands the possibilities of a company with complementary capabilities and resources. The fifth and last strategy is about engaging in policy dialogue with governments. This is an important part, as companies entering the BoP are typically first movers and much of the business environment has yet to be built. Market constraints usually are in the domain of public policy (UNDP 2008: 7ff.).

Mendoza and Thelen (2008) developed a typology of strategic changes to make markets more inclusive for the poor (see Table 4.3).[15] Based on case study research, they distinguish between production strategies, distribution and marketing strategies, retail and pricing strategies, as well as cross-cutting business strategies. The strategies are not mutually exclusive (Mendoza and Thelen 2008: 437ff.).

Table 4.3 **BoP strategies**

Source: Mendoza and Thelen 2008: 438f.

Traditional business strategies	Business strategies that could improve market inclusivity*
Production, distribution and marketing strategies	
• Applying skill- and technology-intensive strategies • Using 'bricks and mortar' strategies • Stand-alone finance	• Deskilling • Leveraging 'soft networks' • Supply chain financing
Retail and pricing strategies	
• Individual consumption • Fixed payment • Undifferentiated pricing	• Joint consumption • Flexible payment • Tiered pricing
Cross-cutting business strategies	
	• Contracting innovations • Dynamic incentives • Partnering • Real options strategy • Total product solutions

* As already mentioned, the impacts BoP ventures have are not yet well researched. Therefore they probably choose the softening term 'could'.

15 As in the case of the UNDP, these strategies are valid for the concept of inclusive business where the poor do not necessarily also have to be consumers.

The different frameworks and listings of strategies to do business with the BoP overlap in many ways. In several aspects, there is more research available. These aspects can be summarised in four categories:

- Financing
- Organisation
- The four As—affordability, acceptability, availability and awareness
- Building on the existing market environment

The next sections describe what is known about each category in more detail.

4.1.3.1 Financing

BoP strategies require companies to re-evaluate price–performance relationships for products and services.

> Imposing the established performance criteria from the top of the pyramid will almost certainly kill the opportunity (Hart 2007: 142).

This demands a new level of capital efficiency and new ways of measuring financial success.

> Companies will be forced to transform their understanding of scale from 'bigger is better' to highly distributed small-scale operations married to world-scale capabilities (Hart 2007: 140).

As the BoP is not a market that allows for the traditional pursuit of high margins; volume and capital efficiency are key. Margins are usually low, but the unit sales account for economic profit (Hart 2007: 142). High volumes are only reached if a product or service is scalable to other regions, countries, cultures and languages. MNCs have advantages there (Prahalad 2006: 32f.). Low capital needs, focused distribution and technology investments, as well as very large volumes at low margins lead to a high return on capital employed (ROCE), which creates value for shareholders (Prahalad and Hammond 2002: 52).

BoP initiatives—like any other corporate project—have to be evaluated for funding using a set of criteria and metrics. Discounted cash flow methods for investment projects usually require an all-or-nothing decision to invest in a project, which is why they are not suitable. It is more beneficial to use a real-options approach (Hart 2007: 203), as it fits with flexible business strategies with feedback mechanisms that allow rapid up- or down-scaling of experimental product lines (Mendoza and Thelen 2008: 451). Real options facilitate strategic decisions in situations where a precise assessment of an investment's profitability is limited due to an uncertain business environment and when management is prompted to consider flexible adjustments to its original strategic plans over time (Busch and Hoffmann 2009: 295f.), which is necessary in a BoP environment (Mendoza and Thelen 2008: 451).

> Without the flexibility afforded by real-options analysis, there will be the inevitable tendency to convert BoP experiments into philanthropy. [. . .] The fact that it is often easier to convert BoP initiatives into corporate donations than it is to make the case for running them as viable business experiments shows how inflexible most MNCs are when it comes to project evaluation and capital budgeting. The solution is to broaden the analytical lens for investment rather than taking the easy way out through the corporate foundation (Hart 2007: 204).

Hart (2007: 204) sees the solution in creating a separate pool of investment capital to fund such low-cost probes as they might fail in the logic of short-term performance in today's business. Companies might create venture groups and internal investment funds that are directed at entrepreneurial effort in BoP markets (Prahalad and Hammond 2002: 53f.).

4.1.3.2 Organisation

Structural changes are also inevitable in order to achieve success. Corporate strategy is viewed as either exploiting economic efficiencies through economies of scale or as encouraging national responsiveness by adapting to local conditions. Often, a mix of the two is chosen (Doz 1980: 27). Focusing on a country-level strategy is potentially representative for effective global strategy in top of the pyramid markets, '. . . but it ignores within-country differences in business environments and implicitly assumes that capabilities developed at the top of the pyramid will be viable across all prospective markets' (London and Hart 2004: 354). The research on BoP practice suggests that small-scale, decentralised initiatives may make more sense in low-income markets than centralisation of control and economies of scale (Christensen *et al.* 2001; Hart 2007: 116, 203).

With relevance to the organisational structure, internationally operating companies relate either on a global or a multinational strategy (Bartlett and Ghoshal 1989). A global strategy means that control is centralised in a head office, and global brands are standardised with limited autonomy for local sites (e.g. McDonald's, Coca-Cola). Multinational strategies, on the other hand, are 'locally responsive' and the individual countries have greater autonomy over businesses, product mix and operating methods (e.g. Nestlé, Unilever). According to research by Sharma and Hart (2006: 13), a multinational strategy positively affects the likelihood of entering into BoP markets. R&D units that are specifically focused on local opportunities and set up in developing countries, for example, can foster innovations for the poor, serving as jumping-off points for innovations (Hart 2007: 234; Prahalad and Hammond 2002: 53). In their research, Keating and Schmidt (2008: 395) found that the spread of innovation to other parts of a company is usually seen as an additional benefit.[16]

---

16 Data gathering through interviews with managers from 22 MNCs in different industries.

4.1.3.3 The four As

To be successful in BoP markets, products and services must be affordable, accepted, available to the target group, and the poor need to be made aware of them.

To be *affordable*,[17] cost and price levels of products and services for the BoP have to be reduced dramatically relative to those directed to the wealthy population to about 10% of what they are today. Altering the price–performance envelope is crucial (Keating and Schmidt 2008: 396; Prahalad 2006: 28ff.). According to Hart (2007: 235), this cannot be achieved by simply fine-tuning current approaches to product development, production and logistics. The focus has to be on functionality rather than on the product itself (Hart 2007: 235). From this perspective, developers must start to look for anomalies from their prior expectations based on their experiences with developed markets (Prahalad 2006: 34ff.). Focused R&D and technology development, as well as the localised nature of most BoP opportunities, offer possibilities for lowering costs (Hart 2007: 235). For example, one successful venture reported by London and Hart (2004: 363) decided to forgo adopting the traditional pricing model of cost plus margin by identifying the appropriate selling price through discussions with local partners. Subsequently, by 'reverse engineering', it designed a product and business model that provided the functionality required and offered profit margins that were acceptable for a high-volume business.

Prices have to match the cash flows of the poor who are often paid on a daily rather than a weekly or monthly basis, and are mostly unable to save money (Anderson and Markides 2007: 84). Subrahmanyan and Gomez-Arias (2008) found that firms should go beyond the mentality of merely removing features or services to make them cheaper. Despite the BoP's income and resource constraints, they are sophisticated and creative consumers. Their buying motivation is driven by seeking to fulfil higher order needs either to build social capital, for cultural reasons or as a compensatory mechanism.

The cash flow problems of the poor can be, for example, matched through flexible payment arrangements or differential ('tiered') pricing whereby the poor pay less (or nothing) than wealthy consumers (Mendoza and Thelen 2008: 445).[18] Tripathi and De (2007: 173f.) call this the 'rational model' where the BoP and the non-BoP are segmented into two parts. Selling smaller units such as single-serve packets can also reduce prices and make products more affordable to the poor. In fact, those examples are often demonstrated as 'BoP innovation' (see Prahalad 2006). However, other scholars criticise this kind of 'innovation'. Karnani points out

---

17 Far more literature and research focuses on the affordability of products and services than on the other As. This is probably due to the fact that companies and researchers first thought that, by lowering the price, the market at the BoP could be easily developed. Single-serve sachets and lower quality were the result. Recently, more and more, scholars and practitioners become aware that acceptability, availability and awareness are likewise crucial.

18 An example is Aravind. For more information see Seelos and Mair 2006: 8ff. or www.aravind.org.

that smaller-sized packets can lead to an increase in consumption by the poor, but that this does not increase affordability, which is a function of per-unit and not per-package price (Karnani 2006: 104). Single-serve packets are also criticised due to their negative impact on the environment. Lowering quality can also reduce the price and therefore raise the affordability. Karnani states that it is often necessary to reduce quality in order to reduce costs and that the challenge is to do this in such a way that the cost–quality trade-off is acceptable to poor consumers (Karnani 2006: 104). It would be helpful if the term 'quality' were better defined in this respect. If quality is referring to international standards (such as ISO 9000), then it does not necessarily have to be reduced. If quality refers to high-quality materials then maintaining a low price is difficult. 'Shared access models' or 'joint consumption' are another way to reduce the price per unit for the poor. This model involves the provision of goods and services to groups and, therefore, widens the customer base and increases asset productivity. Typically, these models can be used with long-life goods such as computers, mobile phones or even cars (Mendoza and Thelen 2007: 438; Prahalad and Hammond 2002: 52). 'Deskilling', another strategy, not only cuts down on costs, but also increases productivity and improves financial viability. Instead of applying skill- and technology-intensive strategies, deskilling is a simplified or standardised procedure (Mendoza and Thelen 2008: 440). According to Prahalad, this is especially important in BoP markets where there is a 'shortage of talent' (Prahalad 2006: 38).[19] Whereas traditionally a 'bricks and mortar'[20] strategy was used to gain new clients, leveraging 'soft networks', such as ICT networks and community or social networks, help to dramatically lower the costs of the final product or service (Mendoza and Thelen 2008: 440).

Acceptability is the degree to which consumers and others in the value chain are willing to consume, distribute or sell a product or service. Products and services that are adapted to the unique needs and circumstances of customers, distributors or both, are predicted to be most successful (Anderson and Markides 2007: 84). Products also have to be culturally acceptable. For cultural, societal, religious or political reasons, products and services that are designed for the developed world may be inappropriate (Anderson and Markides 2007: 85).

Products and services have to be *available* to new customers who must be able to acquire and use them. Basic infrastructure for distribution is often not available in BoP markets and companies may have to establish distribution channels first (Anderson and Markides 2007: 84ff.). New strategies in distribution are as critical as product and process innovations (Prahalad 2006: 43f.). While considering both

---

19 Prahalad here talks about a 'shortage of talent'. Earlier we have seen that he describes the poor as 'resilient and creative entrepreneurs'. The knowledge base of the poor is considered important by BoP scholars, as we will see later. It remains questionable from which point of view 'talent' is judged.

20 The 'bricks and mortar' strategy refers to business that is handled in the physical world rather than in the online world (see, for example, www.encyclopedia.com/doc/1O999-bricksandmortar.html, accessed 20 August 2009).

local companies and future customers, companies can create benefits by localising supply chain activities and involving local actors (Kirchgeorg and Winn 2006: 182).

Customers have to be *aware* of the products or services that a company sells (Anderson and Markides 2007: 84), as well as of their appropriate use and benefits (Prahalad 2006: 40ff.). Given the fact that many poor people cannot read or do not own a TV/radio (Prahalad 2006: 40ff.), companies also need to learn to use alternative communication media and channels (Anderson and Markides 2007: 84). Where common communication media does not exist, tapping into community meetings and personal networks ('word of mouth') can offer solutions. Companies need to develop innovative ways to make use of the existing infrastructure and informal communication channels. It is also critical that message and media choices are rooted in accurate and appropriate marketing research that anticipates unexpected behaviour of poor segments (Kirchgeorg and Winn 2006: 182).

4.1.3.4 Building on the existing market environment[21]

> Business strategies that rely on leveraging the strengths of the existing market environment outperform those that focus on overcoming weaknesses (London and Hart 2004: 350).

BoP markets are often situated in a hostile environment with inadequate infrastructure. But products, services and business models must work there (Prahalad 2006: 42f.). Therefore, companies must adapt to an environment where social, and not legal, contracts dominate (De Soto 2000). Companies that value and leverage existing social capital and informal rules have achieved success (London and Hart 2004: 352). According to London and Hart (2004: 350), these strategies include developing relationships with 'non-traditional partners', 'co-inventing custom solutions' and 'building local capacity'.[22] These strategies suggest the importance of the development of a global capability of 'social embeddedness'. After mentioning some general points on building on the existing environment, the three strategies mentioned by London and Hart are described here in more detail.

Contracting innovations usually build upon the existing market environment. A contract can, for example, be made with a group (as is common in micro-financing), which builds on the strong informal networks within the communities (De Soto 2000: 172; Hart 2007: 210ff.; Mendoza and Thelen 2008: 446). A contract can also entail commitment mechanisms in order to make the product more useful to the poor. This is the case when restrictions on access to savings until a target date are fixed in the contract to avoid a situation whereby the poor are tempted to

---

21 Many of these issues target the core part of this chapter—innovation with the BoP (Section 4.2.2)—and are therefore treated in more detail there.

22 In the company sample of Bruni Celli *et al.* (2010: 41), the ventures that featured relational innovations were the ones that had not yet managed to assemble a working business model. A reason might be that this takes longer.

draw on their savings prematurely (Mendoza and Thelen 2008: 448).[23] 'Dynamic incentives' fall within the same category. Incentives such as these encourage the poor and help to mitigate the effects of constraints related to information asymmetry (Mendoza and Thelen 2008: 449).

'Total product solutions' where complete products are designed, are a better fit for the environment of BoP markets and the characteristics and the tastes of BoP consumers (Mendoza and Thelen 2008: 451). At least as important is the design of the interface so that it fits with the knowledge base of the poor. Especially as most BoP customers are first-time users of products and services, knowledge on their use needs to be gained fast (Prahalad 2006: 43). Prahalad (2006: 30ff.) opts for hybrid solutions to satisfy the market opportunity at BoP markets. Although the BoP market must be addressed by the most advanced technologies, these should be creatively combined with the existing (and evolving) infrastructure.

Companies are used to partnering with the minority of individuals and businesses in the developing world who participate in the formal economy, understand the global capitalist system and value Western products. However, reaching out to new and unfamiliar partners can be an effective strategy for companies. Partnerships come in myriad forms and help to address collective-action challenges (Hart 2007: 208ff.; Mendoza and Thelen 2008: 450). Companies can join with businesses and local entrepreneurs that are already established in those markets, as well as with NGOs and community groups. They are key sources of knowledge about local market conditions and customers' behaviour (Prahalad and Hammond 2002: 54), and can help reduce uncertainty about which knowledge is useful (Hart and Sharma 2004: 9). According to Dahan *et al.* (2010: 326), companies and NGOs can even co-create new innovative business models.

Seelos and Mair (2006: 12) recommend, based on their research, that corporations should consider the social entrepreneurs already in place and include them in their business models. They distinguish between three forms of organisational structures between two companies (e.g. between MNCs and local social entrepreneurs): symbiotic model; the complementary model; and the integrated model. Even though they foster an approach where local small and medium-sized enterprises play an important role, they do not go as far as Karnani who wants the MNCs to keep out:

> [. . .] it is usually small to medium-sized local enterprises that are best suited to exploit these opportunities (Karnani 2006: 105).

Engaging local partners has proven to be more successful than partnering with national ones as they have more knowledge of the local conditions (Hart 2007: 208). In the selection process of partners, companies should also pay attention to the potential partner's existing relationships with other important participants in the value chain (Gradl *et al.* 2010b). Another option is to partner with other corporations

---

23 It is questionable though if this gives the poor more dignity and choice, as mentioned by Prahalad (2006: 20).

and enter as consortia. These powerful synergies can also mitigate risk, save costs, offer access to scaled social assets and reduce individual effort (Bruni Celli *et al.* 2010: 56; Prahalad and Hammond 2002: 54*)*. By building on existing networks the strengths of the poor can be leveraged. Business can benefit by collaborating with the communities to leverage informal contract enforcement, expand risk-sharing arrangements and to coordinate investments into common goods (UNDP 2008: 73).

To access the context-specific information needed, companies have to partner with the target group itself, the poor. This extends far beyond the idea of adapting existing solutions to local conditions (London and Hart 2004: 362). Successful strategies, which really serve the needs of the poor, co-design products and services from the bottom up (as opposed to top down) with local partners who understand which set of functionalities are most important to BoP customers (London and Hart 2004: 363, Mendoza and Thelen 2008: 441). Local managers in developing countries are often as unfamiliar with the context of the poor as Western managers are, so it is not enough to rely on them to penetrate the BoP markets (London and Hart 2004: 359).

In London and Hart's research, a manager noted: '. . . it was important to contrast the perspective of "impoverished markets, our view of the base of the pyramid" with "impoverished mindsets, [which reflects] our lack of knowledge" ' (London and Hart 2004: 359). Learning from the poor is crucial (London and Hart 2004: 359). However, sometimes situations can occur in which local knowledge and capacity is not sufficient for successful business. Sharing of resources outside firm boundaries—local capacity building—can lead to success. Experiences showed that incorporating capacity building into the business models was a more effective way in which to proceed than through the more conventional approach of corporate philanthropy as an activity separate from the business (London and Hart 2004: 363).

Building on the local environment and developing products and services together with the poor is an important strategy to reach success at the BoP. This issue needs to be addressed in the innovation process to develop suitable products and services for the BoP. The next sections are therefore dedicated to innovation at the BoP.

4.2 **Innovation at the base of the pyramid**

Companies fail to employ suitable innovations when they lack the 'customer competence', which includes understanding of customers' needs, their buying process, communications and distribution channels to reach them (Danneels 2004). Most corporate attempts to reach the BoP have been 'alien' in nature and companies only adapted their current business models by repacking existing products into smaller serving sizes or extending product distribution into shanty towns and rural areas (Hart 2007: 195). In consumer-led markets, managers experience a top-down approach to be counter-productive (Munnecke and Van der Lugt 2006: 1).

[. . .] a top-down approach to implementation can seriously limit and even damage the company's hopes of realising the opportunity (Hart 2007: 231).

These strategies are called 'first generation' or 'BoP 1.0' strategies which represent attempts to quickly tap into a new market without an understanding of the real needs of those living there (Hart 2007: 195; London and Hart 2010). Simanis and Hart (2008: 1) express it in even stronger terms. In their view, the rush to capture the fortune at the BoP resulted in the perspectives of the poor themselves being lost. Instead, they advocate for 'BoP 2.0' strategies that require a deep dialogue with the poor, co-development and the creation of mutual value.[24] Companies have to learn how to co-invent and co-evolve—in participation with the poor—products and services that are appropriately embedded in the local ecosystem and culture from the start (Hart 2007: 203). Table 4.4 summarises the differences in approach between the two strategies.

Table 4.4 **From BoP 1.0 to BoP 2.0**

Source: HART, STUART L., CAPITALISM AT THE CROSSROADS: NEXT GENERATION BUSINESS STRATEGIES FOR A POST-CRISIS WORLD, 3rd Edition, © 2010, p.230. Reprinted by permission of Pearson Education, Inc., Upper Saddle River, NJ.

BoP 1.0	BoP 2.0
• Different price point	• Deep dialogue
• Redesign packaging	• Put the last first
• Low cost production	• Build capacity
• Extended distribution	• Leapfrog solutions
• Partner with global NGOs	• Ecosystem of local partners
'Selling to the poor'	'Creating mutual value'

After a short foray into the concepts, terms and types of innovations used in literature, the different BoP 2.0 approaches are now explained in more detail.

4.2.1 The process of innovation

Companies that aim to tackle the opportunities at the BoP must be innovative—in terms of products, services and business models as well as management processes.

---

24 The design and development of a BoP 2.0 strategy process is the goal of the BoP protocol. It contains a pre-field process (selection of sites, formation and training of field team, selection of local community partners), an in-field process (opening up, building the ecosystem, enterprise creation) and a third step, scaling out. For details and examples in practice see Simanis and Hart 2008. When markets first have to be created, Simanis (2010) proposes a similar process based on a value proposition for products or services that is open-ended and does not define a product's value specifically from the beginning.

> The methodologies for innovation at the BOP are different from, and more demanding, than the traditional approaches (Prahalad 2006: 100).

Drawing from basic literature on innovation, this section describes innovation *for* the BoP and paves the way for the core of this part of the book, innovation *with* the BoP.

Generally, after Tidd *et al.* (2005), and extended by Krämer and Belz (2008: 216), innovation can occur in five areas:

- **Process innovations**: change the way in which products and services are produced and delivered

- **Product innovations**: refer to changes in products and services offered.

- **Position innovations**:[25] change the way and context in which products and services are introduced to the market.

- **Paradigm innovations**: represent changes in the underlying mental maps that frame what the organisation does.

- **Partnerships innovations**: are changes in the way an enterprise cooperates with partners and networks to acquire knowledge and technology to innovate

There are two types of innovation.[26] One is incremental, whereby existing products and services are improved on a small scale. The other is radical, as products and services differ significantly from former solutions and mostly imply revolutionary changes (Tidd *et al.* 2005). The literature about innovations for the BoP contains both types. If existing products and services are adapted to local circumstances, as proposed within the strategies of the UNDP (2008), we can call those incremental innovations. Indeed, many examples from practice mentioned throughout BoP literature move in this direction (e.g. single-serve sachets).[27] Radical innovations fit within existing product lines but bring new benefits to the market. This is the direction which Hart, Christensen and Sharma argue for innovations at the BoP (Hart 2007; Hart and Christensen 2002; Sharma and Hart 2006: 7).

According to Hart (2007: 233) it is critical to think in terms of 'creative destruction'[28] rather than continuous improvement. Creative destruction is usually driven by waves of scientific and technological discovery and/or major periods of socio-

25 As Krämer and Belz (2008: 216) note, process and position innovation both encompass technical and managerial processes, but the former takes place during the production process and the latter refers to processes concerning marketing and sales.

26 Hart and Sharma (2004: 6f.) even speak about five types: incremental; sustaining; radical; architectural; and disruptive. They are not, however, clearly distinguished.

27 See also the results of the research by Bruni Celli *et al.* (2010: 38).

28 Joseph Schumpeter initially invented the term 'creative destruction' more than 70 years ago (Schumpeter 1934). He used it to describe the process of transformation that accompanies radical innovation.

political upheaval (Hart 2007: 88). Disruptive innovations improve a product or service in ways that the market does not expect, through lower pricing or design for a different consumer market. They usually introduce products and services with attributes that are not valued in the mainstream markets of a company. Disruptive innovations can be classified into low-end and new-market. A new-market disruptive innovation is mostly aimed at non-consumption (consumers who would not have used the products already on the market), whereas a lower-end disruptive innovation is aimed at mainstream customers for whom price is more important than quality (Christensen 1997). Before a disruptive innovation destroys industry leaders and incumbent technologies, a long period of 'creative creation' typically occurs (Hart 2007: 119; Hart and Christensen 2002: 52). Disruptive innovations are initially perceived as inferior to those already in use and can only take root within non-traditional consumer markets.[29] For Hart and Christensen, the BoP may be the best place to incubate disruptive innovations for two reasons. First, business models that are forged in low-income markets can be diffused well geographically. Second, the poorly served BoP is already content with a more modest version of what is available in high-end markets (Hart and Christensen 2002: 52). To be successful, companies have to manage disruptive innovations separately from their mainstream business (Hart 2007: 136). As empirical evidence shows (Abernathy and Utterback 1978; Christensen 1997), incumbent firms have difficulties with radical and disruptive innovations as they are usually focused on exploiting their current investments. In order to develop disruptive innovations, an experimental or exploratory strategy is useful (Jagtap and Kandachar 2009: 9).

An innovation process contains different stages: idea generation; idea screening; concept development and testing; business analysis; development; testing; launch; and post-launch review (Cooper 2003; Kotler and Armstrong 2004). Krämer and Belz (2008: 217) suggest four major stages for the innovation process of new products and services at the BoP: invention; incubation; introduction to the market; and diffusion.[30] This means that the innovation process goes further than idea generation, as one would expect. Schumpeter (1934) has already differentiated between invention and innovation. An invention is an idea that might be used in production, whereas innovation is the process of turning an invention into an actual product. Mendoza and Thelen (2008: 437) also associate the term 'innovation' with the features of a product or service as well as the method of providing it (i.e. producing, marketing, selling, etc.). In a way closely related to Krämer and Belz and Mendoza and Thelen, this research builds on the following four phases as depicted in Figure 4.8.

29 Innovations that are seen first, or are likely to be used first, in the developing world before spreading to the industrialised world are also called 'reverse innovations' or 'trickle-up innovations' (see Immelt *et al.* 2009).
30 In the literature, there are a great variety of innovation process steps. Gruner and Homburg (2000: 6), for example, use the following six stages: idea generation; product concept development; project definition; engineering; prototype testing; and market launch.

Figure 4.8 **The innovation process**

The whole process is a product/service innovation process, but within each step one can find one or more of the other types of innovations previously mentioned (process, position, paradigm and partnerships innovation).

Further, Chesbrough (2003) distinguishes between an open and a closed innovation paradigm. In a closed innovation process firms are strongly self-reliant, while in an open innovation process firms should additionally use external sources for ideas and input. Consumers, for example, are then integrated actively into one or more stages of the innovation process, which means that the innovation process may no longer be dominated solely by the company.

Innovation usually comes as technology-push or customer-pull. For domestic companies in developing countries, technology-push (introducing new products based on cutting-edge research) has, so far, rarely been an option. Far more often, there is a need to find ways to solve customers' dilemmas without relying on novel science (Sull *et al.* 2003: 3) and deal with scarcity conditions (Srinivas and Sutz 2008). To be able to do this, getting closer to the potential consumer—in this case the poor—is a very important criterion, as elaborated in the next section.

4.2.2 Innovation with the base of the pyramid

> [. . .] we cannot know in advance what is required to serve the real needs of those who have been bypassed or damaged by the globalisation process (Hart 2007: 176).

Companies must get closer to the markets they wish to serve. Getting closer to the target group, the poor, within innovation processes can be achieved in three ways: by integrating the poor as individuals; by integrating groups and networks; and, finally, by embedding the company into communities. This section describes the various existing concepts and buzzwords used in BoP literature.

4.2.2.1 Consumer integration

Even though BoP consumers seem not to have played an important role in the innovation process in many practice examples so far (Hart 2007: 195; Krämer and Belz 2008),[31] this is considered a key component of success of any BoP venture

---

31 Not only in BoP innovation processes, but also in innovation processes for the wealthy, customers are often (if they are at all) integrated into late stages of product development—as prototype testing or market launch (Gruner and Homburg 2000: 11).

(London and Hart 2004: 364). Consumers are one of the most important sources of information and ideas for new product and service development processes as they have need-related information, application information and, sometimes, also solution-related information (Krämer and Belz 2008: 217).[32] The role of the consumer has changed from isolated to connected, from unaware to informed, and from passive to active (Prahalad and Ramaswamy 2004: 4).

Companies are used to 'one-size-fits-all' products and services offered on the global market. Also so-called locally responsive strategies are often simply little more than pre-existing corporate solutions tailored to fit local markets. The results are inappropriate products and business models that fail to effectively address real needs. So far, the unmet needs of the poor are mostly identified through conventional market research methods such as secondary data (Hart 2007: 21).[33] Krämer and Belz (2008: 219) claim that the integration of the poor into market research is a better route to take because quantitative data (if available at all) is often misleading or wrong and consumer integration unveils important qualitative data such as information about latent needs and tacit knowledge. Consumer integration is typically costlier than conventional methods, as more time and resources are required. But it is of more value, especially when the local knowledge resources are important to the firm.[34] This is more often than not the case in BoP ventures, as companies are usually unfamiliar to the BoP environment (Krämer and Belz 2008: 219).

In their research,[35] Gruner and Homburg (2000) analysed customer characteristics and the performance impact of the intensity of customer interaction at different stages of the new product development process. The results indicate that customer interaction, particularly during the early and late stages of the new product development process, has a positive impact on new product success.[36] Integration into the project definition and engineering process, in turn, do not have a positive impact on success (Gruner and Homburg 2000: 10). Equally, the characteristics of the customers play an important role for product success: lead users; financially attractive customers; and close (i.e. loyal) customers are attractive interaction partners. 'Technically attractive'[37] customers do not necessarily lead to a successful new product (Gruner and Homburg 2000: 11). Even though this study focused on

---

32 Summary of a literature review.
33 According to Krämer and Belz (2008: 217), there are two groups of methods to gain knowledge about a market: conventional market research methods; and methods that enable active integration of, and interaction with, consumers.
34 Local knowledge is considered important concerning, for example, the use of products, processes in the informal local market, information exchange, etc.
35 The research builds on inductive field research followed by a survey (Gruner and Homburg 2000: 5).
36 New product success consists of: quality of new product; financial success; quality of the new product development process; and inexpensiveness of new product ownership (Gruner and Homburg 2000: 6).
37 'Technical attractiveness' refers to customers' innovativeness and know-how (Gruner and Homburg 2000: 9).

top-of-the-pyramid customers, it can give us hints for the integration of customers at the BoP. As the financial attractiveness of customers involved is related to their representativeness in the target market and their reputation within that market, we can conclude that for BoP innovations people representing the BoP ('financial non-attractiveness') need to be integrated in order for new products to be success-ful. As we will see later, local know-how is very important for innovations at the BoP, especially because it is significantly different from the know-how a company already has. The same study within a BoP market could therefore show different results in this regard.

4.2.2.2 Engaging fringe stakeholders

Companies tend to focus only on known and powerful stakeholders; those who can directly impact the firm's current success.[38] But to reach the BoP, and to invent disruptive innovations, managers need to put out their feelers a little further and proactively seek out the voices of previously ignored fringe stakeholders (for exam-ple, the poor) who had been invisible to the company or disconnected from it (Hart 2007: 20, 178; Hart and Sharma 2004: 9; see Fig. 4.9).

According to Sharma and Hart (2006: 11), generating knowledge through fringe stakeholders requires that companies develop a capability to tap into new types of knowledge to meet the unique challenges in the new contexts. These new types of knowledge can include:

- An in-depth understanding of the needs and aspirations of the potential customers

- A deep understanding of the complex interactions among the socio-cultural, economic and environmental concerns

- An understanding of the factors that will afford credibility and build long-term relationships

This is only possible by listening intently to the voices of the poor.

4.2.2.3 Radical transactiveness and deep listening

Hart argues for 'radical transactiveness' (see Fig. 4.10). Radical, in this context, refers to the ability to engage with fringe stakeholders possessing radically different views and transactiveness means entering into a two-way dialogue (Hart 2007: 177). As suggested by Hart and Sharma (2004: 11ff.), radical transactiveness consists of two capabilities: the ability to extend the scope of the firm (fan out); and the ability to

---

38 Core economic stakeholders often have an interest in the survival of the current business model and core social stakeholders are focused on mitigating current negative impacts of a company. Focusing on stakeholders with interests in the current business and products can therefore lock the firm into incremental and sustaining innovations rather than the disruptive innovations needed for BoP markets (Sharma and Hart 2006: 10).

Figure 4.9 **Fringe stakeholders**

Source: Hart and Sharma 2004: 10

integrate diverse and disconfirming knowledge (fan in).[39] There are two avenues for extending the scope of the firm (fan out): Networking from the core to the periphery, and putting the last first. The former means that companies identify parties immediately beyond the core of salient stakeholders and follow the networks of each of these stakeholders to the periphery. The latter notion—'putting the last first'—comes originally from Chambers (1983),[40] and requires a conscious effort to reverse the rules of stakeholder saliency by identifying actors who are powerless, non-legitimate, isolated or disinterested with respect to the company (Hart and Sharma 2004: 12). As a second step, the diverse and disconfirming information discovered in the fanning out process ought to be integrated into practical and usable strategies (fan in). The transfer of tacit or unwritten knowledge residing in people and their traditions requires intense interaction, and often a reframing of a firm's dominant logic. With reference to fanning in, again two steps are described: generating complex interactions; and reconciling contradictions (Hart and Sharma 2004: 14). A pre-commercial period of engagement at the BoP is essential for the deep listening required to develop empathetic understanding (Hart 2007: 197). According to Hart and Sharma (2004: 14), the interactions can be developed through managers spending time in homeless shelters or rural areas in developing countries. They can then transfer tacit knowledge about the needs of consumers who they do not cater to with their existing products. Before immersion, however, managers should

---

39 For a more extensive overview see Hart and Sharma 2004.
40 There is more about Chambers and his approach in Chapter 5.

receive suitable cultural and ecosystem sensitivity training. Reconciling contradictions involves incubating disruptive innovations in a transactive mode with fringe stakeholders. It is this last step that focuses on the articulation and implementation of practical solutions to the problems and opportunities identified in the fan-out process (Hart and Sharma 2004: 15f.).

Figure 4.10 **Radical transactiveness**

Source: Hart and Sharma 2004: 11

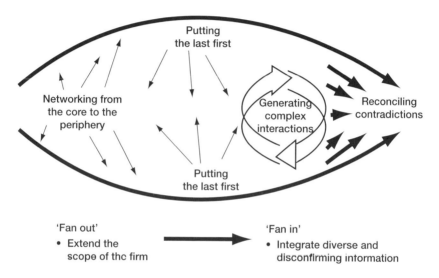

This approach, according to Gardetti (2009: 55ff.), calls for a shift in the paradigm away from the idea that people living in poverty are victims and towards a situation in which their knowledge and wisdom is accepted.

4.2.2.4 Co-creation

Co-creation implies that companies, together with the poor (and shared resources), develop products and services. It includes working together with people living in poverty in an equal partnership to innovate and provide sustainable win–win scenarios in which the poor are actively involved and committed (Gardetti 2009; Gardetti and D'Andrea 2010: 79; London and Hart 2004: 364). This means neither a transfer nor outsourcing of activities to customers, nor does it mean a marginal customisation of products and services. The change companies must make '. . . involves the co-creation of value through personalised interactions that are meaningful and sensitive to a specific consumer . . . The market begins to resemble a forum organised around individuals and their co-creation experiences rather than around passive pockets of demand for the firm's offerings' (Prahalad and Ramaswamy 2004: 6).

Key building blocks in the process of co-creation are dialogue, access to informa-tion, risk assessment (referring to the probability of doing harm to the customer) and transparency. Prahalad and Ramaswamy (2004: 6f.) call this the DART (**d**ialogue, **a**ccess to information, **r**isk assessment, **t**ransparency) model of value co-creation. London and Hart's research (2004: 362) showed, for example, that corporate entry into BoP markets benefited from identifying local partners who could actively con-tribute to venture conceptualisation by adding local content to the product design. An infrastructure for interaction—so-called 'experience environments' and 'expe-rience networks'—between companies and consumers should be built (Prahalad and Ramaswamy 2004: 6).

User innovations (e.g. from lead users) can play an important role here as well (Krämer and Belz 2008: 231; Von Hippel 1986). They are innovations invented by the consumers themselves and are an important part of overall innovative activ-ity in the economy. Krämer and Belz (2008: 231) introduce the idea, that—as BoP consumers are told to be creative entrepreneurs (Prahalad 2006: 1)—screening the BoP market itself for user innovations would be an attractive field of investigation. Discovering how BoP consumers have found innovative solutions to bypass weak or non-existent infrastructure and how this potential can be integrated into future innovation processes or harnessed for common partnerships can be a fruitful source of innovation.

4.2.2.5 Developing native capability and becoming indigenous

Companies must view the poor as partners and colleagues rather than as clients and consumers.[41] This shift in mind-set requires the development of 'native capa-bility', which means learning to engage extensively with local people on their terms in a 'true spirit of mutuality' (Hart 2007: 219). It is about '. . . the development of new "native" capabilities that enable a company to develop fully contextualised solutions to real problems in ways that respect local culture and natural diversity' (Hart 2007: 21f.). This requires corporations to expand their conception of the glo-bal economy to include economic activities that occur outside of the formal, wage-based economy and that strengthen local communities. According to Gardetti and D'Andrea (2010), at a field level, this calls for skills in facilitation and the practice of humility, building trust and close ties across different classes and settings, and co-evolving value propositions and business models through action learning approaches. At the corporate level, native capability requires a 'white space' for R&D to maintain a certain independence from the routines, metrics and structures that usually govern the core business. Also, patient capital and performance met-rics that can support experimentation and learning in the field are required (Gar-detti and D'Andrea 2010: 77). With native capability, companies become part of the local landscape. As Hart (2007: 24) states:

---

41 This is the same paradigm shift development has made: from development aid to devel-opment partnerships.

> Learning to become indigenous, I argue, is the next strategic challenge on
> the road to building a sustainable global enterprise.

Native capability can enable companies to become truly embedded in the local
context.

4.2.2.6 Embeddedness

In the informal sectors, where most poor are active, relationships are primarily
grounded in social, not legal, contracts. It is therefore not only important to co-
create products and services together with the poor, but also to keep in mind the
importance and benefits of the existing social infrastructure, where the innovations must fit. Business models can be based upon social capital and trust (Hart
2007: 211). It is necessary to conduct R&D and market research focused on the
unique situations and requirements of the poor, by region and by country (Hart
2007: 233). According to the research of London and Hart (2004: 364), companies
that are 'socially embedded' enter more successfully into BoP markets than companies without this capability (London and Hart 2004: 364). Bruni Celli *et al.* (2010:
38,), however, found in their research, that it was not an important element in the
business model of many of the companies in their sample. Social embeddedness
can be defined as follows:

> Social embeddedness is the integration into diverse local networks that
> leads to the development of long-term and cooperative relationships and
> which may result in the achievement of common benefits for all the play-
> ers involved in the network (Sánchez *et al.* 2007: 20).

This means that the company integrates itself in the local context and not the
other way around (i.e. by integrating the poor into company processes). The
research by Sánchez *et al.* (2007)[42] focused on factors that influence social embeddedness in low-income markets and suggests that a firm has a stronger incentive
to build embedded ties and partnerships under three conditions: an under-devel-
oped market-oriented system; the high psychic distance of a firm in regard to low-
income markets; and a high degree of personalised co-creation experiences offered
by the firm (Sánchez *et al.* 2007: 22ff.).[43] Even though all the successful case studies
had a high level of social embeddedness (Sánchez *et al.* 2007: 22), the researchers
conclude that becoming socially embedded is not, in every circumstance, a necessary factor for success. However, firms that have developed this ability might create higher levels of total value for all involved, which is of critical importance in
low-income markets (Sánchez *et al.* 2007: 36). This research also shows that distribution and marketing are the two business activities in which embedded ties

---

42 The method was a multiple-case inductive study because of the lack of prior theory on
   social embeddedness in low-income markets. They chose three successful case studies,
   one that failed and one with mixed results (Sánchez *et al.* 2006: 21).
43 This means that a company moves away from its core competencies.

and partnerships seem to be more relevant. The reason could be that developing a distribution channel is extremely costly and challenging for a company to do alone (Sánchez *et al.* 2007: 25).

Recently, Simanis and Hart (2009) elaborated on the 'embedded innovation paradigm' in which companies and communities can jointly construct a new, shared identity and which builds on the potential of the poor. Companies must step away from the 'structural innovation paradigm' they are used to, and re-embed consumers and producers back into society (Simanis and Hart 2009: 83).

Figure 4.11 **The embedded innovation paradigm**
Source: Simanis and Hart 2009: 82

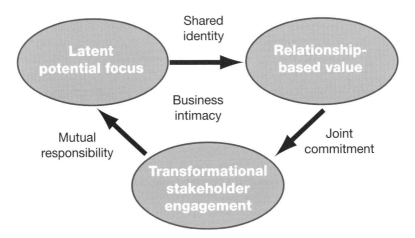

Based on their experience with the BoP Protocol, Simanis and Hart define a 'business model intimacy' that has to be developed. Business model intimacy '. . . is a kind of relationship in which the identity of a community is fused with that of the company. The glue that binds this shared identity is a jointly constructed vision of a better life and community—a strategic community intent—anchored around a new business' (Simanis and Hart 2009: 79). In this case, innovation is not enabled by new relationships. Innovation is the relationship. As we see in Figure 4.11, the new paradigm consists of three main attributes. A latent potential for generating an infinite number of new varieties of businesses and markets exists within diverse economies. It can be formal or non-formal in nature. Relationships create the context in which community members define themselves and form their aspirations. Stakeholder engagement is a transformational process that creates new stakeholder behaviour, habits and identities that are necessary to realise a new enterprise and strategic community intent. In this case, engagement '. . . is a personal change process that instills responsibility and commitment in business partners, breeds dedicated customers and creates an ecosystem of people and institutions that embrace the enterprise's values' (Simanis and Hart 2009: 83). The embedded innovation paradigm is applied within companies that participate in the BoP Protocol.

4.3 **Bottom-up development in BoP literature**

As we saw in the preceding sections, innovation processes for the BoP should integrate the poor to the point at which the process becomes driven from the 'bottom up'. This perspective is not new: development literature has followed this idea for almost three decades. Extracts from so-called 'bottom-up development approaches', where the poor are the centre of projects and processes, are indeed mentioned several times in the literature on serving the BoP, especially concerning methods of doing so.

Hart (2007: 200), for example, states that companies interested in serving the BoP can learn a lot from techniques such as participatory rural appraisal (PRA) (Chambers 1983, 1997), rapid assessment processes (Beebe 2001) and quick ethnography (Handwerker 2001) as they open up valuable ways to hear the marginalised voices of the poor. The participatory approach from Chambers (1983) is also mentioned in London and Hart (2004: 362). Key principles, techniques and methods of the BoP Protocol (Simanis and Hart 2008: 3) have been adapted from the fields of PRA (e.g. Chambers 1983, 1997) and asset-based community development (e.g. Kretzmann and McKnight 1993). 'Immersion', as suggested in the BoP Protocol (Simanis and Hart 2008) has its origins in anthropological research and development practice. Sharma and Hart's (2004: 12) radical transactiveness implies 'putting the last first'. This concept also comes, originally, from Chambers (1983). Simanis and Hart (2009: 77) in their new article 'Innovation from the Inside Out' even claim that '. . . aspiring creators must act on what non-profits already know: you get the best answers by burying yourself in the questions'. Gardetti and D'Andrea (2010: 89) consider bottom-up development as a fundamental feature of the BoP concept, albeit difficult to implement. For Hart (2007: 194), the objective is the creation of indigenous enterprises, co-creating technologies, products and services to meet local needs, and building local businesses from the bottom up. Local knowledge plays an important role.

> For MNCs, the best approach is to marry their global best practices with newfound local knowledge and understanding gleaned from widening the corporate bandwidth (Hart 2007: 194).

Simanis and Hart (2006) state that it is now well accepted that sustainable poverty alleviation must recognise the poor as central agents in that process, and make the link to development literature.

The right level of engagement of the BoP into the innovation process, however, is subject to debate and an area that certainly warrants further attention. According to principles set by London, the involvement needs to be higher than 0%, which would indicate a completely top-down approach, but also should be lower than 100%, which indicates no external participation (London 2007: 27). In fact, London uses the principle of co-creation as a differentiation criterion of the BoP approach compared to traditional poverty alleviation programmes.[44]

> Rather than co-created with poor, these [traditional] poverty alleviation initiatives are designed and managed by professionals trained in the developed world (London 2007: 18).

It might be true that traditional poverty alleviation programmes still use top-down approaches in *practice*[45] but the development *literature* continuously suggests a bottom-up approach. Furthermore, this means that development literature gives a more profound picture of what 'bottom-up' means than does BoP literature.

The next chapter is dedicated to bottom-up approaches in development literature where we will move on to a discussion of the potential application in BoP ventures (of the connections between the two) in order to discover what can be adopted in BoP approaches.

---

44 Programmes of governments, international organisations or NGOs.
45 BoP practice cannot yet give many bottom-up examples either (Hart 2007: 231). We need to support companies in taking a bottom-up approach, so that this idea does not remain in literature only as this is apparently often the case in traditional development projects.

5

Bottom-up development approaches

This chapter builds the reference frame for the case study research. Even though the 'bottom-up' buzzword is mentioned several times in BoP literature, some hints to development theories are given and a couple of methods are applied in practice, the extracts chosen seem very selective. No detailed information is given on what a bottom-up development approach contains and BoP research has never tried to combine the two fields.[1] This research suggests that the BoP concept can profit a great deal more from the knowledge in bottom-up development literature than it has thus far, and BoP research is therefore examined from the perspective of bottom-up development approaches. After a short foray into development research in general, this chapter seeks to summarise the vast knowledge in bottom-up development literature where this is connected to the BoP approach. Relevant questions that lead to assumptions will be posed.

The term 'development' has different meanings.[2] Definitions are contextual and contingent upon the ideological, epistemological or methodological orientation of their purveyors (Simon 1997: 184). The so called 'development as history' approach even goes so far as to state that every country or community should decide itself what development means for them and that this cannot be defined by outsiders.[3] There has never been consensus or unanimity about the meaning or content of

---

1 For the first paper criticising current BoP approaches for under-appreciating issues from development studies—heterogeneity among the poor, and participation—see Arora and Romijn 2009.

2 This book focuses on development in the sense of development of people, communities and countries. Originally, the terms 'progress' and 'evolution' were used. After World War II, 'development' became the most commonly used term (Martinussen 1997: 34).

3 For a short overview see Martinussen 1997: 45.

development research (Simon 1997: 184). There is not even a consensus on what the subject of development research covers or agreement on whether development research is a distinct subject with its own approaches, methods and theories (Martinussen 1997: 3). However, Martinussen (1997: 4) defines the subject area of development studies and research as follows:

> [. . .] the societal reproduction and transformation processes of the developing countries, in conjunction with the international factors that influence these processes.

Research in the developing world therefore only becomes development research, when expressly related to societal conditions and processes (Martinussen 1997: 5). When talking about development, the objectives are generally articulated at three principal levels (Simon 1997: 187f.):

- By the populations of poorer countries

- By nation states, in terms of their political programmes and national development plans

- By international financial institutions and donor agencies, in terms of their overarching discourses, lending criteria and funding priorities

Many of the original theories of development were about economic growth and economic transformation; and they were rarely concerned with political or cultural dimensions in a local context.[4] The corporate economy typically dominated the agenda for development processes (Martinussen 1997: 293). On the other hand, the few theories that considered cultural or political factors were weak in terms of economic analysis.[5] According to Martinussen (1997: 7), there is still a long way to go before economic and non-economic factors are systematically integrated, but there is a noticeable tendency to move in this direction.

It is not easy to make generalisations regarding development theories. The developing world is by no means homogenous (Martinussen 1997: 9), but on the other hand development cannot be universalised from particular case studies (Simon 1997: 190). It is also characteristic that development problems are treated as though they were objective and value free. Martinussen critiques that hardly any normative considerations have been taken, on the basis that development goals are never value free. Typically, they are linked to the 'Western ideal' (Martinussen 1997: 347f.). For decades, Westernisation or Northern theories and policies have dominated development literature. Simon and others label this trend as 'misguided', arguing that it is responsible for current problems in development's lack of success (Simon

---

4 The main protagonists were Adam Smith, Thomas Robert Malthus, David Ricardo, John Stuart Mill, John Maynard Keynes and Joseph Schumpeter. For a detailed overview see Martinussen 1997: 19ff.

5 The main protagonists here were Auguste Comte, Emile Durkheim, Karl Marx and Max Weber. For a detailed overview see Martinussen 1997: 25ff.

1997: 184f.).[6] Hart even states that the Western post-war development fixation with industrial production as the only path to prosperity and its one-size-fits-all solutions has created the BoP as we know it today (Hart 2007: 175). The so-called 'dialectical modernisation theory', which goes way back to the beginning of the 1960s, conveyed to all notions and theories more respect for the developing countries' unique circumstances. This implied a dismissal of the notion that development is something universal, defined solely by the greatest possible similarity to the Northwestern countries. Instead, an open conception of development goals was proposed (Martinussen 1997: 41).

BoP scholars are somewhat divergent on the issue of 'Westernisation' when providing products and services to the poor. Prahalad and Lieberthal (2003: 109) state that companies (especially MNCs) must move beyond their 'imperialist mindset' that requires everyone to look and act like 'Westerners'. BoP markets should not be seen as new markets for old, Western products. However, some strategies proposed to enter the BoP market (e.g. smaller packet size) and giving out free samples (e.g. whitening skin cream) in effect move towards what can be called 'Westernisation'. Landrun (2007: 7), based on her research that brings together existing critiques of Prahalad's book *Fortune at the Bottom of the Pyramid* (Prahalad 2006), criticises the underlying assumption that companies can determine what BoP consumers want and that they just have to find a profitable way of providing it. Landrun opts for the approach taken in the BoP Protocol, which starts with deep listening and mutual dialogue—a bottom-up approach. Simanis, however, one of the 'fathers' of the BoP Protocol states in an article published in the *Wall Street Journal*:

> They [the poor] haven't been **conditioned to think** that the products being offered are something one would even buy. And they haven't adapted their behaviors and budgets to fit the products into their lives [. . .] Companies must create markets—new lifestyles—among poor consumers. They **must make the idea of paying money for the products seem natural**, and they **must induce consumers to fit those goods** into their long-held routines (Simanis 2009).[7]

This seems notably similar to 'Westernisation' and a top-down perspective. The domination of Western theories in development is criticised frequently within development literature, as we have seen above, and can be seen as a main driver for the emergence of bottom-up approaches. But is it also a driver for choosing a bottom-up approach in BoP ventures?

Even though there will probably never be a 'grand theory' of development (Simon 1997: 197), we can note that a paradigm shift occurred during the 1980s and 1990s from top-down approaches (external technologies, national governments) to bottom-up approaches (people-centred and -driven processes) (Ellis and Biggs 2001: 437ff.; Guijt and Shah 1998: 1).

---

6 See also Norgaard 1994.
7 Words in bold indicate where there are conflicts with a bottom-up perspective.

> Reducing poverty requires not only broad-based growth and improved governance at the national level, but also support to bottom-up approaches focusing on poor people and their roles and experiences in the development process (Narayan 2002: ix).

These approaches envisage development as a participatory process that empowers the poor to take control of their own priorities for change (Ellis and Biggs 2001: 443). Simon (1997: 185) puts it as follows:

> [...] human development is the process of enhancing individual and collective quality of life in a manner that satisfies basic needs (as a minimum), is environmentally, socially and economically sustainable and is empowering in the sense that the people concerned have a substantial degree of control (because total control may be unrealistic) over the process through access to the means of accumulating social power.

Specifically related to rural development, but also useful for development in general, is the distinction that Chambers (1983: 147) makes between top-down and bottom-up development. This suitably illustrates the difference with relevance to rural development. The original definition (which is considered top-down) comes from the World Bank (1975: 3):

> Rural development is a strategy designed to improve the economic and social life of a specific group of people—the rural poor. It involves extending the benefits of development to the poorest among those who seek a livelihood in the rural areas.

Chambers (1983: 147) changed the definition to bottom-up as follows:

> Rural development is **a strategy to enable** a specific group of people [...] to gain for themselves and their children more of what they want and need. It involves helping the poorest among those who seek a livelihood in the rural areas **to demand and control more of the benefits of development**.[8]

In this book, we can therefore conclude that development can be defined as follows in the BoP concept:

> Development is a process to enable the BoP to create livelihoods where they demand and control the benefits of their development to a substantial degree.

This chapter presents the main ideas of bottom-up development approaches and—even though it is difficult to generalise—explains the different elements which the approaches have in common. This will help to demonstrate the relation between these findings and the BoP approach.

---

8 Words in bold indicate the changes.

5.1 **Historical background of bottom-up development approaches**

The basic premise of bottom-up development is that the poor have to be the key actors in planning and implementing their own development (Binswanger 2004: 2). Community development movements with 'self-help approaches' can be traced back to the 1920s and have their roots in the cooperative movement and Gandhian notions of village self-reliance and small-scale development in India (Gandhi 1962). Also, Paulo Freire argued that the 'oppressed' needed to unite to find a way to improve their own destinies (Freire 1970). This first wave of, called here, participatory development in the 1950s and 1960s led to the initiation of programmes in over 60 countries in Asia, Africa and Latin America, but soon came to an end (Korten 1980: 482). The approach was mostly used to develop public goods, and economists long remained sceptical because of the free-riding problem (Hardin 1982; Olson 1973). Korten (1980: 482) summarises a set of other characteristic weaknesses of the approach during that first wave:

- Existing power structures were taken as a given and no attempt was made to change them

- Responsibility for implementation had been placed in administratively separate ministries, which paralleled the established line agencies of government

- Greater emphasis tended to be placed on the expansion of social services rather than on increasing real incomes

- Implementation was done through conventional bureaucratic structures, with programmes and targets formulated centrally

- Little was done to build independent member-controlled local organisations able to solve local problems

Table 5.1 sets out the contradictions between poverty-focused development projects and donor preferences, as identified by Korten (1980).[9]

---

9 Even though Korten focuses on rural development, these tendencies can be seen in development in general.

Table 5.1 **Poverty focus and donor preferences**
Source: Korten 1980: 484. This material is reproduced with permission of John Wiley & Sons, Inc.

Poverty-focused development projects	Donor preferences
Small	Large
Administrative and personnel-intensive	Capital- and import-intensive
Difficult to monitor and inspect	Easy to monitor and inspect
Slow to implement	Quick to implement
Not suitable for complex techniques of project appraisal	Suitable for social cost-benefit analysis

By the mid-1980s, however, critics of 'big development' were complaining that many large-scale, government-initiated development programmes—from schooling to health to credit to irrigation systems—were performing poorly and creating significant negative impacts on poverty (Mansuri and Rao 2004: 4f.). This time, critique came not only from post-colonialists and anti-globalisers such as Wolfgang Sachs, David Korten or Arturo Escobar, but also from development insiders such as Joe Stiglitz, George Soros, Jeffrey Sachs and William Easterly. Many called for more reliance on civil society as opposed to governments (Hart 2007: 175). Interest in the local management of resources and decisions was reawakened and a new participatory development movement was born (Mansuri and Rao 2004: 4f.). Under the participatory development movement led by Chambers (1983), these ideas were applied to small-scale and decentralised development in ways that would allow the poor to become informed participants in development, with external agents acting mainly as facilitators and sources of funds. Support came from social scientists (e.g. Escobar 1995; Scott 1998) who argued that top-down perspectives were both disempowering and ineffective (Mansuri and Rao 2004: 5). Amartya Sen's influential effort to shift the focus of development from material well-being to a broad-based 'capability approach' also deeply influenced the development community in this sense (Sen 1985, 1999). Central to this shift in focus were strategies to empower poor people, an agenda taken on by the World Bank and other donors as part of their response to critiques of top-down development.[10] It led to the inclusion of participation as a crucial means of allowing the poor to gain control over decisions, again in large-scale projects (Mansuri and Rao 2004: 5). This second wave of interest in community-based approaches to development—a movement that originated in revolutionary goals that were anti-colonial and anti-modernisation—has been absorbed into the mainstream of development and also into development economics (Mansuri and Rao 2004: 6; Martinussen 1997: 41). According to a study by Narayan *et al.* (2000) based on interviews with 60,000 poor people in 60 countries, poor people demand a development process driven by their communities.

10 See, for example, Madavo 2000.

In recent years, bottom-up approaches evolved in terms of not focusing solely on people, but also considering the environment in which they live and factors that usually cannot be influenced by the poor themselves, such as gender, age, class or religion (Scoones and Thompson 1994: 21). The sustainable livelihood approach (e.g. Farrington *et al.* 1999; Scoones 1998) is probably the most well-known in this sense.[11]

5.2 **Basic assumptions and paradigm shift**

A basic assumption made is that if the poor are central to the design and implementation of the development process, they are more responsive (Marsden 1994a: 53). Top-down approaches with a high concentration of power in bureaucracies are unsuited to motivate people outside these organisations (Gran 1983: 14f.). It is also assumed that people-managed bottom-up learning process approaches can impede 'Westernisation' (Martinussen 1997: 348) and lead to a better fit between the programme design, beneficiary needs and the capacities of assisting organisations (Korten 1980: 490).

While top-down approaches are centralised in terms of power and decision-making, bottom-up approaches pay attention to decentralisation and the development of local institutions that are small enough to command authority and promote participation (Marsden 1994a: 53). Top-down approaches also show a high degree of consensus that implementation should happen through existing bureaucratic organisations, while bottom-up approaches emphasise the role of local people (Martinussen 1997: 331). There is a shift from national to local level and from authorities to citizens (Martinussen 1997: 42). Overarching theories are rejected. Instead, the uniqueness of local and individual experience becomes the central focus (Booth 1994). Martinussen (1997: 41f.), for example, therefore calls this kind of development 'development by people' or 'people-managed development'. Gran (1983) has laid the foundations for a comprehensive strategy of 'people-managed development'.[12] The emphasis is shifted away from simply copying the industrial countries towards a focus on building the capacity within poor populations themselves to make and implement decisions in their particular circumstances (Martinussen 1997: 41). Civil-society dynamics are more strongly manifested and have to be given more attention (Martinussen 1997: 341). Instead of seeing Western knowledge as superior, the validity of indigenous technical knowledge, and their ability

---

11 The sustainable livelihood approach is in fact people-centred, but not necessarily driven or managed by the poor (Ellis and Biggs 2001: 442; Mathie and Cunningham 2003a: 7). This is why it is not part of this book. Nevertheless, it would also be interesting to have a closer look at this approach with regard to BoP ventures.

12 The UNDP incorporated this paradigm shift for the first time in its Human Development Report 1993. Other proponents at that time were Korten, Chambers and Friedmann.

to contribute solutions to the problems they confront, is given importance (e.g. Antweiler 1996): the 'voices from below' are considered important (Simon 1997: 183). With this in mind, advocates of the new paradigm are convinced that the poor can lift themselves out of poverty, but in order for them to do so it is important to 'build the capacity to aspire' (Apparundai 2004).

Chambers (1994: 953) mentions three major changes in development:[13] from top-down to bottom-up; from centralised standardisation to local diversity;[14] and from blueprint (planning) to a learning process.[15] The importance of a learning process is also a focal point in Korten's research (1980). Successful programmes emerge out of a learning process with teamwork containing villagers and programme personal. They embrace error, plan with the local people and link knowledge building with action (Korten 1980: 497f.).

However, all these paradigm shifts do not mean that external influence must be removed completely. Endogenous and exogenous approaches are not necessarily mutually exclusive (Nemes 2005: 7f.). A proportion of resources can come from the external side and a central unit, at least for coordination, is mostly still used (Helmsing 2001: 3). In this sense, networks play an important role (Nemes 2005: 7f.).

5.3 **The different approaches**

Martinussen (1997) distinguishes between 'development concept', 'development process', 'development theory' and 'development strategy' (Fig. 5.1).

Figure 5.1 **Systematisation development**
Source: Martinussen 1997: 15

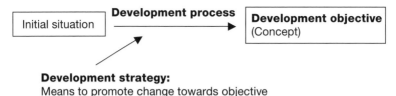

Development theory: hypotheses about promoting and obstructing conditions

Initial situation → **Development process** → **Development objective** (Concept)

Development strategy:
Means to promote change towards objective

---

13 These changes are related to rural development but apply also to urban development.
14 See also Martinussen 1997: 337f.
15 Within blueprint approaches, the project plan is treated as the basic unit of development action. Blueprint approaches have an appealing sense of order, specialisation and recognition of the superordinate role of the intellectual, which makes them easily defensible in budget presentations (Korten 1980: 496f.).

Development concepts contain the answer to what development is for the inventor. This could be the process to move towards greater resemblance with the developed, Western countries. Other concepts focus more on the given conditions in developing countries and define development in terms of bringing out and unfolding what is potentially contained in these societies. Development theories are the stage for expounding how social reality is actually structured—as opposed to development concepts that focus on how it ought to be structured. Theories therefore contain significant normative elements. Development strategy refers essentially to the actions and interventions that can be used to promote development objectives. The development process is the way to reach the set objectives (Martinussen 1997: 14f.).

There is no shortage of bottom-up perspective approaches in development research (Ashley and Maxwell 2001: 396).[16] This is due to influences from different disciplines (e.g. economics, geography, ethnology), different think-tanks, governments and NGOs (Ellis and Biggs 2001: 437). It is not always clear to which category an approach or a theory belongs, as most of the theory construction in development studies has been introduced with no explicit considerations concerning basic ontological, epistemological or methodological positions (Martinussen 1997: 345f.). It should also be noted that much development research is aimed at strategies and practice; there is a lack of reflection on the underlying assumptions of development research (Martinussen 1997: 347). Additionally, no structured overview exists, not even in single disciplines. Approach names are used in some instances as umbrella terms and, at other times, as characteristics of an approach. Furthermore, there is generally no evidence of a clear path in practice; a mix of approaches are used.[17]

Nevertheless, the following predominant approaches are evident in bottom-up literature:[18]

- Community-based/-driven development

- Participation

- Asset-based community development

- Empowerment

- Capacity building and local knowledge

Systematisation is not simple, as it risks oversimplification. Community-based approaches (used synonymously with 'bottom-up') could probably be used as an umbrella term. However, in order not to 'disorder' the literature, this review will be

---

16 Researchers also call their approaches concepts, strategies or theories; but these are not consistent with the terms defined by Martinussen (1997) or those within development literature in general.

17 Statements of NGOs such as Intercooperation and GIZ.

18 Depending on the author, the terms are used as an approach or as part of an approach (term). There are many more development approaches that claim to be 'bottom-up', but to keep it from becoming too complex only the most important ones are described.

consistent with the approach names given by the researchers. The following sections show the basic ideas of each approach and the relationships between the different approaches and terms.

5.3.1 Community-based/-driven development

Community-based development (CBD) is—in line with the World Bank's research—an umbrella term for projects that actively include beneficiaries (the poor) in their design and management, so that they can participate.[19] The concept of community-driven development (CDD) was originally coined by the World Bank[20] and refers to CBD projects in which communities have direct control over key project decisions, including management of investment funds (Mansuri and Rao 2004: 1f.). Mathie and Cunningham (2003a: 13) define the essence of CBD as follows:

> [. . .] community-based development works towards social and economic justice by strengthening the collective power of the disadvantaged and drawing on the strengths of the larger community of which they are a part.

A CBD programme must fulfil the following criteria (Mathie and Cunningham 2003a: 13f.):

- Address the economic and social conditions of people's lives

- Initiate and strengthen the various institutional forms of people organising at a local level

- Link local initiatives to regional, national and global institutions that further local level interests

- Lead to a restructuring of economic and political systems that prejudice those interests

CDD can be defined as follows:

> CDD gives control of decisions and resources to community groups. These groups often work in partnership with demand-responsive support organisations and service providers, including elected local governments, the private sector, NGOs, and central government agencies. CDD is a way to provide social and infrastructure services, organise economic activity

---

19 We will talk about the term 'community' in more detail in Section 5.4.3.
20 According to a conservative calculation, the World Bank's lending for community-driven projects has gone up from US$325 million in 1996 to US$2 billion in 2003. When lending for community-based projects and the enabling of an environment for CDD is included, the amount rises to US$7 billion in 2003 (Mansuri and Rao 2003: 2). Helping to build an enabling environment with the goal of empowering the poor can be crucial for the success of community-driven projects (Binswanger 2004).

and resource management, empower poor people, improve governance, and enhance security of the poorest (Dongier *et al.* 2002: 303f.).

It is an approach that aims to empower communities and local governments with resources, and assign them the authority to use these flexibly (Madavo 2002: 1). Poor people are often viewed as the target of poverty reduction efforts. CDD, in contrast, treats poor people and their institutions as assets and partners in the development process (Dongier *et al.* 2002: 303).

The objective of CDD is to reverse power relations in a manner that creates agency and a voice for the poor, allowing them to gain more control over development assistance:

> This is expected to make the allocation of development funds more responsive to their needs, improve the targeting of poverty programs, make government more responsive, improve the delivery of public goods and services, and strengthen the capabilities of the citizenry to undertake self-initiated development activities (Mansuri and Rao 2004: 2).

CDD has many advantages over other kinds of development approaches. It: enhances sustainability; improves efficiency and effectiveness; allows poverty reduction efforts to be taken to scale; makes development more inclusive; empowers poor people; builds social capital;[21] strengthens governance; complements market and public sector activities; reduces information problems; expands the resources available to the poor; and strengthens the civic capacities of communities (Dongier *et al.* 2002: 304ff.; Mansuri and Rao 2004: 2). CDD does, however, have its disadvantages. If the organised communities are not appropriately strengthened or they exclude the poor, if they cannot finance recurrent costs, if they crowd out local government or are manipulated by vested interests, CDD may not be the optimal strategy (Dongier *et al.* 2002: 308). But:

> While clear rules, transparency, and accountability are important safeguards to prevent corruption or the capture of community resources by elites, the speed and directness with which CDD empowers poor people is rarely matched by other institutional frameworks of poverty reduction (Dongier *et al.* 2002: 308).

In community-driven approaches there is no need for an external initiator (Simanowitz 1997: 129) as local governments and communities are put in the driver's seat with new powers, rights and obligations (Binswanger and Nguyen 2005:

---

21 Social capital can be differentiated between 'bonding' and 'bridging' social capital. While bonding social capital can be detected in the close-knit relations of friends and families, bridging social capital provides leverage in relationships beyond the confines of one's own affinity group, or even beyond the local community (Woolcock and Narayan 2000: 227). Social capital compromises the ability of individuals in a group to form relationships of trust, cooperation and common purpose (Lal 2002). Strengthened social capital helps to reduce household exposure to risk (Dongier *et al.* 2002: 308).

2).[22] There are highly successful projects that do not necessarily access external resource flows. To scale up community-driven approaches, support can be given, for example in terms of information or capacity building and clear rules (Dongier *et al.* 2002: 307–9). But, where appropriate, capacity building should build on existing community strengths, including local organisations, local knowledge and culture-based skills, so that existing capacity is strengthened rather than undermined (Dongier *et al.* 2002: 325).

Community-driven approaches also empower poor people:

> The objective of development is not merely to increase incomes or to improve poverty indicators, but also to expand people's real freedoms (Dongier *et al.* 2002: 307).[23]

Empowerment is widely recognised as an important element of poverty reduction:

> The intent of CDD is to help empower local communities [. . .] to shape their future by giving them more resources and the authority to use these resources to improve their standards of living. Empowering communities is a smart and dignified way to go, and is an integral part of effective poverty reduction strategies (Madavo 2000: 1).

With relevance to empowerment, the World Bank (Madavo 2000: 8ff.) identifies five main dimensions of CDD: empowering communities; empowering local governments; realigning the centre; improving accountability; and building capacity.[24]

The potential of CDD is greatest for projects that are small in scale, not particularly complex and that require local cooperation. Local cooperation is necessary when the project implementers need local know-how or if the project has to be sustained by the communities afterwards. Usually, CDD is used for common pool goods, public goods and civil goods. For private goods, it might be better to rely on individuals rather than on collective community action and use market-based approaches. However, CDD can fill gaps where markets are missing or imperfect (Dongier *et al.* 2002: 304).

5.3.2 Participation

In contrast to CDD, 'participation' must be in relation to something—for example, an external agent or other sections of a community. The concept of 'community participation' relates mostly to the involvement of people in externally initiated and facilitated development interventions (Simanowitz 1997: 128). A useful distinction

---

22 When they are initially put in the driver's seat an external initiator needs to be present.
23 See also Friedmann 1992.
24 Even though the paper of the World Bank (Madavo 2000) is more a 'call' than a 'paper', the five dimensions mentioned were assimilated by other scholars such as Binswanger and Nguyen (2005: 2).

can be made through the goal towards which participation is directed. It can be seen as a means by which something may be improved (for example, project efficiency, cost-effectiveness or sustainability) or as an end in itself (for example, to develop a process where the community controls its own development) (Nelson and Wright 1995: 1). The motivation for this approach is, according to Simanowitz (1997: 128), essentially '. . . based on the premise that communities are not capable of managing their own development'. The active involvement of members of a defined community in at least some aspects of project design and implementation is expected to lead to better-designed projects, better targeted benefits, more cost-effective and timely delivery of project inputs, and more equitably distributed project benefits (Mansuri and Rao 2004: 6). The key objective is the incorporation of local knowledge into the project's decision-making processes (Mansuri and Rao 2004: 6). Oakley *et al.* (1991: 6) even state that real participation involves equality in decision-making throughout the whole project cycle—assessment, planning, implementation and evaluation.

The main characteristics of participation are, according to Mansuri and Rao (2004: 6), the following:

- Active involvement of beneficiaries

- Incorporation of local knowledge

- Beneficiaries make decisions, which leads to empowerment

Participatory rural appraisal (PRA) is probably the best known method of fostering participation by the poor. It '. . . describes a growing family of methods and approaches to enable local people to share, enhance and analyze their knowledge of life and conditions, to plan and to act' (Chambers 1994: 953). Even though PRA is a process mainly used for problem analysis in a certain community, it can be extended into analysis, planning and action. It is seen to be a cost-effective method for integrating the poor (Chambers 1994: 956). Mathie and Cunningham (2002: 15) also propose to use this method for the identification and mobilisation of community strengths and capacities, as well as for research and analysis of the community development process. Even though the method is called 'rural' appraisal, it can also be used for urban areas (Chambers 1994: 959).

There are also challenges posed when the poor participate in projects. The process of including the 'voices of the poor' can be timely and costly. Participation may lead to psychological stress for the most socially and economically disadvantaged, as they may want to take positions that are contrary to the interests of powerful groups, but are afraid to articulate them (Mansuri and Rao 2004: 6f.). Cooke and Kothari (2001) edited a book in which they criticise the practice of participation due to its potential to reinforce existing inequalities, and the limited knowledge of power relations.[25] In general, participatory projects are more successful in more developed economies than in less developed as the broader institutional environ-

25 This issue is described in further detail in Section 5.4.2.

ment plays an important role and institutional support is important (Mansuri and Rao 2004: 15ff.).

5.3.3 Asset-based community development

Asset-based community development (ABCD) is an approach, a set of methods for community mobilisation and a strategy for CBD and CDD (Mathie and Cunningham 2002: 5). It arises from criticism about need-based approaches. Kretzmann and McKnight's criticism (1993) is that the needs and problems of the poor are focused in order to attract resources. This in turn can lead to a feeling of hopelessness and a situation in which the poor subsequently view themselves as incapable of initiating positive change. Additionally, community members no longer act like citizens. Instead, they begin to act like 'clients' with no incentive to be producers. The argument of Kretzmann and McKnight in turn is that communities can drive the development process themselves by identifying and mobilising existing but often unrecognised assets. These assets can contain personal attributes and skills, relationships between people, and informal networks (Kretzmann and McKnight 1993). A focus is put on social assets—the gifts and talents of individuals, and the social relationships that fuel local associations and informal networks (Mathie and Cunningham 2002: 3). Therefore, ABCD takes as its starting point the existing assets and strengths of a community (Mathie and Cunningham 2003b: 474).

First, the poor must be aware of their situation and possibilities. Gran (1983: 150) understands underdevelopment as a 'state of mind' and opts for 'conscientisation', which is a process through which people—not as passive recipients but as knowing and active citizens—achieve a deeper understanding of the social reality that shapes their lives and of their capabilities to transform that reality (Gran 1983: 155ff.). These capabilities and assets have to be recognised within a perspective in which communities can '. . . begin to assemble their strengths into new combinations, new structures of opportunity, new sources of income and control, and new possibilities for production' (Kretzmann and McKnight 1993: 6). Within an ABCD approach, communities are transformed from 'clients' of services to 'designers' of community programmes and, finally 'producers' of community (Kretzmann and McKnight 1999).

Assets are more than just resources with instrumental value for economic purposes. Drawing on the work of Amartya Sen, Anthony Giddens and Jürgen Habermas, Bebbington (1999) argues that assets also give people the capacity or potential to act, and thus are a source of engagement with the world. However, to activate the assets, the poor need to have access to them. That is why social capital is of crucial importance to provide access to other assets.

5.3.4 Empowerment

The goal to empower the poor has already been mentioned in some of the approaches above, but empowerment is also itself considered an approach. It builds on the premise that the poor have been widely excluded from state and economy and goes in the same direction as CDD. It places the emphasis on autonomy in the decision-making of territorially organised communities, local self-reliance (but not autarchy), direct (participatory) democracy and experiential social learning. Its starting point is always the locality, because civil society is most readily mobilised around local issues (Friedmann 1992).

> Empowerment is the expansion of assets and capabilities of poor people to participate in, negotiate with, influence, control, and hold accountable institutions that affect their lives (Narayan 2002: xviii).

Empowerment expands the freedom of choice and action to shape one's life. This implies control over resources and decisions (Narayan 2002: xviii). Taking the traditional model of power, the process of empowerment is about people gaining the ability to undertake activities, to set their own agendas and change events (Crawley 1999: 26).

5.3.5 Capacity building and local knowledge

To give more power to the poor in their development processes, they need to have the capacity to make and implement decisions. According to these notions of development, a society exhibits development primarily in the form of better abilities and greater capacity to make decisions and implement them effectively (Martinussen 1997: 41). The attention given to building autonomous capacity can be viewed as an attempt to reduce the ethnocentrism that so strongly characterises top-down approaches (Martinussen 1997: 41f.). The World Bank (1998: i) points out that no single definition exists in literature for local knowledge. Nevertheless, some factors distinguish it from knowledge in general: it is unique to a particular culture and society; it is embedded in community practices, institutions, relationships and rituals; it is the basis for local decision-making; and it is essentially tacit knowledge that is not easily codifiable (World Bank 1998: i). Local knowledge refers to a '. . . dynamic process of acquisition and integration of contemporary information and experience' (Antweiler 1996: 7). It consists of factual knowledge, skills and capabilities. It is culturally situated and best understood as a 'social product' (Antweiler 1996: 1). As Chambers (1983: 83) points out, knowledge refers to the whole system of knowledge, including concepts, beliefs and perceptions, the stock of knowledge, and the processes whereby it is acquired, augmented, stored and transmitted. Local knowledge is often only transmitted orally, is experimental rather than theoretical, often learned through repetition and is constantly changing (World Bank 1998: 2). Local knowledge does not have to refer to a specific location but it has to be culturally and ecologically integrated (Antweiler 1996: 17). Local knowledge is constructed through people's practices as 'situated agents', where 'situated' refers to the cultural context and 'agents' refers to actively generated (Scoones and Thompson 1994: 19). Local knowledge also provides the basis for problem-solving strategies in local communities. Learning from local knowledge can improve understanding of local conditions and provide a productive context for activities designed to help communities (World Bank 1998: i).

Scoones and Thompson (1994: 17f.) detect three ways in which the knowledge of the poor can be seen:

- Local knowledge is 'primitive', 'unscientific' and 'wrong'. Outsiders must 'educate', 'direct' and 'transform' such knowledge in order to 'develop' it

- Local knowledge is a 'valuable and under-utilised resource' and needs to be intensively and extensively studied so that it an be 'incorporated' into formal research in order to make development strategies more 'sustainable'

- Neither local knowledge nor Western science is superior. They represent contrasting multiple epistemologies produced within particular contexts

After years of assuming that Western knowledge is superior to all other knowledge, the value of local knowledge—along with its significant development potential—has been acknowledged by most scholars since the late 1970s (Agrawal 1995: 1; Antweiler 1996: 1; Scoones and Thompson 1994: 18; Sillitoe 2004: 6; Simon 1997: 185). Internationally, the term 'indigenous knowledge' is widespread and has come to be used in a political context as 'non-Western' or 'anti-Western' knowledge, or the knowledge of minorities (Agrawal 1995: 2; Antweiler 1996: 4). Originally, however, 'indigenous' was equivalent to 'local' or 'folk' or, when applied to knowledge, 'informal knowledge' (Antweiler 1996: 4).[26] Local knowledge is local to the extent that it is acquired and applied by people with respect to local objectives, situations and problems. Problem solutions, which are based on local knowledge, draw on locally available resources (Antweiler 1996: 17).

While in capacity building, knowledge comes from outside and is 'taught' to the poor, local knowledge focuses on working with the poor and extracting the knowledge already in place (Simon 1997: 185). To what extent external knowledge (and information) needs to be introduced and integrated into local knowledge systems has to be defined in every context (Antweiler 1996: 2).

What implications do bottom-up development approaches have for the BoP concept? BoP literature does not articulate when a bottom-up approach is appropriate and when it is not. The literature that advocates bottom-up approaches implies that this is the strategy to use in general (e.g. Simanis and Hart 2008). Is a bottom-up strategy more successful in more developed countries and regions? For what kind of goods and services is a bottom-up approach the route? The various

---

26 In line with Antweiler's (1996: 4f.) and Agrawal's (1995: 2) theses, in this book the term 'local knowledge' is used, even if original articles talk about 'indigenous knowledge'. The term 'indigenous' has political connotations leading to a clear separation between 'Western' and 'indigenous' knowledge. There are several reasons, however, why the two forms of knowledge are not as different as assumed. For an overview of different terms used see Antweiler 1996: 5.

elements contained in bottom-up development approaches will be examined in further detail in the next section.

5.4 **Bottom-up development elements**

The bottom-up development approaches presented above show many similarities and the general mindset appears to be the same. Some distinctions can be detected, however. Nevertheless—no matter how the approaches are labelled—certain elements are present within them all:

- Real participation
- Power relations and 'elite capture'
- Community and targeting
- Local knowledge as base for capacity building
- Ownership
- Networks
- Scaling up the process

Based on an extensive literature review, these fields were defined because of their frequency of appearance in development literature. Practically all input from bottom-up development literature fits into those categories. While some areas focus more on the initial situation for development (power relations and elite capture; community and targeting; local knowledge as base for capacity building; networks), others focus more on the development process (real participation; power relations and elite capture; capacity building; scaling up the process; networks) or on the development objectives (real participation; ownership; scaling up the process).[27] Bearing in mind the research questions and the objectives of this research, the seven elements mentioned above can be assumed to play an important role when establishing a BoP venture. Potential drivers, circumstances and success factors when applying a bottom-up development perspective in BoP ventures can be identified within all elements. It is along this line that further questions (derived from bottom-up development literature) will be developed (in order to test them in BoP ventures) in the following section.

27 These are the categories already mentioned in Section 5.3.

5.4.1 Real participation

The different approaches in bottom-up development treat the poor and their institutions as assets and partners in the development process, not only as targets of
poverty reduction efforts (Dongier *et al.* 2002: 303). Within the ABCD approach, the
identity of communities shifts from 'clients' of services to 'designers' of community
programmes and, finally, to 'producers' of community (Kretzmann and McKnight
1999). However, Long and Villareal (1994) state that most approaches that promote
development 'from below' do not escape the managerialist and interventionist
undertones inherent in development work, tending to evoke the image of 'more
knowledgeable and powerful outsiders' helping 'the powerless and less discerning
local folk' (Long and Villareal 1994: 51).

Chambers (1983: 141) also criticises the practice of participation as a 'paternal
trap':

> However much the rhetoric changes to 'participation', 'participatory
> research', 'community involvement' and the like, at the end of the day there
> is still an outsider seeking to change things. Marxist, socialist, capitalist,
> Muslim, Christian, Hindu, Buddhist, humanist, male, female, young, old,
> national, foreigner, black, brown, white—*who* the outsider is may change
> but the relation is the same. A stronger person wants to change things for
> a person who is weaker.

Chambers sees no complete escape from this 'paternal trap', but nevertheless
there is partial remedy. to respect the poor and what they want, starting with their
priorities and wishes, and to make an effort to detect them (Chambers 1983: 141).

Real participation involves equality in decision-making throughout the whole
project cycle. Citizens have to be involved at every stage and level (Binswanger and
Aryar 2003: 10; Oakley *et al.* 1991). This involvement leads to collective choices of
development plans and expenditures (Binswanger and Aryar 2003: 9). Empowerment even places the emphasis on 'autonomy in the decision-making of territorially organised communities' (Friedmann 1992). It is necessary that no information
gaps exist between the poor and the facilitators so that decisions are made on the
same basis. In the same way, choices should be made from a fully informed perspective in which a full representation of all interests exists (Binswanger and Aryar
2003: 10; Dongier *et al.* 2002: 307; Mansuri and Rao 2004: 14). For participatory
approaches, it is important that the host country is itself committed to become
more participatory, responsive and transparent (Mansuri and Rao 2004: 29).

'Putting the last first' (Chambers 1983) is the notion taken within participation.
But this alone is not enough:

> [. . .] to put the last first is the easier half. Putting the first last is harder
> (Chambers 1997: 2).

External facilitators and development workers have to step back and be 'disem-
powered' at the same time (Chambers 1997: 2). Mathie and Cunningham (2002: 15)
call this 'leading by stepping back'. With the goal of empowerment in mind, where

people's capacity to transform their lives is increased, participation must be more than merely participating in meetings (Guijt and Shah 1999: 11).

In BoP 1.0 literature the poor are seen essentially as consumers—as a target group (e.g. Prahalad and Hammond 2002). However, Hart (2007: 156) and Seelos and Mair (2006: 11) defend a broader role for the poor within the BoP concept where they are seen not only as customers but as a vital and integral part of the business model. This is also consistent with the conclusion of Gardetti and D'Andrea (2010: 87) who state that early BoP strategies are based on a 'basic needs' development approach, which defines poverty and underdevelopment as a form of material deprivation below a given level. Developing supplementary and broader programmes in which the poor also participate promotes skills, in addition to income. Thus, BoP 2.0 strategies move in the same direction as bottom-up development approaches by having the poor participate in the innovation process and seeing them not just as a target group. However, it is not only about integrating the poor; the way in which they are integrated is also important. Thus far in BoP literature, only the BoP Protocol discusses in more detail how the poor are, or should be, integrated: this is principally about their participation in workshops and in project implementation (Simanis and Hart 2008). According to (Prahalad and Ramaswamy 2004: 6) co-creation means neither a transfer nor an outsourcing of activities to customers. But should the poor be integrated into the *whole* innovation process? How much participation is feasible? To what extent can equality in decision-making and the related information sharing be assured? Is it possible to transfer activities completely to the BoP? Are company representatives willing to step back in order to let the projects be led by the BoP?

The BoP participants have to represent the entire breadth of the community (Binswanger and Aryar 2003: 10). Guijt and Shah (1999: 3) highlight the importance of gender issues within participation;[28] the presence of women at community gatherings does not mean that their issues and meanings are being included. For real participation, therefore, the representing individuals do not only have to be present but also must articulate their real opinions. Participation addresses the issue of structural inequalities within communities. However, very powerful sections of the community often dominate these processes and it is difficult to overcome the prevailing inequalities (Simanowitz 1997: 131).[29]

To have an impact, the act of participation has to be well defined in projects.[30] Usually, anything participatory is assumed to be synonymous with 'good' and 'empowering' (Guijt and Shah 1999: 9). Participation of the poor can vary between 0% and 100%—where 0% is no participation and 100% would mean total local control over the whole process. However, according to Guijt and Shah (1999: 10), the concept of 100% participation is a myth. The local political context will strongly

---

28 This research is not dedicated to gender issues and does not go into detail here. For an in-depth overview on gender issues and participation see Guijt and Shah 1999.

29 More on this issue in Section 5.4.2.

30 Possibilities for typologisation in Guijt and Shah 1999: 9f.

influence both the intensity and form of participation. While clustering the myriad forms of participation into categories can hinder innovation, it is more important to describe how different players are participating and why those forms have been chosen. Participation in a research context, for example, is different to participation in an action context (Guijt and Shah 1999: 10).

Most BoP authors do not mention the degree of integration of the poor into innovation processes. According to London's principles (2007: 27), participation should be higher than 0% (as 0% would mean no local participation at all) but lower than 100% (as 100% would mean absolutely no external participation by a company). Moreover, bottom-up development literature does not stipulate how much participation is necessary or its form. Does success therefore depend not so much on the grade of participation but, rather, on the form and representativeness of the community within the process? Can the representation of *all* interests be assured?

The more the communities and their individuals participate, the more they lead the process and the more important governance becomes. With governance comes the impact of power relations and the avoidance of elite capture.

5.4.2 Power relations and elite capture

In the extreme, decentralisation of poverty programmes can worsen local inequality and perpetuate current local power relations. This is especially the case in communities where mobility is low and power hierarchies are deeply entrenched. Institutions and mechanisms to ensure local accountability, and a deep sense of the local structures of power, are therefore crucial (Apparundai 2004; Mansuri and Rao 2004: 9f.). Parties involved in development processes can be differentiated in terms of relations of power. Development can be seen as a transaction process involving different actors and negotiation over divergent goals (Scoones and Thompson 1994: 20ff.). This involves a shift away from the focus of empowerment to one that views empowerment more as 'management of power when in the hands of the powerful' (Leal 1997). The incentives for project implementers (local or external ones) should be aligned with the needs of the project—something that is often not the case in practice (Mansuri and Rao 2004: 2). Clear rules, transparency and accountability help to prevent corruption (Dongier *et al.* 2002: 308).

As already critiqued by Black (2006: 52), the issue of power is not well addressed in BoP literature, raising some intriguing questions. Is a deep sense of local power structures needed in BoP ventures? Do managers need to manage the power when it is shifted to communities? Are incentives important to align the activities with the needs of the project?

There are many links between powerlessness and poverty. Those who have power at the local level are often described as 'the elite'. They are relatively well off in assets and income, are physically strong and healthy, have security, and are at the local centre of things—spatially, socially and politically. Local elites stand as barriers between their poorer neighbours and the outside world (Chambers 1983: 131).

Inequalities, oppressive social hierarchies and discrimination are often overlooked, and instead, enthusiasm is generated for the cooperative and harmonious ideal promised by the imagery of 'community' (Guijt and Shah 1999: 7f.).

Studies show that the more educated, better-networked and better-informed members of a community—the elite—profit more from bottom-up development projects (Simanowitz 1997: 129). When resources and benefits are caught and trapped, this can be termed 'elite capture' (Chambers 1983: 131; Mansuri and Rao 2004: 19). Donors want the poor to become organised, but they usually do not know much about the local hierarchies. This information gap can be misused by the local elites (Platteau and Gaspart 2003: 1691). The risk is especially high when self-conscious, organised local communities do not exist prior to new programmes (Platteau and Gaspart 2003: 1689).

Local governments can easily become an instrument for elite capture and corruption at the local level. In strong, empowered communities with a strong local private sector, this risk is minimised (Binswanger 2004: 6). The analysis of World Bank projects shows the main limitations to be the lack of capacity building and a lack of ownership of the projects by the beneficiary groups. This is often due to time constraints and impatience—which is necessary for bottom-up projects. In this way, benefits are likely to be largely pre-empted by local elites (Platteau and Gaspart 2003: 1687). Especially in community-driven development programmes, where mostly all resources are channelled down to the local level, problems of elite capture may arise. Because of the limited time available, when communities are asked to choose a leader to receive resources to distribute they often choose a member of a local elite. Furthermore, there is often an explosive growth of local NGOs created by educated unemployed individuals, politicians or state employees who may have been laid off and who now act as local 'development brokers' to receive distributed funds (Platteau and Gaspart 2003: 1688).

To hinder the richer members of a community capturing the benefits of bottom-up development projects, financial incentives should be kept low (Jalan and Ravallion 2003: 22). The poor have to be enabled to '. . . mobilise and organise, to demand, gain and maintain control over assets and income' (Chambers 1983: 140). However, the acceptability to local and other elites of programmes to combat powerlessness is often weak, as they do not want to lose their status (Chambers 1983: 164). Platteau and Gaspart (2003) suggest a leader-disciplining mechanism (LDM) framework, which is based on game theory, to control the leader. This includes an option to punish him (or her) and the game must be repeated.[31] Also, to avoid elite capture, training for the less informed and educated members of a community is crucial (Simanowitz 1997: 129).

The BoP literature has, so far, not spoken much about elite capture. Individuals pertaining to the 'elite' are called 'gatekeepers' in the BoP Protocol. Simanis and

---

31 For details see Platteau and Gaspart 2003.

Hart (2008: 21) point out that, by choosing a project team, a company has to be sure to enquire into, and highlight, the community's unique strengths and knowledge. To ensure they do not create a group of 'gatekeepers', the team should use PRA techniques such as social and institutional mapping. This highlights the variability in the community across poverty, caste, occupation, access to resources and age.

Thus, we can assume that elite capture is also an issue in BoP ventures. Is the risk of elite capture also higher when self-conscious, organised local communities do not exist prior to new programmes? Can one avoid elite capture by selecting a variety of persons that represent the pluralism within the targeted community? Is the risk lower within strong, empowered communities with a strong local private sector? Are transparency, accountability, capacity building, more ownership and low enough wages effective instruments to avoid elite capture?

To know more about power relations and the potential of elite capture, one has to take a closer look at the community. This leads to more precise targeting of the beneficiaries and their needs.

5.4.3 Community and targeting

Community

Bottom-up projects are usually implemented in a unit referred to as a 'community' which is the target group of poverty alleviation efforts. Most literature on development uses the term without much qualification to '. . . denote a culturally and politically homogeneous social system or one that at least implicitly is internally cohesive and more or less harmonious, such as an administratively defined locale (tribal area or neighborhood) or a common interest group (community of weavers or potters)' (Mansuri and Rao 2004: 8). This superficial notion of community is problematic as it obscures local structures of economic and social power that are likely to influence project outcomes. Community is itself an abstract social construct (Mansuri and Rao 2004: 8f.).

Advocates of bottom-up development often describe indigenous communities as sites of social homogeneity, harmony and consensus (Natcher and Hickey 2002: 350). As scholars have shown, communities are not homogenous entities but rather sites of pluralism with a range of ideological positions, and that is why several parts of the community have been previously overlooked, leading to a softened top-downism (Natcher and Hickey 2002: 351). Communities are seen as fluid, dynamic and differentiated, rather than static and homogenous (Mathie and Cunningham 2003a: 14).[32]

---

32 In fact, there is substantial literature that examines the relationship between heterogeneity and the capacity for collective action. Certain types of inequality might even favour the provision of public goods. Collective action is more difficult to mobilise in very homogenous groups, because no individual can make a significant difference. More unequal groups might do better, even though those with fewer interests would free-ride (Baland and Platteau 1999; Oliver *et al.* 1985; Olson 1973; Platteau 2003).

According to Binswanger and Nguyen (2005: 1), a community can be a group of people with a common residence or a group of people with a common interest. Guijt and Shah (1999: 268) put it as follows:

> It refers to a geographic collective (as compared to a generic use of community such as in 'the global community', 'the gay community', etc.): a group of people who live (full and/or part-time) in a locality and are connected by a web of emotional, economic and/or relational bonds and a culture, and share a set of values, norms, and meanings. Within the community, there are, of course, social sub-groups who share sub-sets of values, norms and meanings.

All the complexity of thought on society and culture of the targeted communities have to be brought in to inform the design of development practice. The question, whether large development organisations can apply these complex notions, remains (Mansuri and Rao 2004: 9f.). To overcome this barrier, local institutions and organisations, which have the experience and knowledge needed to adapt the general rules to the local context, should be integrated. If outsiders themselves want to learn more about a poor community, 'total immersion' seems the best way to go. This means spending a lot of time living in communities to understand them better (Chambers 1983). Conning and Kevane (2002) discovered that communities with relatively egalitarian preferences, relatively open and transparent systems of decision-making or clear rules for determining who is poor will tend to be more effective.

Expressions such as 'engaging the community' (Mendoza and Thelen 2008: 442) or 'targeting the community as customer' (Hammond *et al.* 2007: 10) in BoP literature suggest that the 'poor community' is seen as one unit and target group. Arora and Romijn (2009: 17) criticise the uncritical use of the term 'community' within the BoP literature:

> Communities of the poor are romanticised as replete with entrepreneurial individuals ready to team up with a TNC [transnational corporation] and its local non-governmental partners.

If we follow the logic of bottom-up development literature, their critique is completely comprehensible. But is sufficient attention paid to this in BoP ventures that take a bottom-up approach? Is there a risk of ignoring sub-groups, which are often the poorest? Are local structures of economic and social power that influence project outcomes obscured? Do managers monitor and evaluate community pluralism and implement an effective and inclusive approach?

Targeting

Development projects are intended to target the poorest areas. Defining where the poorest areas are is not always easy. Chase (2002), in his research about the Armenia Social Fund, determined that areas with the poorest infrastructure, for example, were not always the poorest areas. The fund under observation required a community contribution. This may have led to a selection bias against the poorest communities, as they are often unwilling or unable to contribute.[33] Badly organised communities are less likely to obtain projects and are more likely to mismanage projects that are allocated to them (Mansuri and Rao 2004: 17). The collective action should not have any negative net benefits for members of a community (Heckathorn 1993: 343), which means that they should not have invested more (time, money) than they will obtain from collective action outputs. But, even if the poorest areas are detected, it does not mean that the poorest households within these areas are targeted effectively (Pradhan and Rawlings 2002).

One of the previously mentioned advantages of bottom-up approaches is that the match between the needs and wants of a community and what they receive is improved. This can be called 'preference targeting' (Dongier *et al.* 2002: 307; Mansuri and Rao 2004: 13) and causes development to be demand-driven. However, there is little reliable evidence on preference targeting in practice as panel data with baseline information on major problems faced by the community would be required (Mansuri and Rao 2004: 13). In a study by Rao and Ibanez (2005) on the Jamaica Social Investment Fund, it transpired that better-educated and better-networked people (i.e. the elite) were more likely to attract projects that matched their preferences. The individuals who were not part of the elite often have less access to project implementers and may be constrained by information gaps (Mansuri and Rao, 2004: 14). Access-type disadvantages are usually visible and quantifiable results of uneven development, which is based on imperfect resources. The varying types of access are physical, economic and political (Nemes 2005: 12). Effective targeting is more successfully reached if communities have a high mobility (no fixed power relations), egalitarian preferences, open and transparent systems of decision-making, clear rules to decide who is poor, are not too isolated and land equality (Mansuri and Rao 2004: 10f.).

Hammond *et al.* (2007) conducted extensive research on the different market segments and sectors within the BoP market. The poorest segment of a population is seldom chosen for BoP ventures. Are they also left out of the innovation process? Is a bottom-up approach in BoP projects chosen to foster the match between what the community wants and what it gets? Who has to be integrated to reach this goal? Which circumstances in the target community are favourable to enter more easily and effectively?

The mechanisms used to identify beneficiaries are crucial in determining whether the poor are targeted (Mansuri and Rao 2004: 13). Involving the community in selecting beneficiaries of development projects has become increasingly common as incorporating their knowledge can improve targeting (Mansuri and Rao 2004: 10). But it is not only the people in the communities in general who are very heterogeneous; this is also true of their knowledge.

---

33 However, as we will see later in Section 5.4.5, asking for a contribution leads to ownership and therefore a more sustainable project. In very poor areas, this contribution could be in the form of time/work instead of a financial contribution.

5.4.4 Local knowledge as a base for capacity building

Local knowledge is relevant to all bottom-up development projects as it begins where people are instead of where others want them to be (Marsden 1994b: 46). Even though development workers often think that their knowledge is superior (Chambers 1983: 76), local assets and knowledge is seen as an important source when it comes to solving poverty problems (Sillitoe 2004: 6). In most developing countries, local knowledge is an enormous and under-utilised resource, and its positive potential for development processes remains widely unused (Antweiler 1996: 3; Chambers 1983: 92). Decentralisation efforts—crucial to bottom-up development—need local capacity, and the base for local capacity is local knowledge (Antweiler 1996: 2). The potential benefits of local knowledge for development projects are not always obvious in a given situation. The World Bank (1998: 8) points out the following advantages of local knowledge:

- Local knowledge can provide problem-solving strategies for local communities

- Learning from local knowledge can improve understanding of local conditions

- Understanding local knowledge can increase responsiveness to clients

- Building on local experiences, judgements and practices can increase the impact of a development programme

- Local approaches to development can help to create a sense of ownership that may have a longer lasting impact on relations between the local population and the local administration

- Local knowledge can provide a building block for the empowerment of the poor

However, local knowledge is often also instrumentalised and idealised as being more sustainable (Antweiler 1996: 3). Chambers (1983: 75) even goes as far as saying:

> Rural people's knowledge is often superior to that of outsiders.

The diversity and dynamics of, as well as changes to, local knowledge have to be understood as part of the respective cultural system (Antweiler 1996: 14), and it is important to see the ecological, cultural and social context in which that local knowledge is located (Antweiler 1996: 6). Local knowledge may compromise fixed and structured knowledge, which can be articulated (what is known) as well as a more fluid process of knowing (how something is known) (Antweiler 1996: 9). Within a broader definition of local knowledge, less conscious or unwritten knowledge can also be included—making it equally important (Antweiler 1996: 17). It is necessary to analyse the ways in which knowledge is generated, exchanged, transformed, consolidated, stored, retrieved, disseminated and utilised (Marsden

1994a: 55). Furthermore, knowledge can be of a declarative, procedural or complex nature. Table 5.2 illustrates the differences.

Table 5.2 **Forms of knowledge**

Source: Adapted from Antweiler/Mersmann 1996: page 11

General forms of knowledge	Examples
1. Declarative knowledge	
1.1 Factual knowledge	Animals, plants, temperature, social status, prices, salaries, administrative levels
1.2 Categorical knowledge	Categories of organisms, colours, kinship, development project types
2. Procedural knowledge	
2.1 General processes, rules	Farming calendar, religious calendar, environmental crises, household cycle, development project cycle
2.2 Specific processes, schemes and plans	Everyday routines, natural resource management, ritual sequences, project request schema
3. Complex knowledge (concepts, belief systems, knowledge systems)	Cosmology, therapies, cropping systems, decision-making procedures

As local knowledge always has a history and is synchronically dynamic, according to Antweiler (1996: 13) it is important with respect to a given community to distinguish between:

- Present knowledge stock, pool and knowledge products
- Present spatial and social distribution of knowledge
- Initial acquisition of knowledge through innovation or diffusion
- Social transmission of knowledge, e.g. by socialisation
- Specific knowledge processes

The poor themselves can also analyse their own situations and possibilities as well as drive development processes using their local knowledge. As they have to survive in extreme conditions, they usually cannot afford inaccurate observations or misleading inferences. For Madavo (2000: 4), existing capacity is best defined as the ability to solve problems:

> People who have survived by trying to solve problems in difficult economic and political conditions have considerable capacity to put their experience and skills to work, once they are empowered.

The experimental nature of their knowledge can be used for innovative solutions (Chambers 1983: 89ff.).

The local population readily accepts solutions obtained through local knowledge as they are linked to familiar information and methods, and the knowledge is diffused via established media, mostly verbal (Antweiler 1996: 28). In contrast to this, external (especially scientific) knowledge is often met with silent opposition from locals, even though they might cooperate in the process (Antweiler 1996: 32). Also, solutions developed through local knowledge tend to be labour-intensive and require less material, which keeps capital costs, external inputs and dependency low (Antweiler 1996: 28; World Bank 1998: 7).

These are actually also advantages for companies entering BoP markets. But even though BoP literature agrees on the importance of building on assets and knowledge available in poor communities (Hart 2007; London and Hart 2004: 350; Seelos and Mair 2006), it scarcely digs deeper into the research on local knowledge and its benefits. Is local knowledge a driver to find innovative, environmentally friendly solutions, or even disruptive innovations with BoP ventures? Should companies take care not to idealise or instrumentalise local knowledge? Do they want to keep dependency low? Only Sharma and Hart (2006: 11) mention that generating knowledge through fringe stakeholders requires that companies develop a capability to tap into new types of knowledge. The needs, aspirations, interactions and factors that will afford credibility can be contained in these new types of knowledge. Knowledge can also be tacit or unwritten (Hart and Sharma 2004: 12). Some of this knowledge is integrated when companies integrate the poor in their processes, as happens in the BoP Protocol (Simanis and Hart 2008). Do companies have to discover and analyse all local knowledge available (tacit and explicit)? Is this easier within a decentralised organisation structure? Is it necessary to analyse the ways in which knowledge is generated, exchanged, transformed, consolidated, stored, retrieved, disseminated and utilised? To be successful in BoP markets, the poor must be willing to consume, distribute or sell a product or service of a company, and the products and services have to be culturally acceptable. Does the target group really accept products and services more readily when they are obtained through local knowledge?

The drawback of using local knowledge, however, is that validity is often locally restricted and cannot (or only with difficulty) be transferred into other local contexts (Antweiler 1996: 28). If local knowledge needs to be disseminated, because of its dynamic nature, it is therefore useful to describe the relevant social, economic, cultural and ecological processes (Antweiler 1996: 19).

> The process of making use of the knowledge available is a societal one, which requires more than documentation or the integration of some local ideas into the respective project concepts of development agencies (Antweiler 1996: 34).

If local knowledge needs to be used in another context, it cannot simply be transferred into that context, but needs to be adapted to fit it (Antweiler 1996: 30).

Do BoP innovations based on local knowledge have to be adapted to be scaled up in a new context? If so, how?

It is often wrongly assumed that local knowledge is evenly distributed within a community and that practically every member of the group shares the same knowledge (Antweiler 1996: 7). The poor's knowledge in a community can be conflicting and divergent (Scoones and Thompson 1994: 21). Depending on the power structures, local knowledge is more visible to outsiders than others (Scoones and Thompson 1994: 22).[34] Knowledge is held, controlled and generated by different people in a community (Scoones and Thompson 1994: 25). Should companies therefore consider carefully the members of the community from whom the local knowledge is gleaned and verify that this favours the poor in their BoP venture?

Local knowledge can be a productive contribution to development as long as the acquisition and social distribution of knowledge within the community takes place effectively (Antweiler 1996: 33). The use of local knowledge should, however, be led by local communities and not by outsiders. It is not enough to simply listen to locals, their active participation throughout the planning and implementation process is also essential (Antweiler 1996: 37). Khwaja (2001) ascertained that community participation in technical decisions reduced the quality of infrastructure maintenance, whereas community participation in non-technical decisions significantly improved maintenance of infrastructure projects.

For outsiders it is not easy to learn from local knowledge due to the difficulties of codifying it and understanding its cultural context (Scoones and Thompson 1994: 21). Western science is often incapable of appreciating the local knowledge of poor communities (World Bank 1998: 13).

> Besides power, professionalism, prestige, lack of contact, problems of language, and sheer prejudice, another factor is the gap between practitioner and academic cultures (Chambers 1983: 83).

Analysing the interfaces between local and 'external' knowledge is therefore crucial (Long and Villareal 1994: 43f.).[35] The World Bank (1998: ii) proposes six steps to exchange local knowledge:

- Recognition and identification (technical and social analyses may be required as some knowledge is unrecognisable at first glance to outsiders)

- Validation (assessment of significance and relevance, reliability, functionality, effectiveness and transferability)

- Recording and documentation (very important because most is tacit)

- Storage in retrievable repositories

---

34 People with more power often hide their knowledge from others in a community (Scoones and Thompson 1994: 27).

35 For more information on interfaces see Long and Villareal 1994.

- Transfer (includes also testing of the knowledge in the new environment and eventually adapting it)

- Dissemination to a wider community

When outsiders perceive a lack of local capacity, this is often a reflection of the fact that what local people want is different from what central planners want. This does not mean that skill development is not required at all, but it should be demand-driven and not imposed from above (Madavo 2000: 4). The goal is that the poor themselves can make 'informed choices' (Mansuri and Rao, 2004: 15ff.). The process of bottom-up development and community control of resources requires a level of local skills and experience in the use of those resources, which is often lacking (Simanowitz 1007: 128). It is necessary to define to what extent external knowledge needs to be introduced and integrated into a local knowledge system (Antweiler 1996: 2). In order to motivate communities for collective action, helping them to understand the collective benefits of participation may be required. Also, at the end of projects, marginal inputs and training to sustain project outputs might be necessary (Mansuri and Rao 2004: 18). Training a core cadre of facilitators—whether locals or outsiders—is, in any case, crucial, as they have a pivotal role in the success of community-based interventions (Mansuri and Rao 2004: 29).

Capacity building should build on existing community strengths, including local organisations, local knowledge and culture-based skills, so that existing capacity is strengthened rather than undermined and the external knowledge is accepted (Antweiler 1996: 32; Dongier *et al.* 2002: 325). This also applies to new technologies introduced into poor areas, as they should be built on current ones. If this is not the case, the poor become dependent on the provider (Korten 1980: 499). The adaptation of global (external) knowledge to a local community only works if it is adapted to local practice. A key factor in the process is the involvement of those community members who possess the local knowledge (World Bank 1998: 3).

Hart (2007: 21f.) argues for '. . . the development of new "native" capabilities that enable a company to develop fully contextualised solutions to real problems in ways that respect local culture and natural diversity'. When combined with MNCs' ability to provide technical resources, investment and global learning, native capability can enable companies to become truly embedded in the local context. But in which kind of projects is it better to build on local knowledge and when is it more important to rely on the company's own knowledge? Is involving the poor's knowledge a more viable strategy in non-technical decisions than in technical decisions? How is knowledge best exchanged? Do managers or the local communities better lead the use of local knowledge? If capacity building is necessary, should it build on existing local knowledge? And should new technologies build on existing ones?

In any case, the more the poor can contribute to projects with what they have (knowledge, skills, time, etc.) the more they will feel responsible for the project. This leads to a certain level of ownership.

5.4.5 Ownership

It is crucial to distinguish between local and external control of development processes. The links and relations between local actors and external actors should be
clearly specified. This approach recasts endogenous and exogenous concerns into
the analysis of power relations (Lowe *et al.* 1995). Empowering the poor means
giving them control over resources, project and programme designs, as well as
selection, implementation and monitoring, and evaluation (Binswanger and Aryar
2003: 10). In a study about water supply, Katz and Sara (1997) ascertained that the
more control communities have, especially over investment funds, the more they
are willing to make investments. Ownership in general is important for project success. The demand of the poor is better articulated when communities contribute to
investment costs and control investment choices (Dongier *et al.* 2002: 305).

Must processes be initiated by an external agent or can the poor themselves initiate them? Gran (1983: 165ff.) argues that, at the least, an external catalyst, who will
take the initiative and facilitate the process of self-organisation, is necessary. In
his view, the most appropriate procedure is to select members of the local target
groups, train them and send them back to their villages and communities. Using
local facilitators also results in cost-savings, even allowing for the additional facilitation time needed in bottom-up projects (Simanowitz 1997: 130). However, catalysts can also be outsiders and come from other regions, countries or segments
of society. What is important is that they are personally respected and do not act
as managers or experts, but rather as facilitators, mediators or brokers. Gran pre-
fers non-government development workers to government-employed experts,
as they are closer to the target groups and are also less bureaucratic (Gran 1983:
166). Gran's opinion is not shared by everyone though. Chambers (1997) claims
that people coming from rich industrialised countries are generally unable to play
decisive roles. Instead, spontaneous local initiatives that are not initiated externally
should be recognised (Mathie and Cunningham 2002:17).[36] It should also be noted
that who is driving development has implications for who is held accountable for
results. Planning, monitoring and evaluation lead to an 'upwards' accountability
(Mathie and Cunningham 2003a: 10).

Ownership is an issue omitted entirely from the theoretical BoP discussions.
BoP literature usually acts on the assumption that companies initiate the projects.
Examples explained in the literature suggest that it is principally companies that
control the processes, even when the poor are integrated and have their role in
the business model. Krämer and Belz (2008: 231), however, mention the idea that
companies could also watch out for lead-user innovations and then start from
ideas previously developed by the poor. Still, is ownership a driver for choosing a
bottom-up approach, because the poor are willing to invest more resources (time,

---

36 This is, for example, what AVINA, an organisation founded in 1994 by the Swiss entrepreneur Stephan Schmidheiny, does. In their projects, they build on existing resources and
ideas that local entrepreneurs have and support them in scaling-up. For more information see www.avina.net.

assets, funds) when they have more control over the process? Who is initiating and managing the projects? Are existing innovations and solutions considered when starting a BoP venture? And when a higher degree of ownership is granted, is it backed up by rules, more accountability and transparency?

5.4.6 Networks

Successful bottom-up development projects usually make use of networks and interaction between public and private actors (Helmsing 2001). On the one hand, such projects can profit from networks and, on the other, bottom-up development projects have a positive impact on social capital.[37] According to Hall (2006: 10), partnerships can be based on resource and skill synergies, risk sharing or can relate to the wish of private companies to contribute to philanthropic activities. Helmsing (2001) found that meso institutions play a central role in development projects as well and were mostly newly created for the projects. Community-based organisations (CBOs) and so-called social movements also play an important role as partners as they are 'on the ground' and know the local circumstances (Simon 1997: 186).

> CBOs are normally membership organisations made up of a group of individuals in a self-defined community who have joined together to further common interests (Dongier *et al.* 2002: 305).

CBOs can be informal or formal in nature (Dongier *et al.* 2002: 305). Existing networks are assumed to be the source of constructive energy in the community and can serve as a mediating force between the responsibilities of government and the power of capital at local, national and international levels (Mathie and Cunningham 2002: 15). Working together with local networks has made considerable contributions to community empowerment and material improvement, but should not be applied uncritically (Simon 1997: 186). Existing CBOs do not always match with the project goals and it might make sense to adapt them or to raise new CBOs (Dongier *et al.* 2002: 305). To impact on poverty alleviation, CBOs therefore need to include poor people as members and represent their needs and interests (Dongier *et al.* 2002: 305).

Dongier *et al.* (2002: 313) elaborated on key design principles for partnerships between CBOs and private support organisations:

- Screening the potential partners and their qualities carefully

- Creating performance incentives

- Forging links between CBOs and local governments

- Supporting growth of competent support organisations

---

37 As we have already seen, social capital can be differentiated between bonding and bridging (Woolcock and Narayan 2000: 227).

- Ensuring that an exit strategy is in place for intermediaries

Also for companies entering BoP markets, building on existing networks and working together with locally embedded organisations should be considered (Hart 2007: 208). Business models for the BoP can be based upon social capital (Hart 2007: 211) as relationships are primarily grounded in social—not legal—contracts in the informal market economy (Hart and London 2005: 33). A company can increase access, trust and accountability by engaging the poor as intermediaries and building on their social networks (UNDP 2008: 7ff.). Embedding a company into diverse local networks may lead to common benefits for all involved (Sánchez *et al.* 2007: 20). Businesses and local entrepreneurs that are already established as well as local NGOs and community groups are the key sources of market knowledge and customers' behaviour (Prahalad and Hammond 2002: 54). According to Seelos and Mair (2006: 11) companies can even build local social entrepreneurs into their business model. Simanis and Hart (2008: 12) also opt for engaging with existing CBOs. According to them, the most important characteristics of a CBO are:

- That it is open to learning new capabilities and using enterprise as a way of advancing its mission

- That its staff are experienced in using participatory development practices

- That it is 'socially embedded' in the community, which includes locating its offices in, and drawing its staff from, the local community

Still, what else do companies have to consider when working together with local partners? Do companies have to make use of bonding and bridging social capital to embed themselves locally? Do they first have to convince potential organisations to partner up? Which criteria should they rely on when choosing partners? Are the characteristics set in BoP literature sufficient?

Networks are especially essential when a multi-sector approach is chosen. A multi-sector approach has the potential to respond better to the priority demands of each community and make services more appropriate and targeted. Efficiency and quality gains in outreach, social mobilisation and community capacity building can be reached. Also, experience shows that multi-sector approaches have enhanced impact on poverty alleviation (Dongier *et al.* 2002: 317). However, single-sector approaches also have their advantages. They can pay greater attention to sector policy and sector institutional issues, and are managed with reduced complexity (Dongier *et al.* 2002: 317f.).

The multi-sector approach is also mentioned in BoP literature when companies partner with different corporations and enter as consortia. These powerful synergies can also mitigate risk (Prahalad and Hammond 2002: 54). Is entering in consortia or choosing a multi-sector approach a valid way to proceed in BoP ventures? Does this have an enhanced impact on poverty alleviation?

5.4.7 Scaling up the process

> Small may be beautiful, but it may also be insignificant (Martinussen 1997: 341).

Bottom-up development projects need a long time horizon. They require slow, gradual, persistent learning through action and a project design that gradually adapts to local conditions by learning from mistakes. Monitoring and evaluation should be a central part of the project design from the start. Projects should start with a carefully selected set of pilot communities (Mansuri and Rao 2004: 28), and should proceed with small steps into what can be foreseen, rather than by long leaps into the unknown. Experience is gained on the way (Chambers 1983: 145).

In practice, bottom-up projects already work quite well on a small scale and at a non-complex level. The focal point of the current discussion is how to scale up successful small projects. Bringing the projects to scale is a very important (Martinussen 1997: 341) but also a very difficult task (Binswanger and Aryar 2003: 5). One has to think about the process beyond the project, and of transformation or transition rather than exit. When scaling up bottom-up development, the whole approach and its core features are intended to be scaled up, not just the outcomes of previous projects (Binswanger and Aryar 2003: 5). So far, there are few scaling-up success stories from practice. Binswanger and Aryar (2003) attribute this to the following problems:

- Total and/or fiscal costs may be too high

- Institutional settings may be hostile to bottom-up projects (e.g. dictatorship, gender/social divisions)

- Difficulties arising from co-production (as different values, unclear functions, etc.) may not be mastered

- Adaptation to a local context may be missing

- There may be a lack of scaling-up logistics (e.g. widely dispersed communities)

Successful scaling-up processes can take up to 10–15 years (Binswanger and Aryar 2003: 35). Binswanger and Nguyen (2005: 1), whose research focuses on multi-sectoral CDD programmes, point out that given the varying governance structures, capacities and social, economic, political and historical specificities of each country, scaling-up—and the programme design to do so—must be tailor-made. The fact that successful pilots have not automatically scaled up in practice shows that they may require adaptation to succeed in different contexts. Lessons can be learnt from successful experiments within a country and from global experience, but project design must be adapted to the local context (Binswanger and Aryar 2003: 33).

Binswanger and Nguyen (2005: 4) develop three principles for scaling up development projects:

- Cost-effectiveness and fiscal sustainability

- Co-production of services and infrastructure by different actors and levels

- Equal access to information, participation and democratic decision-making

Cost-effectiveness and fiscal sustainability can best be achieved by using and further developing existing local institutions, capacities and people; by avoiding intermediaries; transferring resources directly to each of the implementing agents and levels; and by relying on, or developing, community-level technical assistants (Binswanger and Nguyen 2005: 4). The more that is made locally, the further costs can be reduced (e.g. use of local materials and contractors, evaluation and monitoring done by communities, train locals to be trainers and facilitators) (Binswanger and Aryar 2003: 28). Co-production often poses problems, as many actors at different levels are involved. Overcoming these problems requires fostering a common culture and vision among stakeholders; assigning and describing all programme functions unambiguously to different participants based on the principle of subsidiarity; and providing incentives compatible with programme objectives. Information, education and communication activities are a crucial requirement to keep access equal (Binswanger and Nguyen 2005: 4).

Drawn from their case study research, Binswanger and Aryar (2003: 7f.) highlight the following factors leading to success for scaling-up projects:

- Strong political commitment, strong NGOs and a lively civil society

- Sophisticated, context-specific procedures, incorporated in manuals with simple transparent messages (manuals/procedures as 'living' documents)

- Good systems for sharing and spreading knowledge

- Appropriate incentives for different stakeholders that are aimed at getting the right outcomes rather than rapid disbursement

- Building on many years of past experience and utilising existing institutions

- As the process is very long, patience and flexibility in sequencing need to accommodate projects

As is the case with pilot projects, the scaling-up process should also start in one district or province. One 'big bang' at the national level is rarely successful (Binswanger and Nguyen 2005: 6). To save fiscal costs and improve ownership and accountability at the community level, communities should be asked to contribute a minimum share of the costs, which may constitute between 10% and 40% of the total. The contribution does not have to be in cash—as very poor communities would not be able to provide this—it can also be in the form of labour or materials (Binswanger and Nguyen 2005: 15). Further annual financial support can be based on performance of the individual communities (Binswanger and Nguyen 2005: 16).

If the scaling-up process works out well in one district, national scaling-up can be attempted. Depending on the number of districts in the country, there may have to be two or more phases to reach national coverage. The focus should first be on the larger districts with better capacity; a programme can then quickly increase the percentage of population reached. Another option is to select a range of districts with different sizes and capacity levels, which allows for fine-tuning of operational approaches and manuals to different situations (Binswanger and Nguyen 2005: 18).

Also in business ventures with the BoP, bringing the projects to scale is considered as one of the biggest challenges, as the multitude of small emerging experiments may not have the level of global impact required to truly move towards a more sustainable world. Accelerating and scaling up BoP strategies requires additional action (Hart 2010: 4).[38] In an uncertain environment, management suggests strategies that can be adapted during the process; for example, using real options for investment decisions (Busch and Hoffmann 2009: 2; Hart 2007: 203; Mendoza and Thelen 2008: 451). Still, do BoP ventures have to start with small-scale and non-complex pilot projects before they can be scaled up? Must successful strategies be open to the outcome and adaptable along the way? To reach the required level of adaptation to local contexts, and simultaneously cut down costs when scaling up, do local institutions, capacities and people have to be involved as much as possible? How can synergies be used when scaling up a venture?

38 The Boston Consulting Group notes that a growing number of entrepreneurs in the emerging world are replacing scaling-up with scaling-out, which means involving a wider range of people in the process. This is mentioned in the article 'Here Be Dragons: The emerging world is teeming with new business models' in a special report on innovation in emerging markets in the *Economist Online*, 15 April, 2010, www.economist.com/node/15879289, accessed 6 October 2010. Besides this, only the IFC has published a report on scaling up inclusive business (Jenkins and Ishikawa 2010).

6
Conclusions from theoretical part

Bottom-up development literature often corresponds with BoP literature. However it unveils additional details and goes further. The knowledge gained and the questions posed in this part can be subdivided into three categories which relate to the research questions:

- **Drivers** to choose a bottom-up development perspective in BoP ventures

- **Circumstances** that help or hinder the application of a bottom-up development perspective in BoP ventures

- **Success factors** when choosing a bottom-up development perspective in BoP ventures

Table 6.1 gives an overview of the issues raised in the theoretical part.

In the next chapters, issues associated with these categories in BoP ventures in Latin America and the Caribbean will be explored. The issues derived from the theoretical part form the reference frame for the case study research. This helps to define the application of knowledge derived from bottom-up development approaches in the innovation process of BoP ventures.

Table 6.1 Overview of issues raised in theoretical part

	Drivers	Circumstances	Success factors
General questions	Avoiding 'Westernisation'	Development level Products, services and sector	
Real participation		Readiness of company representatives to step back	• Integration into the whole innovation process • Amount of participation • Equality in decision-making and information sharing • Transferring entire activities to the BoP
Power relations and elite capture		Risk of elite capture depends on existence of self-conscious, organised and empowered communities with a strong local private sector	• Deep sense of local structures of power • Need to manage power relations • Importance of incentives • Avoidance of elite capture when considering pluralism, transparency, accountability, capacity building, ownership, low enough wages
Community and targeting	Match between demand and receipt	Circumstances in the target community that favour easy and effective entrance	• Romanticising communities • Risk of ignoring sub-groups and obscuration of local structures of economic and social power • Monitoring and evaluating community pluralism • Selection of persons to integrate
Local knowledge/ capacity building	Local knowledge leads to innovative, environmentally friendly solutions Acceptance of products and services	Decentralised organisational structure favours working with local knowledge Non-technical vs. technical decisions Building on existing technologies	• Idealisation and instrumentalisation of local knowledge • Keeping dependency low • Discovering and analysing local knowledge • Adapting local knowledge to scale up in different contexts • Careful verification of local knowledge • When to build on local knowledge • Exchange of knowledge • Local knowledge should be led by community
Ownership	Poor are willing to invest more resources with higher ownership	Consideration of existing innovations and solutions	• Initiating and managing the projects • Necessity of rules, accountability and transparency with higher ownership
Networks		Acceptance of company and its partners	• Points to consider when working with local partners • Use of social capital and local embedding • Convincing potential organisations to partner • Criteria to rely on when choosing partners • Entering in consortia
Scaling up the process			• Start with small-scale and non-complex pilot projects • Strategies need to be open to the outcome and adaptable • Involvement of local actors in the process of scaling-up

Bottom-up development elements

Part III
The bottom-up development perspective in BoP practice

Chapter 7 explains the methodology applied in order to determine which knowledge provided by bottom-up development literature is applicable in the innovation process of BoP ventures. Chapter 8 provides an overview of the situation in Latin America and the Caribbean (LAC), while Chapter 9 summarises the companies and projects that participated in the case study research. Finally, Chapter 10 provides an analysis of the results.

7
Methodology

The goal of the systematic literature review in the theoretical part of this book was to understand the bottom-up development perspective, its approaches and success factors. By combining the concept of the BoP and the respective innovation processes with the elements of bottom-up development, further possible links became evident, and 'a priori constructs' could be pictured. However, to find out what is applicable and already applied in practice, what is possible and what is not, qualitative research was necessary and a multiple-case inductive analysis of BoP ventures was applied. The objective was to build empirically validated constructs that help to build theory on applying a bottom-up development perspective in the innovation process of BoP ventures.

The first section focuses on the research questions. This is followed by a justification of why case study research was chosen and an explanation of how the case studies were selected. The research phases, the methods and tools used in the case study research are described in detail in this chapter. The research primarily followed the process of building theory from case study research by Eisenhardt (1989) and Yin (1984).

7.1 Questions addressed

For case study research, the initial definition of research questions and, if possible, a priori constructs are important in order to build theory. The a priori specification of constructs can help to shape the initial design of theory-building research. If the constructs prove important as the study progresses, researchers have a firmer empirical grounding for the emergent theory. However, no construct is guaranteed a place in the resultant theory, and the research questions may shift during the research (Eisenhardt 1989: 536). The questions developed in Chapter 6 form the a priori constructs, and were arranged within the following three key research questions:

- What are the **drivers** to choose a bottom-up development perspective in BoP ventures?

- What **circumstances** help or hinder the application of a bottom-up development perspective in BoP ventures?

- What are the **success factors** when choosing a bottom-up development perspective in BoP ventures?

Eisenhardt (1989: 536) recommends that investigators should formulate a research problem and, possibly, specify some potentially important variables with reference to extant literature, during, and especially at the outset of, the process. The theoretical background and the key research questions helped to guide the case study research**.**

7.2 **Why case study research?**

In the theoretical part, concepts and theories from different research areas were combined—or, more specifically, assumptions were drawn out of bottom-up development literature that might be applied to the innovation process of BoP ventures. In order to empirically investigate the drivers, the circumstances and success factors of a bottom-up development perspective in BoP ventures, a qualitative research method was chosen over a quantitative research method. This research can therefore deliver propositions (informed assertions), but not seek empirical support by testing these propositions quantitatively. Defining a representative sample would not have been possible for quantitative research as not enough cases, which see the poor as consumers *and* integrate them into the innovation process exist in practice.[1] A qualitative research design is particularly useful for exploring implicit assumptions and examining new relationships and abstract concepts (Patton 1990; Weick 1996). Implicit assumptions about the application of bottom-up development knowledge in BoP ventures were developed in the last chapter. This research examines new relationships between two concepts, which are both, as yet, relatively abstract.

Within qualitative research methods, an explanatory case study research strategy was selected over a descriptive case study research design. The explanatory case study research is used to explore causation in order to find underlying principles (Yin 1981: 59), which is the objective of this research in terms of a bottom-up

---

1 See Section 7.3 for the challenges associated with selecting the case studies.

development perspective in BoP ventures. Although case studies cannot attribute impact[2] they can provide a more nuanced picture of BoP ventures in particular contexts, and yield insights that are difficult to generate through quantitative techniques (Mansuri and Rao 2004: 3). The combination of bottom-up development and BoP concepts is—as previously mentioned—a very new topic in literature as well as in practice. Little is known about the bottom-up development perspective in BoP ventures and researchers have never tried to connect both concepts to this extent. A theory of, or further empirical research on, a bottom-up development perspective in BoP ventures therefore does not exist. In early stages of research on a topic, case study research is, according to Eisenhardt (1989: 548), most appropriate:

> In these situations, theory building from case study research is particularly appropriate because theory building from case studies does not rely on previous literature or prior empirical evidence.

Even though the case study research relies on issues derived from bottom-up development literature, it cannot rely on literature with a bottom-up development perspective in BoP ventures.

The qualitative approach chosen helps to better describe the applicability of a bottom-up development perspective in practice, and it helps to develop the assumptions further into a valuable theory. In fact, much research on BoP ventures has used the case study approach (e.g. London and Hart 2004; Sánchez *et al.* 2005). For BoP research in general, Sharma and Hart (2006: 28) opt for a field-based, case-comparative methodology in order to identify and document this emerging activity.

> Understanding why and how companies pursue the BOP and succeed in these markets could [. . .] be an important contribution to management theory in the coming decade.

This is exactly what this research aims for: understanding *why*, *where* and *how* companies currently use a bottom-up development perspective in the innovation process of their BoP ventures.

To elaborate on propositions regarding drivers, circumstances and success factors associated with a bottom-up development perspective in BoP ventures, two different types of case studies were used: Three in-depth case studies (intensive cases) and eight less intensive cases involving a questionnaire (following Pettigrew 1990: 276). While the in-depth case studies were used to develop preliminary conclusions on possible propositions as a first step, the purpose of the questionnaire was to verify and fine-tune the propositions.[3]

---

2 It would be desirable to measure the impact on poverty alleviation and the company's success by applying a bottom-up development perspective quantitatively. This could be part of further research.

3 More on the two phases in Section 7.4.1.

7.3 **Selection of case studies**

The case studies were selected from a severely limited field of possible ventures. The concept of a population is crucial in case study research, as the population defines the set of entities from which the research sample is drawn. This also helps to define the limits for generalising the findings (Eisenhardt 1989: 537). For the purpose of this research, cases needed to comply with the following criteria:

- Being (part of) a MNC, active in more than one country[4]

- The project/venture under consideration needed to be located in Latin America and/or the Caribbean (local subsidiary of company desirable)

- The project/venture needed to target the poor as consumers

- The project/venture needed to integrate the target group into one or more steps of the innovation process (idea generation, product/service development, production, distribution/marketing)

That the venture itself is profitable was not a criterion for several reasons. Most companies have only recently started to integrate the poor into their innovation process for BoP ventures and therefore lack experience. As a result, the ventures cannot be profitable yet, or might never be. Furthermore, some companies did not want to disclose whether their BoP business is profitable or not. Others define success within their BoP projects in a different way to solely 'making profit'. 'Market reach', 'preparing the market', 'growth', or 'getting to know the BoP' were other goals mentioned. Also, the goal of this research was to look at the processes. The companies learn what works and what does not in their projects, regardless of whether it is already profitable. It is an analysis about the current state the companies are in at the moment rather than about 'successful best practice'.

Case study research can involve either single or multiple cases and numerous levels of analysis (Yin 1984: 27ff.). There is no ideal number of cases, but according to Eisenhardt (1989: 545), between four and ten usually work well.[5] However, there can be some flexibility in these numbers if distinctions are made between major (intensive) cases and minor (less intensive) cases (Pettigrew 1990: 276). For the purpose of this research, three cases were chosen for in-depth case study research (intensive cases). In the second less intensive questionnaire round, eight more projects were included. A total of 11 cases can therefore be considered sufficient and, with the distinction made between major and minor cases, complexity could be kept within reasonable limits.

---

4 This criterion had to be dropped for the questionnaire as there were not enough MNC cases available. This did not make a difference to the conclusions drawn.
5 Fewer than four cases lead to empirical grounding which is likely to be unconvincing. With more than ten cases, however, complexity and volume of data become difficult to cope with (Einsenhardt 1989: 545).

The selection of the cases is a very important step. Random sampling—as often used for quantitative research—is not desirable in case study research (Eisenhardt 1989: 537). Given the limited number of cases that can usually be studied, it makes more sense to use purposive sampling whereby the sample is based on cases that are appropriate for the study and the process of selection is transparently observable (Pettigrew 1990: 275f.; Silverman 2006). This allows the choice of strategic and information-rich cases in order to illustrate features and processes which the study aims to explore. The goal of theoretical sampling is thus; to choose cases which are likely to replicate or extend the emergent theory (Eisenhardt 1989: 537), and where high experience levels as well as evidence can be found (Pettigrew 1990: 276).

Choosing conflicting cases (for example, a successful case which didn't integrate the poor into the innovation process, or projects that failed even though they integrated the poor) would have been a possibility too. As Mason (1996) suggests, this can help in overcoming the tendency to select cases that are likely to support the argument. Yet many BoP projects are still in pilot phases and it is difficult to determine whether they will fail. During the search phase for the case studies, two cases were detected that, despite integrating the poor, had been abandoned, although it was not possible to find out why.[6] Choosing cases that did not integrate the poor made no sense, as the research question is not whether a bottom-up perspective in BoP ventures should be applied or not. Rather, the question is about *why* and *how* companies apply the bottom-up development perspective (when they decide to do so). Also, the goal of this research is to build a theory for a new phenomenon, so using cases that fit with the phenomenon is appropriate. In a later phase it would be interesting to compare companies using a bottom-up development perspective with companies not using it, according to the impact of their activities on corporate success and development.

It was quite difficult to find cases that comply with the criteria mentioned above. First, because there are, in general, few such cases[7] and, second, because some were not reachable, did not reply, were being restructured, or simply did not have the time. Some also promised to participate but then did not, even after several reminders. Another reason for difficulties in finding suitable BoP ventures in LAC could be that many initiatives in the region build—for historical reasons—on vol-

---

6 Amanco, now Mexichem, in Guatemala (Irrigation Systems for farmers), P&G in Nicaragua (NutriStar).

7 Hart (2010) claims in the preface to the special issue of *Greener Management International* on BoP in Latin America that Latin America has been a particularly fertile ground for the emergence of BoP strategies. There are BoP Learning Labs in Mexico, Brazil, Venezuela, Colombia and Chile. The IDB estimated that by 2007 there were in excess of 500 companies working at the BoP in the region. However, the well over 200 initiatives screened either failed to consider the poor as producers and not just consumers (which still counts as 'inclusive business'), or did not integrate them in other parts of the innovation process (purely targeting the BoP as consumers). Another problem was that many projects were from not-for-profit NGOs or foundations. Nor were many cases from MNCs. This is the reason why locally operating companies were also included in the survey.

untarism with no intention of making a profit.[8] The following activities helped to find cases:

- Searching for cases in publications, websites or blogs and contacting the companies[9]

- Contacting people already known (professionals, consultants, professors)

- Contacting new networks and exposed persons directly [10]

- Writing blog posts on nextbillion in Spanish and English,[11] combined with a call for participation

- Making a call for participation at the BoP conference in Delft,[12] November 2009, following a presentation

A fact sheet containing more information and a call for participation was developed in English and Spanish and distributed widely. For many companies, an in-depth case study (involving the researcher in a stay of two to three weeks) was too much. They were then integrated in the second phase of the case study research—the questionnaire. For the questionnaire, people and networks were approached again with an information fact sheet on the research and the questionnaire.

In spite of these difficulties, three very innovative initiatives for the in-depth case studies were acquired, and eight more completed the questionnaire for the second stage.[13]

8 Due to the Catholic tradition in Latin America, projects that are intended to have a positive impact for the poor should be of philanthropic nature and not expect to bring in revenue. Reficco (2009) criticises this as it leads to less professionalism in inclusive business ventures.
9 When possible, the researcher contacted a person in charge of the project directly. If this was not possible, contact was made with the corporate sustainability/responsibility department and if this was not successful then the company's head office was contacted.
10 For example, the regional network of the WBCSD, BoP Learning Labs, IDB, nextbillion. org, negociosinclusivos.org, the Social Enterprise Knowledge Network (SEKN), Ashoka, World Resources Institute, Movimiento BdP, UNDP Growing Inclusive Markets, IFC, SNV, Fundes, Avina, CSR Europe BoP Laboratory and the World Bank.
11 espanol.nextbillion.net/blog/co-creacion-de-productos-en-empresas-multinacionales; espanol.nextbillion.net/blog/2010/05/15/escalando-desde-abajo; www.nextbillion.net/ blog/2010/07/16/bottom-up-scaling.
12 www.bopimpact.nl.
13 There were three more completed questionnaires received but they could not be used because they did not comply with all criteria. However, they still provided valuable input that could be considered in the research.

7.4 **Research design**

7.4.1 Stages

In order to discover more about the bottom-up development perspective which companies apply in practice, the fieldwork took place in two stages. Three in-depth case studies paved the way to formulate an initial draft for propositions. To broaden the research findings and make them more robust, a questionnaire, involving different companies than were involved in the first stage, was developed.

7.4.1.1 Stage 1: in-depth case studies

This stage took place from February until July 2010. Following a study of all documents on the case study available in advance, the individual(s) responsible for coordination at each company received a research plan describing the areas of research, the methods to be used, the different research stages, a list of potential interviewees, an action plan and a note on confidentiality. The company coordinator could then organise the interview appointments and meetings.

In qualitative research, the researcher's role receives greater critical attention than in quantitative research. In each case about half the time was spent with company personnel involved in the project (mostly the CEO or those working in the areas of corporate responsibility/sustainability or innovation/business development) and half of the time was spent with the integrated poor and the company's customers. Throughout the research process it was crucial to spend as much time as possible with the poor who were involved individually—without company representatives—in order to avoid any undue company influence on their responses. This was normally feasible but sometimes, inevitably, other people were present (such as community leaders or representatives from local NGOs) when the researcher visited the communities. In order to choose the poor who would be involved, and with whom the researcher would spend the most time, attention was directed towards those who were well known and accepted in the community. This was important for the researchers' safety. Also, the poor who were selected represented different income levels and ages, and had different levels of engagement and time involved with the project.

The range of data collection methods for building theory from case study research is wide. Typically, different methods are combined. Interviews, observations, documentations and archival sources are particularly common, but researchers are not limited to these methods alone (Eisenhardt 1989: 537; Yin 1984: 79ff.). For this research, the following data collection methods were used:

On the company side:

- Face-to-face[14] semi-structured[15] key informant and focus group interviews[16]

- Informal conversational interviews[17]

- Participant and direct observation

- Document analysis/information from other sources (internet)

- Presentation and discussion (validation workshop)

On the side of the target group:

- Immersion (passing time in the life of the poor involved in the project)[18]

- Informal conversational interviews[19]

The methods were used simultaneously within each stay at the case study locations. The iterative process of using multiple sources of information ('data triangulation') draws on the particular and different strengths of various data collection methods (Pettigrew 1990: 277; Yin 1984: 89ff.). This also reduces the potential biases of using only one method of data collection, increases the validity of the studied cases, and provides stronger substantiation of constructs and hypotheses (Denzin 1970: 300; Eisenhardt 1989: 538; Moran-Ellis *et al.* 2006: 55). Whenever possible, individual responses were double checked with other people involved (snowballing).

Table 7.1 sets out the five phases involved in carrying out a case study.

14 Problems of data collection and reliability of responses may be exacerbated in developing/emerging countries. When the researcher comes from a different context (language, understanding of management concepts, etc.), a face-to-face interview leads to the most reliable responses because this provides the ability to check and probe aspects of behaviour (Hoskisson *et al.* 2000: 258).

15 The interview guide approach was used (according to Mikkelsen [1995: 103]).

16 The author started recording the interviews but then soon came to the conclusion that this did not make much sense as the most interesting information often came out in informal conversation before or after the interviews (lunch, dinner, city trips, etc.). Transcribing interviews would have only shown a small portion of the information gained and it would not be possible to draw conclusions based on that material.

17 According to Mikkelsen (1995: 102). The interview guide approach and the informal conversational interview method are considered as participatory methods (Mikkelsen 1995: 103).

18 'Total immersion', as done by development experts, as recommended in the BoP Protocol, was not possible due to time constraints. However, as the goal was not developing a new product/service but research on what is already there, this seemed a good way to go. Also, it was important as a researcher to not get over-involved or 'go native' as this would have damaged objectivity (Pettigrew 1990: 278).

19 Individual interviews were undertaken with an opportunity sample of purposely selected respondents to obtain representative information (as recommended by Mikkelsen 1995: 104).

Table 7.1 **In-depth case study phases**

Phase	Day(s)[a]	What	Objective
1. Introduction	1	Introduction to the company, the people in charge, the product and the project as well as presenting the research and its goals.	Build a common base for the case study investigation
2. First-round interviews	1–3	First round of interviews with key informants[b]	Receive a first impression of the opinions of the informants
Time for analysis			
3. Immersion	2–10	Spend time with the target group	Understand the opinions of the target group
Time for analysis			
4. Second-round interviews	1–3	Second round of interviews with key informants[c]	Gain a deeper understanding of opinions to the propositions. Cross-check information received and ensure all relevant information has been collected
Time for analysis			
5. Finalisation	1	Presentation of first impression followed by a discussion (feedback and validation workshop)[d]	Give the company a first impression of the results and a chance to discuss them, as well as the opportunity to gain new inputs and ensure internal validity

a The days varied according to the time available (determined by the participating company).

b See Annex 1.

c See Annex 2. The questions in the second round were further elaborated after every case. In the annex, the questions for the first in-depth case study can be found.

d Pettigrew (1990: 278f.), for example, even recommends one-day 'research in action workshops' for 10 to 15 key people in the organisation. However, this was not possible given the limited time of the people on site. With the validation workshop, the researcher tried to make at least a 'small version' of this.

The questions posed in the first round of the interviews were semi-structured and the interviews lasted around 1.5 hours each. After a short explanation about the research project and the definition of a 'bottom-up development perspective', some introductory questions about the position and role of the interviewee in the venture were posed. The three key research questions were then elaborated upon, building the core of the interview, and extended into conversations. The interviewer facilitated the process. The purpose of open-ended questions is to '. . . enable the researcher to understand and capture the points of view of other people without predetermining those points of view through prior selections of questionnaire categories' (Patton 2002: 21). The information collected in this first round gave a good base for the further phases.

This research is not only *about* a bottom-up development perspective, but is also an attempt to *apply* this perspective within the research and listen to the 'voices of the poor'. The second phase, in which the researcher spent time with the poor involved in the innovation process and the company's customers, was mostly informal. Methods for research about the poor must be eclectic, inventive, adaptable and open to unexpected information (Chambers 1983: 47). Experience from development research shows that formalised interviews (e.g. sitting at a table, posing questions and writing down the answers) do not produce the desired results in this environment; people feel under pressure to say what the interviewer wants to hear. Open and simple questions, relevant to the current context, were posed. Therefore, the conversations mostly took place while people were completing their daily tasks. The researcher tried to adhere to the following principles:[20]

- Being transparent about the process and objectives

- Respecting and adapting to local norms, values, attitudes and habits

- Keeping an open mind and not being judgemental

- Listening more than talking

- Trying to make people feel comfortable (e.g. through supporting them in their daily tasks)

- Trying to be unobtrusive

The second round of interviews took place with key company personnel who dealt with the projects; these were mostly the same interviewees as in the first round. In this second round, semi-structured interviews were applied. The framework for this round was built on the assumptions detailed in the theoretical part as well as on new input that came from phases one and two. For each case, the content of this interview round was adjusted (propositions were changed or added) in accordance with the case before. The final presentation and discussion with the whole team helped to ensure internal validity.

To get a comprehensive sense of the projects, it was very important to establish trust—both on the side of the company but, especially, on the side of the poor. Where possible, the author lived in the houses of people involved in the project and shared their life, cooked and ate with them, went to work with them, and sometimes also spent the night there.[21] This established a very good base for trust; not to mention the huge amount of information that could be transferred in this way.

---

20 These principles derive from the experience shared in a 'deep listening' workshop at the BoP conference in Delft, November 2009. Many match with what Chambers (1983) recommends for development research.

21 This was not possible in some cases, as people did not have enough space for one more person. Especially in urban environments, up to five people slept in one room.

In all conversations the native language was used (Spanish[22]) and a familiar environment was chosen, in order to increase the authenticity of the information received. If desired, the coordinator could cross-check the interview transcripts, as well as the original thesis, to check and correct facts and to ensure the researcher did not divulge commercially sensitive information (as mentioned by Pettigrew 1990: 278). This process led to greater precision rather than to wholesale changes to statements.

Case study research can involve qualitative data only, quantitative data only, or both (Yin 1984: 82). The combination of data types can be highly synergistic. Quantitative data can strengthen the theory developed. However, in the cases involved in this research, only a small amount of quantitative data was available or disclosed, and, in addition, it was not of great importance for the research subject. For this reason, the results rely, for the most part, upon qualitative information.

Throughout the researcher's stay, field notes were taken—especially also because the majority of conversations/interviews were not formal in nature. Due to the amount of time spent in the projects, a lot of field notes were gathered. As recommended by Eisenhardt (1989: 539), whatever impressions occurred were written down—instead of sifting out what may seem important. This is key to useful field notes. However, the author mostly stayed within the key questions of this research and used the assumptions as a reference frame, so that research would not become overloaded with data (as recommended by Yin 1981: 60f.).

7.4.1.2 Stage 2: questionnaire

The purpose of this second phase was to verify and fine-tune the results of the previous research. According to the analysis of the in-depth case studies, and based on the assumptions from the theoretical research, propositions were developed. These built the base to develop the questionnaire[23] for the second stage of the case study research, targeted at more companies. Assumptions that did not apply to all in-depth case studies were dropped and not included in the questionnaire. The assumptions where a mixed picture could be drawn from the in-depth case studies were included in the questionnaire to back up these uncertain impressions.

This phase took place between August and September 2010. The companies were selected based on the same criteria as used in the in-depth case studies, except they did not have to be MNCs, they could be national companies. The same sources and contacts were used as in the search for the in-depth case studies. As the issue is a burgeoning one, there were additional sources that had not been available when searching for the in-depth case studies. Finally, eight completed questionnaires were received that could be used to further develop the propositions.

---

22 The exception was Nestlé in Brazil. However, even there the researcher got along quite well with a mix between Spanish and Portuguese. When necessary, an assistant provided support.

23 See Section 3 of the Annex.

The questionnaire was sent to the companies, along with an information sheet that explained the research project, the methods applied and the goals of the survey. If needed, support was given via email and Skype. The questionnaire contained two parts. The first consisted of general questions about the company, the respondent and the project/venture. In the second, respondents were asked to assess the propositions on a four-point Likert scale ('strongly agree'; 'somewhat agree'; 'somewhat disagree'; 'strongly disagree'). 'Undecided' was not an option because many propositions were heavily dependent upon the context or product/service offered or innovation process step. Therefore, for each proposition, respondents could elaborate further on the reasons for the conclusions they had reached based on their experiences and points of view.

7.4.2 Data analysis

> Analyzing data is the heart of building theory from case studies, but it is both the most difficult and the least codified part of the process (Eisenhardt 1989: 539).

A special feature of research to build theory from case studies is the frequent overlap of data analysis with data collection (Eisenhardt 1989: 538). While data collection and data analysis were carried out separately, so as not to influence the process too much, analysis began when in the field.[24] This helped to shape the assumptions from each phase to the next and unveiled open questions. It left room to make adjustments (e.g. to add interview partners, visit other areas, add interview questions) during the data collection process. These kinds of adjustments enabled emergent themes to be probed and for special opportunities to be explored. Alterations are legitimate in theory-building research because investigators are trying to understand each case individually and in as much depth as possible (Eisenhardt 1989: 539). This flexibility is, however, '. . . not a license to be unsystematic. Rather, this flexibility is controlled opportunism in which researchers take advantage of the uniqueness of a specific case and the emergence of new themes to improve resultant theory' (Eisenhardt 1989: 539).

The data gathered in the in-depth case studies was analysed in two ways: *within-case* and *cross-case*. The within-case analysis is important for reducing the volume of data received (Eisenhardt 1989: 540) and took place during, and immediately after, the stay in the field so the propositions could be adjusted and enhanced for the following case study. The observations and information of each case study were organised around the substantive topics of the case study research (the assump-

---

24 In between the five phases within each case study, the researcher always had some time for analysis, which was carried out separately from observation and interviews/conversations.

tions mentioned in the theoretical part) as recommended by Yin (1981: 60).[25] This accelerated *cross-case comparison*, the second step, was done after all the in-depth case studies were finished.[26] Various tendencies for false conclusions exist when searching for cross-case patterns. These can be limited, however, by looking at the data in many divergent ways (Eisenhardt 1989: 540). The three research questions mentioned earlier were selected as dimensions to look for within-group similarities coupled with inter-group differences. The assumptions made in the theoretical part guided the researcher as well. Also, the similarities and differences of the in-depth cases were listed. The idea behind these cross-case searching tactics is '. . . to force investigators to go beyond initial impressions, especially through the use of structured and diverse lenses on the data' (Eisenhardt 1989: 541).

According to Yin (1981: 61), an explanatory case study research strategy consists of:

> (a) an accurate rendition of the facts of the case, (b) some consideration of alternative explanations of these facts, and (c) a conclusion based on the single explanation that appears most congruent with the facts.

The assumptions most likely to be confirmed, added or denied when applying a bottom-up development perspective in the innovation process of BoP ventures became clear during the analysis process. However, there were always certain cases that did not correspond to the findings of the others. In that case, the researcher tried to find out why and the explanations became more detailed. The emergent frame was consistently compared with the evidence from each case in order to assess how well or poorly it fits with case data (following Eisenhardt 1989: 541). The assumptions were refined and propositions elaborated according to the analysis. Analysing the in-depth case studies also resulted in new propositions that could be added.

The emergent frame with the propositions built the base for the second phase of the case study research—the questionnaire. The answers from the questionnaire were used to support the evolving theory from the analysis of the in-depth case studies. They also helped to shape the propositions more precisely and elaborate them further. The results are 28 propositions in three categories, with evidence from the case studies that can prove the propositions in each case (following Eisenhardt 1989: 541). The process of analysis came to an end when the incremental improvement to theory was seen as minimal (following Eisenhardt 1989: 545).

25 Another possibility would have been to write each case up separately. Such an approach can be central to the generation of insight because it addresses the enormous volume of data early in the analysis process. The overall idea of this process is '. . . to become intimately familiar with each case as a stand-alone entity' (Eisenhardt 1989: 540). A detailed write-up of all case studies separately only makes sense when the study specifically calls for publishing this material (Yin 1981: 69). All the cases are briefly summarised in this book, but they are not described in detail.

26 Yin (1981: 62) calls this the case-comparison approach, as opposed to the case-survey approach.

7.5 **Limitations**

Eisenhardt (1989: 538) recommends the use of multiple investigators as they enhance the creative potential of the study, and—when the observations are convergent—confidence in the findings. There was only a single investigator involved in this research. As the cases were few, it was manageable for one person. Also, the selected companies would not have had the time to involve a second person and explain/show everything twice. It could, however, have been useful to have more investigators present when communicating with the poor.

At first, during the research conducted in Brazil, the language barrier presented a problem for this author, although this was ultimately overcome. Also, due to the scale of the Nestlé project, it was not possible to see everything in the time available. The author did not visit a factory to talk with the poor involved on the production side (as it was at a different location) or assist with an idea generation workshop (which did not take place during the field visit).

As not all possible companies took part in the research, a bias may be evident due to the fact that only very engaged companies are included in the study. None of the in-depth case studies had been part of other published BoP research, when the case study research took place, and therefore the reasons for participation could also have been visibility and new input.

In two cases, the questionnaires were not completed by a company representative.[27] However, these informants did have a comprehensive knowledge of the projects and had been heavily involved in them from the start.

27 In the case of Gas Natural, the questionnaire was filled out by representatives of the Fundación Pro Vivienda Social, which was heavily involved in the implementation of the project. In the case of TIA's Multiahorro Barrio Stores, a professor from the IDE Business School, who is continuously involved in the process, filled out the questionnaire. Nevertheless, in both cases, a company representative revised and confirmed the answers.

8
Portrait of Latin America and the Caribbean

This chapter gives an insight into the region of Latin America and the Caribbean (LAC), in order to understand more about the environment within which the research took place.[1] With respect to the focus of the book, different issues are summarised. The first section explains the region's economy, the main economic sectors and activities. This is followed by a closer look at the people, their poverty issues and other social problems. There are significant differences between urban and rural regions, and the subsequent section contains more about this issue. Finally, the chapter addresses the core of this research, presenting further detail surrounding the specific market at the BoP in the region.

---

1 Latin America contains the following countries: Argentina; Bolivia (Plurinational State of); Brazil; Chile; Colombia; Costa Rica; Cuba; Dominican Republic; Ecuador; El Salvador; Guatemala; Haiti; Honduras; Mexico; Nicaragua; Panama; Paraguay; Peru; Uruguay; and Venezuela (Bolivarian Republic of). The Caribbean contains the following countries: Anguilla; Antigua and Barbuda; Aruba; Bahamas; Barbados; Belize; British Virgin Islands; Cayman Islands; Dominica; Grenada; Guyana; Jamaica; Montserrat; Netherlands Antilles; Puerto Rico; Saint Kitts and Nevis; Saint Lucia; Saint Vincent and the Grenadines; Suriname; Trinidad and Tobago; Turks and Caicos Islands; and United States Virgin Islands. In fact, there is only one case study located in the Caribbean, but the vast majority of literature and reports cover the two regions together, including in terms of data.

8.1 **The economy**

In the last few years, the LAC region has had a favourable economic performance. In 2006 all countries, with the exception of Haiti, reached a growth per capita of more than 2% (CEPAL 2008: 52), which is unprecedented in the last two decades. In 2008, the total GDP increased by 4.1% which is equal to 3% per capita (CEPAL 2009a: 51). For 2009, the forecast was a decrease to 1.8% GDP (2.9% per capita) as from the end of 2008 the global economic crisis affected all countries in the region (CEPAL 2009b: 13).[2] The interruption of growth led to a higher rate of unemployment, estimated at around 8.3% for the region in 2009 (7.4% in 2008). Remittances and tourism activity decreased, which especially affected Mexico, Central America and the Caribbean. Direct foreign investment fell by an estimated 37% (CEPAL 2009b: 9). The H1N1 virus affected Mexico's economy negatively, dengue fever negatively influenced Bolivia, and natural disasters (floods in Brazil and El Salvador), as well as an excess in humidity, hurricanes, storms and increased seismological activity in Central America, adversely affected economic activities. Because of global climate change, it is expected that the agricultural sector in particular will be affected more by severe weather events in the future (CEPAL 2009b: 60). However, during 2009 the economy picked up again. Industrial activity (domestic as well as in terms of export markets) recuperated, and there was an increase in the construction and commerce sector (CEPAL 2009b: 61). Inflation also decreased from 8.3% in 2008 to 4.5% in 2009 (CEPAL 2009b: 13) which led, in most countries, to an increase in real income (CEPAL 2009b: 61). A higher growth rate is expected in South America than in the rest of the region because of its larger size and the improved diversification of its export markets (CEPAL 2009b: 10). This offers favourable conditions for companies to engage in the region.

In recent years, most countries in LAC have opened up their economies to foreign competition, de-regulated markets and privatised economic activities. Even though Latin America has an abundance of land, it differs from most other developing regions in its small share of rural workers in the labour market, and in the small share that agriculture represents in the economy. Over 45% of the population of some of the smaller economies (e.g. El Salvador, Guatemala, Honduras, Paraguay and Jamaica) live in rural areas. But in most larger countries (e.g. Argentina, Brazil, Chile, Colombia, Mexico, Peru and Venezuela) less than 30% of the population live in rural areas. Agriculture's share in GDP is consistently below 25% throughout the region and is less than 15% in the larger economies (López and Valdés 2000: 198f.). Even though the employment rate has decreased in the agricultural sector, the proportion of women participating in this sector has increased. Around 40% of labour in agriculture is provided by women (Echeverria 1998: 7; Quang Dao 2004: 503).

---

2 Many countries still had a positive GDP although aggregated the GDP was negative (CEPAL 2009b: 57).

Also, women own and operate from 30–60% of all micro-enterprises, the region's fastest growing sub-sectors (Echeverria 1998: 7).

Household incomes come from different sources—from working, from public transfers (social security, poverty reduction programmes), private transfers (remittances, donations, gifts from other households), income from capital and other incomes. The majority of income, however, comes from the labour market, regardless of whether the household is poor or not (CEPAL 2009a: 63). More than half of all jobs in LAC are provided by enterprises with fewer than 10 employees, and 50% of these are family-run businesses (Echeverria 1998: 21).

LAC countries feature high levels of informality. The average size of the informal economy in South and Central America is slightly growing and accounted, in 1999–2000, for more than 41.5% of GDP (Schneider 2005: 609). More than half of the labour force earns its living in the informal economy. Workers active in the informal economy often become more vulnerable to exploitation and poor working conditions, with scarce protection from the law and institutions (Marquez *et al.* 2010: 12f.). During the economic crisis, when less 'formal' jobs were available, more people switched to an informal income generating activity (CEPAL 2009b: 65). This means that companies wishing to engage in BoP markets definitively have to cope with the informal economy—be it by integrating new people into the formal market or by working together with informal business models.

8.2 **Poverty and other social problems**

In terms of income poverty, LAC is not the poorest region in the world. The HDI is high or medium in all countries.[3] The lowest levels of poverty, with poverty rates below 22% and extreme poverty rates between 3% and 7%, can be found in Argentina,[4] Chile, Costa Rica and Uruguay. Brazil, Panama and Venezuela have a poverty rate below 30%. In Colombia, Ecuador, El Salvador, Mexico, Peru and Dominican Republic, the poverty rates are between 35% and 48%. The highest levels of poverty are in Bolivia, Guatemala, Honduras, Nicaragua and Paraguay, where over 50% live in poverty and over 30% in extreme poverty (CEPAL 2009a: 54).

2008 was the sixth consecutive year in a row that showed a reduction in poverty. From 2002, the poverty rate decreased by 11% (to 33%) chiefly due to an increase of

---

3 Dominican Republic, Saint Vincent and the Grenadines, Belize, Jamaica, Paraguay, El Salvador, Honduras, Bolivia, Guyana, Guatemala, Nicaragua and Haiti (in order of rank) show medium human development (HDI). Chile, Antigua and Barbuda, Argentina, Uruguay, Cuba, Bahamas, Mexico, Costa Rica, Bolivarian Republic of Venezuela, Panama, Saint Kitts and Nevis, Trinidad and Tobago, Saint Lucia, Dominica, Grenada, Brazil, Colombia, Peru and Ecuador (in order of rank) have a high HDI, Barbados has a very high HDI (hdr.undp.org/en/statistics, accessed 1 September 2010).

4 Data only from urban areas.

the median income and a higher occupancy rate, complemented by better distribution in some countries (CEPAL 2009a: 51).[5] A lower dependency ratio or 'demographic bonus' supported the idea that more people could escape poverty (CEPAL 2008: 67).[6] 180 million people count as poor, including 12.9% of the population (71 million) that live in extreme poverty (CEPAL 2009a: 52). The largest concentrations of poverty are in Central America and north-eastern Brazil. Of the indigenous people, 80% live below the poverty line (Echeverria 1998: 2, 7). For 2009 it is estimated that the poverty rate increased again by 1.1% (poverty), respectively 0.8% (extreme poverty) due to the worldwide financial crisis (CEPAL 2009a: 69).

However, the fact that poverty rates have been decreasing over recent years does not mean that a problem no longer exists, and companies can still become active at the BoP. The region suffers from huge inequality in the distribution of income (Lustig and Deutsch 1998: i). The Gini coefficient varies from 0.412 in Venezuela to 0.594 in Brazil (CEPAL 2009a: 269f.). Wage disparities in LAC are among the largest worldwide. In total, 10% of the richest people in the region concentrate 34% of total income. The highest rates of income disparity can be found in Brazil and Colombia where the richest 10% concentrate over 40% of total income; the lowest rates are in Bolivia, Venezuela and Uruguay where the richest 10% have less than 27% of total income. Even though the concentration of income remains high, from 2002 until 2008, almost all countries had a diminishing concentration.[7] Colombia, Guatemala and the Dominican Republic were the only countries with an increasing concentration over that period (CEPAL 2009a: 58f.). Inequality has often been associated with uneven earnings growth owing to differences in human capital (e.g. in education) and in characteristics of jobs (e.g. managers vs. blue-collar workers, modern sectors vs. traditional sectors, informal vs. formal employment) (Lustig and Arias 2000: 33). The longer such conditions persist, the greater the possibility for socio-economic conflicts. Inequality can easily lead to increasing violence and crime rates (Marquez *et al.* 2010: 12). Also, because of the high inequality, people mistrust political institutions and the government. They believe that they serve the rich elite, as opposed to the majority of the population (CEPAL 2009a: 75). The World Bank came to the conclusion that the UN MDG poverty goal will be hard to reach if income inequality cannot be overcome (World Bank n.d.).

5 The poverty line is defined as the level of income beneath which a person cannot meet their daily nutritional requirements and other basic needs. The absolute poverty line is defined in terms of income insufficient to meet minimum daily nutritional requirements. The levels are set differently depending on country and region. They range from US$45–161 in urban areas and from US$32–101 in rural areas (local currency converted into US$, level of income per month). The line for extreme poverty ranges from US$23–81 in urban areas to US$18–58 in rural (level of income per month, CEPAL 2008: 59).

6 Big families are often dependent on one salary. So even someone with a good income can still be poor, depending on how many dependents they have. Family size has, however, decreased over the last few years. This is called the 'demographic bonus'.

7 In Venezuela, for example, the Gini coefficient decreased by 18%. In Argentina, Peru, Bolivia, Nicaragua, Panama and Paraguay it decreased by 8–10% (CEPAL 2009a: 59).

When looking at the other UN MDGs, it can be said that the region has made considerable progress in meeting some targets, albeit with differences between countries. However, the likelihood that most of the countries will achieve many of the targets is small. The pace of hunger reduction has been slow, even though the food produced surpasses around 40% of what would be needed to fulfil the people's basic requirements. In 2004–2006 8.7% of the population lacked access to sufficient food. Only one-third of the countries are estimated to reach the targeted reduction of child mortality. Achieving the maternal mortality ratio goal is likely to be difficult for the region. The land area covered by forest continues to decrease—the LAC region has the highest rate of deforestation in the world—and CO_2 emissions are increasing. On the other hand, goals in education and gender equality are on track. The prevalence of HIV has been stabilised in LAC, and the incidence of malaria and tuberculosis has diminished. Also, the proportion of the population using an improved drinking water source and an improved sanitation facility has increased (UN 2010b).

8.3 **Rural and urban disparities**

In total, around two-thirds of the poor in LAC are urban and one third live in rural areas.[8] Between 2002 and 2008 poverty in LAC has been reduced by 28% in urban areas and 16% in rural areas. Extreme poverty has been reduced by 39% in urban areas and 22% in rural areas (CEPAL 2009a: 54). In all, aggregating the countries together, the relative number of rural to urban poor has decreased,[9] although this is mainly due to population shifts rather than successful rural poverty reduction interventions, while the absolute number of urban poor has risen. Economic growth has reduced rural poverty primarily through urban migration.[10] A high percentage of the poor living in cities are new or recent arrivals from rural areas (Echeverria 1998: 2, 8). Still, a large fraction of the rural poor is relatively immobile due to low skills, age or ethnic characteristics such as language barriers (López and Valdés 2000: 198).

By 2020 the LAC population is estimated to grow to 670 million. The number of rural inhabitants will remain unchanged at 125 million, which means that population growth will be happening in urban areas (Echeverria 1998: 12). According to

8 Data from 2008.
9 This trend hides considerable heterogeneity between countries, and is dominated by successful rural poverty reduction in Brazil. For many other countries, the incidence of rural poverty has been constant or rising (De Janvry and Sadoulet 2000: 390).
10 In the decade 1970 to 1980, migration explained 76% of rural poverty reduction, while 28% could be explained by poverty reduction in situ. Between 1980 and 1990 it was 61% due to migration and 7% in situ, and between 1990 and 1994 95% was due to migration and 61% to rural decline. (De Janvry and Sadoulet 2000: 399).

the Social Enterprise Knowledge Network (SEKN), the main problems of the urban poor are over-crowding, everyday violence, insufficient basic services and poor urban infrastructure (Marquez *et al.* 2010: 11). The spatial segregation of the poor in many big cities in LAC leads to a polarisation whereby the poor usually live in informal settlements (slums) and the richer in closed apartment buildings or even 'closed communities'. This has important impacts on social cohesion as it highlights the erosion of opportunities in the life of the poor and deepens the disparity between them and the rest of society. It also leads to segregated access to work and education. These contribute to even bigger gaps between classes (CEPAL 2009a: 80).

Still, the incidence of rural poverty is considerably higher than the incidence of urban poverty.[11] In 2008, of the rural population in LAC, 52.2% lived in poverty, compared to 27.6% in urban areas. Rural poverty is usually also more extreme than urban poverty (Echeverria 1998: 1), with 29.5% living in extreme poverty in rural areas versus 8.3% in urban areas (CEPAL 2009a: 54). Over 60% of the poor in Mexico, Central America and the Andean countries live in rural areas. Living conditions—in terms of access to education, healthcare, clean water and sanitation—faced by the rural poor are usually much worse than those faced by the urban poor (López and Valdés 2000: 197; Quang Dao 2004: 500). Rural poverty is the result of a long history of unequal development and comes in part from low productivity of the assets, low quality assets (e.g. schools), government failures and market imperfections. Even though LAC has an abundance of land, there is a large proportion of landless rural workers who work as hired workers, and a high concentration of land in which a small number of large commercial farms coexists with a much larger number of small farms (López and Valdés 2000: 198). The rural poor face several problems: few employment opportunities; inadequate nutrition/health/education; and a lack of sufficient levels of organisation to lobby (Echeverria 1998: 2). On the other hand, rural poverty is less sensitive to aggregate income growth and to downturns than urban poverty (De Janvry and Sadoulet 2000: 394). Small farmers represent the largest share of the rural poor,[12] while the landless population and indigenous groups account for the remainder, and many rural poor do not have enough access to land and productive resources with which they could generate sufficient earnings from agricultural production itself (De Janvry and Sadoulet 2000: 3ff.). In rural LAC, education levels are lower than in urban areas. Individuals in rural areas complete about half the average years of schooling of those in urban areas. However, the impact of education on farm output and rural incomes is small, although it does

---

11 For these poverty measurements only income is relevant, and as many rural poor have some land available to grow their own food they do not suffer necessarily from hunger but rather from a lack of other basic goods and services.

12 In LAC relatively few small and medium-sized farmers have legal title to their land (López and Valdés 2000: 207).

have a positive effect on non-farm employment (López and Valdés 2000: 199).[13] According to the study of De Janvry and Sadoulet (2000), the most important path out of rural poverty for the region should be pluriactivity, a path that combines the cultivation of a small plot of land with access to off-farm sources of income. Also, López and Valdés (2000) point out that the availability of non-farm employment is important for poverty reduction in rural areas of LAC, not least because the rural exodus leads to high social costs.

8.4 **The market at the BoP**

As the majority of poor people in LAC live in urban areas, the BoP markets are more urban than rural. However, in the poorer BoP segments the rural poor constitute the majority in Bolivia (BoP1000[14] and lower), Colombia (BoP500), Honduras (BoP1000 and lower), Mexico (BoP1000 and lower) and Peru (BoP1000 and lower). In Guatemala and Paraguay the rural BoP market is already in the majority at US$2,000 PPP/year, in Jamaica at US$2,500 PPP/year. The only exception is Brazil,[15] where the urban poor form the majority of the market in all BoP segments (Hammond *et al.* 2007). Figure 8.1 shows the distribution in the respective BoP segments for the whole region.

Figure 8.1 **The BoP in LAC**

Source: Hammond *et al.* 2007: 19

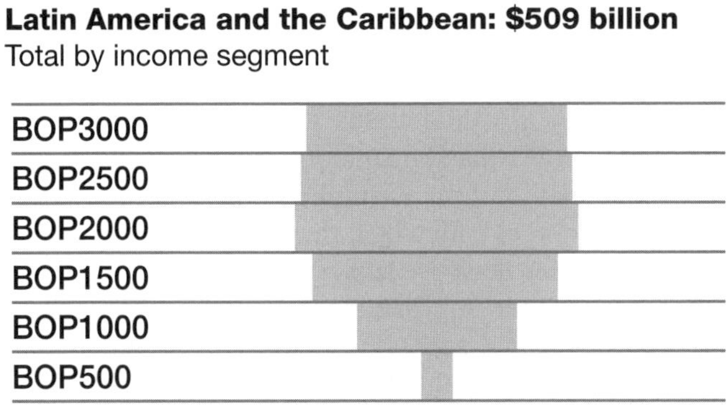

Latin America and the Caribbean: $509 billion
Total by income segment

BOP3000	
BOP2500	
BOP2000	
BOP1500	
BOP1000	
BOP500	

---

13 In general, a higher farm output does not necessarily mean more income. There has to be a market for the products (López and Valdés 2000: 205).

14 BoP1000 is people earning up to US$1,000 PPP per year and so on (Hammond *et al.* 2007).

15 Exception from the countries analysed in detail by Hammond *et al.* (2007).

We can see that the majority of the BoP live on US$1,500 PPP/year and above; only a small portion of the BoP lives below that level. One reason could be that—as mentioned before—due to economic growth over recent years many were lifted up the ladder. The upper segments are made up of almost the same number of people. Still, the distribution in the respective BoP segments varies between countries, so companies need to take more detailed statistics into account.

When defining the BoP as those living below US$3,000 PPP/year, the BoP market[16] in LAC consists of 360 million people having US$509 billion PPP to spend. Although this represents 70% of the region's population it is only 28% of aggregated household income.[17] This is a smaller share than in other developing regions (Hammond *et al.* 2007: 19). The BoP share of total income in the region ranges—in line with the amount of poor—from 13.4% in Argentina to 62.9% in Haiti (Hammond *et al.* 2007: 111). The majority of people in the LAC region suffer from a 'BoP penalty' in several forms: lack of access to essential goods and services; higher prices for goods and services; and/or poor quality of goods and services. However, this also means that there is significant potential for enterprises to enter the market. The rate of increase in sector-specific spending is highest in financial services and ICT. Technology innovation is also driving the growth in the ICT and financial sectors by reducing the BoP penalty (IDB 2006: 3). Hammond *et al.* (2007) took a closer look at the different BoP sector markets. Table 8.1 gives an overview of the total market size in the LAC region.

Table 8.1 **Expenditures BoP LAC**

Source: summarised from Hammond *et al.* 2007

Sector	Total market size (in US$ billion PPP) per sector
Food	199
Housing	56.7
Energy	30.5
Water	4.8
Health	24
ICT	13.4
Transportation	45.9

For most sectors, the average BoP household spending is significantly higher in LAC than in other regions (Hammond *et al.* 2007: 29). The BoP in LAC buys less than higher classes, but the portion of income spent on food and consumer

16 70% of the population of the 21 countries in LAC were included in the survey and then extrapolated (Hammond *et al.* 2007: 19).

17 As we have already seen, the informal market represents more than 40% of the official GDP in LAC. The household surveys of Hammond *et al.* (2007) reflect this issue.

products is significantly higher.[18] The remaining income usually goes into housing or rent, transportation and communications (D'Andrea and Herrero 2007: 26[19]). Latin America has its share of poverty, but infrastructure is often better than in other developing regions. Many households have reasonable access to electricity and tap water (Banerjee and Duflo 2006: 18), and to basic appliances that impact on purchasing behaviour. Household expenditure has a much greater meaning to developing/emerging consumers and women derive considerable self-esteem from managing this spending in the best way possible (D'Andrea and Herrero 2007: 27). D'Andrea and Herrero (2007) found that BoP consumers showed strong preferences for leading and intermediate brands over low-priced, economy brands. Because they have less disposable income, they also have a smaller margin for error in their purchases, and steer their preferences toward established, proven brands. This is an advantage for companies that have established a well-known brand in these countries. Low-income consumers buy more basic goods, but are willing to pay more for intermediate and leading brands in basic categories. The more expensive, higher-value-added categories (e.g. frozen food, ready-to-eat meals, yoghurt or flavoured milk drinks) are less prevalent in these households (D'Andrea and Herrero 2007: 27). The buying behaviour of BoP consumers differs from that of richer customers with the shopping process driven by day-to-day needs. Low-income consumers in LAC are price-sensitive, but purchasing decisions are generally driven by a desire to minimise total purchasing costs. They include the costs for transportation, how to bring the purchases home, finding childcare and the time needed. The trade-off between physical proximity and pricing is a key determinant of store choice. Street and open-air markets are perceived as having better quality and price, and they enable social interaction with neighbours. A wide product assortment and the ability to pay with credit cards are less important to low-income consumers (D'Andrea and Herrero 2007: 29f.). Barki and Parente (2010), in their study on the BoP in Brazil, found the following characteristics in consumer behaviour among less well-off customers:

- A perception of value not solely determined by lower prices

- A need to compensate for a dignity deficit and low self-esteem

- A stronger preference for personalised relationships

- A high aspiration to feel socially included in society

- A preference for stores with a crowded and overstocked atmosphere

18 On average, for the whole population in LAC, consumer products make up roughly 30–35% of spending. Emerging consumers spend 50–75% of available income on consumer products but amongst the lowest strata this is often 100% (D'Andrea and Herrero 2007: 26).

19 The research covers six countries of LAC (Argentina, Brazil, Chile, Colombia, Costa Rica and Mexico), home to 71% of the region's population and 81% of the region's GDP (D'Andrea and Herrero 2007: 26).

In Chapter 9 we will look at the companies involved in the research and their initiatives to target the BoP market in LAC.

9
Companies participating in the case study research[1]

This section describes the projects of the three companies that participated in the in-depth case studies, and provides a summary of the companies participating in stage two (the questionnaire stage).

9.1 **In-depth case studies**

The three companies that participated in the in-depth case studies and their BoP projects are summarised in the following sections.[2]

9.1.1 Sucromiles (Cali, Colombia)

Type of company	A joint venture between a local economic group (Ardila Lülle) and a MNC (Tate & Lyle)
Start of the project	2009
Sector	Health/nutrition
Type of product/service	Micronutrient (calcium powder)
Where the project is anchored in the company	Corporate Social Responsibility
Integration of target group	Distribution and, to a lesser extent, ideas generation. People from lower classes also work in the production facilities

---

1 Company data was valid at the time the case study research was conducted.
2 In order of date when the author conducted the case study fieldwork.

Sucromiles S.A., located in Cali Palmira-Valley, Colombia, is a joint venture between Ardila Lülle[3] and the UK company Tate & Lyle, a global provider of distinctive, high-quality ingredients and solutions for the food, beverage and other industries. Sucromiles is a biotechnology company, producing and selling raw materials to the chemical, pharmaceutical and nutrition industry. Their products are sold in the national, as well as international, markets (US, Europe, Latin America, Central America, Caribbean, Asia, Japan and Australia).

Over ten years ago, Sucromiles got involved with the foundation Trascender, an organisation focused on the education of children from vulnerable households in Colombia. To finance its activities, the foundation sold different consumer products. As part of its CSR,[4] Sucromiles then developed TriCaltone, a calcium powder based on calcium citrate, which was launched in November 2006. 100% of the profit made by the product goes into sustaining the foundation's education programmes.

TriCaltone is targeted at an identified health need. Around 80% of the population in Colombia has a calcium deficit, which can lead to osteoporosis and high health-care costs.[5] Furthermore, calcium supplements may reduce the risk of dying from heart disease and cancer. The final price of the product can be kept very low mainly due to reduced product functionality. There is no advertisement, it comes in powder (not tablet) form, it has no imprints, no R&D costs, no colour, etc. Even though costs are kept low, the quality of the product is high, conforming to ISO 9001:2000 and the normal quality procedures at Sucromiles. TriCaltone is sold in pots of 160 doses (around US$11) and in 80 doses (with or without vitamin D at around US$8.50), as well as in boxes containing 30 one-dose sachets (around US$5.50). It has to be taken once or twice daily.

The product has been—apart from established partnerships with supermarkets—sold since June 2009 via a network of so-called *TriCaldamas*. There are currently more than 170 *TriCaldamas* who are mostly women from strata one to three—the BoP in Colombia.[6] To start, they have to buy a 'kit' costing around US$27.50 which contains a bag, products, selling material and elements to identify themselves as *TriCaldama*. They continuously order the products they need by calling the team at Sucromiles[7] and get 21 days credit to pay for them. The products are delivered once a week. When they start, they usually sell first to their family, neighbours and friends. Later, they develop their own strategies in order to identify sales locations.

3 A major Colombian conglomerate active in the beverage sector, sugar and biofuels, packaging and telecommunications, and which also controls entities such as RCN TV (a TV station), the Postobon soft drinks company, and the Atlético Nacional football team.

4 The six-person team dedicated to the project at Sucromiles is called 'mercadeo social' (social marketing).

5 WFP and ICBF (2005): La ENSIN: Encuesta Nacional de la Situación Nutricional en Colombia.

6 Of the around 44 million population in Colombia, approximately 70% can be counted to the BoP (with the limit of US$3,000 PPP/year according to Hammond *et al.* 2007: 122).

7 The team is in continuous contact with the *TriCaldamas*. They also talk about how sales are going, where problems are and can bring in suggestions.

Sucromiles supports them in the organisation of so called *brigadas* where people's calcium levels can be measured, thus far mostly with groups of elderly people.[8] Around once a month, all *TriCaldamas* can attend a *capacitación*, which covers computer skills, selling techniques, health and nutrition, and activities aimed at fostering personal development.[9] The margin the *TriCaldamas* can keep is 30% for each product sold.

The potential market for TriCaltone is very big, not only in Colombia, but also in other countries. It can be divided into two groups: those who already take calcium and usually get it from the public health system, mainly pregnant and elderly women;[10] and those who are not yet aware of the importance of calcium to health.

The project is innovative in several ways. As it is in powder form, TriCaltone is easily absorbable and can be mixed into food. Its low price means that it reaches groups of people who are usually not within the company's focus. The inclusion of the target group as a distribution channel is also something that is fairly new. But the biggest change for Sucromiles, which is more used to business-to-business activities, is in producing something directly for a mass market. The next steps now focus on increasing sales and scaling-up.

9.1.2 Nestlé (São Paulo, Brazil)

Type of company	MNC based in developed country
Start of the project	2006
Sector	Nutrition
Type of product/service	Food products and beverages
Where the project is anchored in the company	Department Regionalização & BOP (Regionalisation & BoP)
Integration of target group	Idea generation and distribution/marketing. People from lower classes also work in the production facilities and suppliers are often small-scale farmers. During the product development process concept and product testing is carried out on BoP consumers

Nestlé was founded in 1866 and has its HQ in Vevey, Switzerland. Today it is the world's leading nutrition, health and wellness company. Sales for 2009 were CHF108

---

8   It is very common in Colombia for older people in different neighbourhoods to meet every morning in groups to do exercise or other activities together.

9   During the time when the author was there, there was a *capacitación* to improve self-esteem and work as a group/network.

10 The products from the government are based on calcium carbonate and not on calcium citrate. Many people are intolerant of this. Other products based on calcium citrate are around ten times more expensive than TriCaltone and not affordable for the BoP.

billion. Around 280,000 people are employed worldwide, and factories or operations are present in almost every country in the world. In Brazil, Nestlé has been
active since 1921 with its HQ in São Paulo and production facilities/operations all
over the country.

Nestlé Brazil has so far mostly targeted social classes A and B.[11] But since 2006,
the intention with regard to 'popularly positioned products'[12] is to increase Nestlé's
presence in the lower classes (C, D and E) by offering products that meet the specific nutritional needs of BoP consumers.[13] Popularly positioned products are also
one of four growth pillars for Nestlé worldwide.

The programme in Brazil, Nestlé até Você, contains, in essence, two distribution channels. 'Partnerships' are intended to make Nestlé products visible and
to become closer to the C, D and E classes (via shops located in metro stations,
the football stadium Morumbí and stores of Casas Bahia). The 'door-to-door system' brings Nestlé products in the form of kits to the C, D and E classes.[14] Also,
products are sold in the 'floating supermarket' in the Amazon and selected stores.
Nestlé's factory in Feira de Santana, in the Bahia region of Brazil, was opened in
2007 and produces Maggi instant noodles (also a popularly positioned product).
Besides bringing direct and indirect employment opportunities to an economically
deprived region, it also helps Nestlé to reach 50 million consumers located in this
area, of which the great majority belongs to the BoP.

The door-to-door system with the so called 'selling ladies' (*revendedoras*) started
in São Paulo and grew to other regions of Brazil. So far, there are more than 7,700
revendedoras, mainly coming from lower social strata. The mission is to establish a
dedicated channel that offers affordability, convenience and credit to BoP consumers. Nestlé delivers the products to micro-distributors who then deliver the kits to
the *revendedoras* to sell from a Nestlé cart at the consumers' locations. Groups of
revendedoras are organised under a supervisor who trains and coordinates them
and is the contact person for any inquiries. All purchases can be made on credit,
which must be paid back within 15 to 30 days. *Revendedoras* earn around 30% of

11 Classes A and B are the richer social classes in Brazil, with C being the emerging middle
   class. Classes D and E, as well as a part of class C, count as the BoP. Of the more than 192
   million population (2009 estimate), around 124 million people are considered as the BoP
   (limit at US$3,000 PPP; Hammond *et al.* 2007: 117).
12 Popularly positioned products include, for example, powdered milk in sachets (Ideal), a
   new sugared instant coffee (Nescafé dolca) and a juice powder (La Frutta). There is also a
   new biscuit made of Canjica, a cereal found in the north-east of the country.
13 Some products are nutritionally fortified according to the nutritional deficits of the
   respective target groups.
14 Kits contain different products of Nestlé. There are, for example, yoghurt kits, breakfast
   kits, chocolate kits, dessert kits, etc.

the retail price of the kits[15] and can usually easily earn more than the minimum wage in Brazil.[16]

Nestlé provides various support and activities to the *revendedoras*, the supervisors and the micro-distributors—recruitment and retention campaigns; big events with prices; sales conventions; promotions; and selling catalogues. The ABC training programme consists of training in sales and health/nutrition. A '*telenovela*', produced especially for this purpose, is used to divulge this information. A new web portal is—among other goals—intended to improve communication with the micro-distributors and leaders as well as accelerate the flow of information.[17]

Nestlé's activities are innovative in several ways. By changing the main focus from A and B to C, D and E class customers, and dedicating a structure working for emerging consumers, Nestlé is achieving a paradigm innovation. Some production process innovations appear as well, such as changing the packaging size and type (e.g. powdered milk in sachets) and with the factory in Feira de Santana. Product innovation can be found in the new developed products. The new partnerships with the Casas Bahia, the football stadium and metro stations can be considered a partnership innovation. However, the biggest innovation can be detected in the position innovation: with the partnerships mentioned, but also with the micro-distributor–supervisor–selling lady system, products are introduced differently to the market.

9.1.3 BAC | Credomatic (San José, Costa Rica)

Type of company	Domestic MNC
Start of the project	January 2010
Sector	Financial services
Type of product/service	Credit
Where the project is anchored in the company	Corporate Social Responsibility
Integration of target group	The target group is controlling the whole process. From the view of BAC	Credomatic it is integrated into the distribution

The privately owned BAC | Credomatic network (BAC COM) dates back to 1952 and now operates in Guatemala, El Salvador, Honduras, Nicaragua, Costa Rica, Panama, Grand Cayman, Bahamas and the US. It has bank locations in the different regions,

---

15 There are recommendations from Nestlé to set the price, but the micro-distributors and the *revendedoras* are free to decide how much they want to sell it for. They can also decide on the composition of the kits.

16 By selling four kits a day, *revendedoras* earn more than the minimum wage.

17 www.nestle.com.br/portalnestle/nestleatevoce/nestle_ate_voce.aspx (accessed 3 September 2010).

offers credit card operations, makes stock positions, manages pension funds and offers insurance services as well as other financial services.

In partnership with the Fundación Integral Campesina (FINCA) and American Express, BAC COM Costa Rica has developed the project 'Microcredit and Financial Education for Adults and Youth in Costa Rica', which aims to facilitate access to financial services, promote entrepreneurship, foster community development and encourage environmental sensibility among micro-entrepreneurs and young people in Costa Rica. While Costa Rica is considered to be a middle-income country, it still struggles with high levels of inequality and poverty.[18] The Central Valley is home to a number of communities where micro- and small enterprises are the predominant source of income for residents, yet these communities have limited access to credit and other financial services. Too often, micro-enterprises fail because the business owner has limited education and/or lacks the basic managerial skills and financial proficiency necessary to succeed.

FINCA was established in 1985 for the purpose of improving the socioeconomic situation of low-income individuals. It utilises a proven methodology in which solidarity groups create corporations as a means to save money, manage their savings and access loans for working capital for group members' income generating activities. FINCA's process entails the formation of groups, called Communal Credit Enterprises (CCEs), of approximately 15 to 30 individuals, which are institutionalised as legal corporations (SA). FINCA trains the groups, collaborates with them and helps determine the amount of money they will seek to manage both as capital and credit. Facilitators of FINCA likewise train the groups on business administration, savings, lending and corporate management. To date, FINCA has formed about 1,200 CCEs, directly benefiting over 50,000 participants and family members. Each year FINCA extends in excess of US$1 million in new credit and promotes US$400,000 in savings.

The CCEs first build their own capital by selling shares. With this money, they give credits, mostly to people from the community. After a while, when they are well established, they can apply for higher credits from 'outside', which are provided by EDESA, a company held by all CCEs.[19] Even though the facilitators accompany the CCEs in their development (at the beginning more and then gradually less, until they no longer need support), the CCEs are free to formulate all their rules (e.g. who to give credit to, share price, interest rates). Around once a month, the CCEs in a specified geographic sector meet to exchange their experiences and learn from each other.

Within its project, BAC COM established a new credit line for 20 selected CCEs to the tune of US$200,000. At least 200 beneficiaries receive a credit via EDESA.

---

18 With a US$3,000 PPP limit, 60% of the population (2.4 million) are counted as the BoP (Hammond *et al.* 2007: 111).

19 Some CCE also apply for/receive credits from other banks.

Besides facilitating access to credit, the project has several other objectives and activities:[20]

- To strengthen the 20 CCEs through assessment, project promotion briefings, signing agreements with neighbourhood groups and providing training in administration, planning, credit, accounting, finance and organisation

- To provide business development training through five-year strategic plans, annual operating plans, training in basic administration, financial analysis, portfolio management and basic managerial skills as well as establishing a marketing plan for each CCE

- To develop youth entrepreneurs through workshops for establishing regulations for the CCEs' educational investment programmes (EIPs), EIP, appointing an EIP committee for each CCE and implementing educational activities for young people

- To foster environmental awareness through a special environmental week, workshops on environmental sustainability and sound business practices, and graduation ceremonies

All these activities took place during 2010. The credit line will remain for at least five years. The strategy of BAC COM with this project is to get closer to the BoP markets and to learn from the experiences they accumulate. Additionally, they want to strengthen the relationship with EDESA for possible future credits. The fundamental reason, however, is to learn to be a 'second-tier bank' (*banco de segundo piso*), as their credits reach the ECCs via EDESA. Thus, for BAC COM this project is mainly a partnership innovation.

9.2 **Questionnaire case studies**

Eight companies with BoP ventures/projects participated in the questionnaire. Table 9.1 summarises the participating cases.[21]

---

20 These activities are funded by BAC COM and have no direct returns for the company or American Express.
21 In alphabetical order.

Table 9.1 **Questionnaire case studies**

Company name	Type of company	Sector	Location of project	Name of project/venture	Description of project/venture	Start of project/ venture	Type of product/service offered	Integration of target group
Cemex	Multinational, large, domestic	Construction	Mexico, Colombia, Venezuela, Nicaragua, Costa Rica, Dominican Republic	Patrimonio Hoy	Patrimonio Hoy addresses the housing needs of low-income families by empowering them through a market-based solution. The project provides services as technical assistance, micro-credits and materials.	2000	Construction materials and specified additional services	Idea generation, product development, distribution/ marketing
Empresas Públicas de Medellín E.S.P. (EPM)	Domestic, state-owned, large	Energy, water	Colombia	Antioquia Iluminada	Under the strategy 'universalisation of services', 42,000 families in remote areas in the state of Antioquia are connected to electricity with this project. It is estimated that 500 new jobs have been created within the project and the new clients are educated about energy use.	2009	Electricity	Product development, distribution/ marketing
Gas Natural Fenosa S.A.	Multinational, large, foreign	Energy	Argentina	Solidarity Network Trust Fund (Cuarte V)	The initiative is focused on expanding the natural gas network to low-income neighbourhoods. It implements a system of financing public works (natural gas) through a community participatory model, incorporating the generation of social capital and returns on investment. Gas Natural works closely together with the Fundación Pro Vivienda Social in this project.	2003	Natural gas networks	Idea generation, product/service development, distribution/ marketing

Company name	Type of company	Sector	Location of project	Name of project/venture	Description of project/venture	Start of project/venture	Type of product/service offered	Integration of target group
Holcim Ltd.	Multinational, large, foreign	Construction	Costa Rica, Colombia, El Salvador, Mexico, Nicaragua	Different housing projects: MiCasa, Provivah, Prefa, Vivienda Segura	All projects are focused on building houses including construction material of Holcim (concrete) and additional services.	1995	Construction materials and additional services	Depending on the project, the target group is more or less integrated, up to the extent of integration in every innovation step.
Mejoramiento Integral Asistido S.A. (MIA)	Domestic, medium size	Construction	Mexico	Vivienda Progresiva Rural MIA	MIA developed a model for the autoconstruction of housing for families with low incomes, mainly in rural areas. Within that model, the company offers access to credit and subsidies, logistics (materials), training and support in construction, as well as complementary programmes	2009	Housing	Production
Siconterra	Domestic, new venture	Construction	Mexico	Adobeterra	Siconterra builds construction blocks (ADOBETERRA) for building homes out of adobe, a tradional Mexican clay paste. This building material is inexpensive, environmentally friendly, and naturally insulating, resistant to weight and humidity. Through a foundation, advice and capacitaciones for the autoconstruction of houses are offered to poor households	2003	Construction materials	Idea generation

Company name	Type of company	Sector	Location of project	Name of project/venture	Description of project/venture	Start of project/ venture	Type of product/service offered	Integration of target group
Tecnosol S.A.	Domestic, binational, medium size	Energy	Nicaragua, El Salvador	Tecnosol as a whole only serves the BoP	Tecnosol is providing renewable energy (water, wind, solar) to homes, farms and small enterprises, mainly in rural areas in Nicaragua. With 17 branch offices around the country, the various services are offered close to the customers.	1998	Renewable energy products	Distribution/ marketing
Tiendas Industriales Asociadas (TIA) S.A.	Binational domestic, family-held, large	Retail	Ecuador	Multiahorro Barrio store	Multiahorro Barrio stores are located in poor areas with high density. The strategy is to sell at the lowest price in the area of influence. The stores provide a limited selection of basic goods such as food, perishable goods and dairy products. A part of products are sold under the brand Multiahorro	2000	Small supermarkets	Distribution/ marketing; most of the people running the stores come from poor areas and are trained by the company

10
Analysis of the results from the case studies

With dependency, there is no development (María Marta Padilla, FINCA).

The illustration of the results of the case study research is grouped around the bottom-up development elements and related questions elaborated in Chapter 5 and summarised in Chapter 6.[1] After some general observations on the bottom-up development perspective in the participating BoP ventures, projects and initiatives of the represented companies in LAC, we dig into the exposure of the bottom-up development elements in the case studies. While the three in-depth case studies formed the initial set of propositions on a bottom-up development perspective applied in BoP ventures,[2] the answers given in the questionnaires helped to verify and fine-tune these propositions.[3] The propositions can be seen as statements that derived from analysing BoP case studies under the perspective of a bottom-up development perspective. Due to their validity in the case studies conducted, they represent initial empirical evidence.[4]

1 The logic to follow the structure developed in Chapter 5 is chosen to make the connections to bottom-up development literature more visible. In a last step (Chapter 12), the results are then grouped around the three research questions.
2 See the questionnaire in Section 3 of the Annex.
3 By discussing the results in this chapter, the in-depth case studies certainly take up more space. Yet information and statements from the questionnaires help to enrich the results.
4 Qualitative, not quantitative; with more cases available, a quantitative methodology could give further evidence.

10.1 **General observations**

The individuals from the companies that were involved in the cases under consideration have often not been aware of applying elements of a bottom-up development perspective, and their application evolved naturally due to the experiences accumulated. In fact, Sucromiles did not even intentionally start a BoP approach or inclusive business; but the project grew into it.

   In some cases, a very high level of responsibility and decision-making power was shifted to the involved poor (e.g. BAC COM/FINCA). In other cases, the poor were given a certain amount of responsibility in a defined field as a starting point, and in other decisions the poor only participated (e.g. Nestlé and Sucromiles). However, most plan to integrate the target group further as the experiences had were successful. The contribution of the target group is seen as valuable to the innovation process and in none of the cases was a disparaging attitude towards low-income consumers detected.

10.1.1 Orientation: West or South?

What is the development aim of BoP initiatives? Should the poor develop like the West/North ('Westernisation') or is there another path to escape from poverty?[5] First, all the poor the author spent time with had a TV and were well aware of products and services offered to the top of the pyramid in their respective country.[6] Especially in urban areas, they desired the products shown in the advertisements and different TV series (such as beauty products, home appliances and clothing) as well as the associated lifestyle enjoyed by the more affluent in their countries. The differentiation between a development path taken in the West/North (meaning developed/rich) and South/East (meaning underdeveloped/poor) was not really understood by the practitioner participants, and cannot be applied within the context given. In LAC many cities (or big parts of them) are not so noticeably different from the West/North in terms of consumerism and a part of the population already live a life comparable to that of people in developed countries. The poor, therefore, cannot take a completely different development path.[7]

   The view and opinions of the companies give a mixed picture. For most, Westernisation is not something bad per se. To some extent, Western achievements can bear opportunities for poverty alleviation and solutions to local problems. Sucromiles and TriCaltone, for example, try to foster what they call a 'cultural change' by focusing on ill-health prevention rather than treatment, the approach followed by the

---

5 This question follows the discussion in development literature of whether development in developing countries necessarily has to take the same path as in developed countries.
6 Even the most isolated poor in rural areas, who did not have a functioning toilet or enough knives for the whole family, owned a TV and a DVD player. The TV was on for more or less the whole day.
7 Exceptions might be very isolated indigenous villages (for example in the Amazon).

rich and educated. However, in Colombia, there is an objective problem with calcium deficiency and even though calcium augmentation is not seen as necessary by the low-income population (symptoms usually appear when it is too late) it is nevertheless advantageous for them to take it. Clearly, having a calcium-rich diet (milk products, green vegetables) would be better, but such a diet is prohibitively expensive for the poor, and people are not used to calcium-rich food. In this case, calcium is an objectively detected (rather than invented) necessity, even though the product idea comes from 'the top'. The potential consumers therefore must be educated about their needs. This is also the case with fortified products from Nestlé. However, the products have to be adapted to local needs.

> A company can use the same brands, R&D, and factories, but marketing and distribution have to be developed locally (Sylvain Darnil, Nestlé).

Also, in the case of BAC COM, the entirety of financial know-how applied is 'Western'. Even though BAC COM state that trying to implant something that comes from the 'rich world' does not generally work and solutions have to be developed together, some knowledge from the 'West'—adapted to the target group—is important (e.g. financial accounting methods). When something is already well established in the developed world it can be brought forward to developing regions. Still, when the target group has superior knowledge, FINCA does not intervene. This also increases the self-esteem of the participating people.

> The best is a combination without dependency (María Marta Padilla, FINCA).

While the in-depth case studies gave a mixed picture on whether 'avoiding Westernisation' is a reason to choose a bottom-up development perspective in BoP ventures, the questionnaire participants did not confirm this proposition. One respondent stated that a project should start without any paradigms. We can therefore *not* conclude that 'avoiding Westernisation' is a driver to choose a bottom-up development perspective in BoP ventures.

10.1.2 Decentralisation

Are bottom-up projects more likely to be successful with a decentralised organisational structure? In the case of the MNCs participating in the in-depth case studies, the more decentralised the company is (multinational strategy) the higher the probability that they come up with BoP projects in general. Nestlé Brazil has a high level of independency from its parent company. BAC COM in Costa Rica is completely independent. Moreover, for project implementation a higher decentralisation is better.

> The higher you go in the pyramid, the more the customers are the same all over the world. The lower you go, the more they are different. That's why

> decentralisation is important when a company wants to reach the BoP
> (Sylvain Darnil, Nestlé).

While we can conclude from the in-depth case studies that a decentralised organisational structure is an advantage in using a bottom-up approach, the participants in the case studies confirmed the assumption. For example, in the case of Cemex:

> More responsibility for local offices and actors foster ownership and
> hence success (Henning Alts, Cemex).

However, central coordination is necessary and there are some limits in terms of economies of scale.

> If the organisation is too decentralised, the decision-making process
> becomes more complicated, since a bottom-up approach has a lot of
> input from local communities. Information technologies make it easy to
> transmit information from the field to a central HQ where decisions can
> be made (Guillermo Jaime Calderón, MIA).

According to the questionnaire responses, the assumption could be specified, and we can state:

> **Proposition**: *A decentralised organisational company structure
> makes it easier to use bottom-up strategies. Central coordination is
> nevertheless important.*

10.2 Analysis of the bottom-up development elements applied in practice

After the more general implications of bottom-up development approaches derived from the case study research, we now discuss the elements of bottom-up development outlined in Section 5.4.

10.2.1 Real participation

Do companies that want to sell their products or services to the BoP also have to integrate the target group into the whole innovation process? How, and how much, should they participate? Who should participate?

All of the projects participating in the case study research integrated the target group somehow into the innovation process (this was also a criterion to participate), and therefore were clearly convinced that this leads to more success or, in the first place, enables a project. However, few projects were seen that integrate the target group into the whole process. Rather, they were integrated to different extents. With consumer products (as in the case of Nestlé and Sucromiles), the poor were mainly integrated into idea generation and distribution/marketing. They were also employed in the production process, where it did not demand high education levels. Opinions were gathered from the BoP primarily during the product testing phase, but also during product development. For the *TriCaldamas* themselves, for example, it was not important to be part of all steps of the innovation process; it was enough for them to be kept informed. The participating poor either wanted to be permanently employed, or their working schedule had to allow flexibility to enable them to fulfil their other daily tasks. In the case of BAC COM, after facilitation the target group was able to manage the whole process. Also, the companies participating in the questionnaire integrated the target group to very different extents—some only in one step of the innovation process, others in the whole process.[8] Overall we can conclude that the level of integration depends very much on the project, the products and services. Ideas and opinions can generally be integrated throughout the whole process, but how much the people are really involved depends upon the step in question. However, we *cannot* conclude that the poor have to be integrated into the whole innovation process.

Even though the level of participation does not necessarily have to be close to 100%, it is important that the participating individuals represent the pluralism, diversity and socio-demographic characteristics of the target community. This does not necessarily mean that they are representative of the whole target group, but it is important that they know the community and the target group well, in order to reflect what BoP means. For example, in the case of Nestlé and Sucromiles, it is more important to have a wide range of *revendedoras/TriCaldamas* ('selling ladies') from different areas than to represent the exact composition of the communities. However, for the processes of idea generation and product testing the representativeness of the target group is important. As strangers are often unable to enter poor communities (especially in urban areas), it is important to gain insight via representative locals. Therefore, it is also very important that those participating are accepted in their respective community. Pluralism in the integrated group is in general less important when a wide variety of products is being offered. In the case of BAC COM and FINCA, other selection criteria were more important than representativeness.[9] As the participants had a very demanding task in managing the CCEs, it was more important that they were motivated to establish a CCE, had an entrepreneurial spirit, were flexible and versatile, reliable, felt settled where they were, and that they were honest. Too much diversity can also lead to less efficiency. From the in-depth case studies, we can therefore conclude that a representation of pluralism is important when working together with the target group. The questionnaire participants confirmed this assumption.

---

8 For details see Section 9.2.
9 However, the inclusiveness of women was important for BAC COM.

Many brains think more than one. It's important to include the diversity of the community into a project (Javier Contreras, Siconterra).

The key point is to understand and know the needs of the target group. That means that you have to be able to constantly include them in your innovative strategies. At the same time it is fundamental to work directly at the local level, involving and giving community actors responsibilities (Henning Alts, Cemex).

We state:

> **Proposition**: *It is important that the people involved in the project represent the pluralism in the targeted community, especially in certain steps of the innovation process.*

Do the projects require equality in decision-making? Giving the participating group some freedom in decision-making is important, as this leads to empowerment. Nestlé's *revendedoras* can decide when, how much and what (composition of kits) they sell. The *TriCaldamas* can decide where, when and how much they sell. The CCEs within the BAC COM scheme decide all their rules (interest rates, how much credit to whom, etc.). However, this does not mean that the poor have to participate in all decision-making. When a new product is developed, for example at Nestlé, only a focus group can be involved, as *revendedoras* generally do not sign a confidentiality agreement.[10] Equality in decision-making is very difficult with big groups if the necessary technology is not available. Nestlé, for example, established a SMS channel[11] for these kinds of processes; for the same reason, Sucromiles is training the *TriCaldamas* in the use of computers and the internet. However, there is a limit to the amount of listening that can be done:

> Too much discussion leads to that nothing is happening. We have to listen up to a certain level and then go forward (Sylvain Darnil, Nestlé).

For BAC COM, it is not only equality in decision-making that counts:

> More than equality, partnership, a true sense of 'being on the same boat' and the acknowledgement of how all parts win and what is in for each is important. This also permits more trust (Laura Porras Alfaro, BAC COM).

We can therefore conclude that equality in decision-making is indeed important in BoP ventures that take a bottom-up approach. But far more important is that the involved poor have freedom of decision in defined areas, and that the communication flow is guaranteed.

This assumption was strengthened by the responses to the questionnaire. In the experiences of Holcim and Multiahorro Barrio stores, for example, equality in decision-making was not very important, but information flow, however, was. To make informed decisions, the information flow is important, but this does not

---

10 The *revendedoras* are independent and not employed by Nestlé or the micro-distributors.
11 Short message service via cellular phone.

necessarily mean *all* information. It is difficult to ensure that the involved poor are informed of everything that is going on.

We can therefore state:

> **Proposition**: *The involved poor need freedom of decision in defined areas and the company has to assure a steady information flow between all partners involved.*

Does everybody in the community have to be integrated or is a selection enough? Part of this has been outlined earlier, but when it comes to sectors there are differences. The companies participating in the in-depth case studies were all involved with private consumer goods. Their experience shows that in a consumer goods market a selection of the target group is acceptable as it is each person's choice whether or not to buy. But it is also sometimes useful to mobilise the whole community in order to fill gaps within missing or imperfect markets. For example, in the case of Sucromiles, the 'cultural change' in terms of paying attention to prevention requires a wholesale mobilisation of the target community. The people who are integrated usually subsequently become clients. Furthermore, in the case of BAC COM, the whole community can sometimes participate in training organised by FINCA.

When including the answers of the questionnaire participants, we see a more detailed picture. The projects in the industry of common pool goods (e.g. electricity and, to a certain extent, construction) all have the goal of mobilising all community members.

> At least, the whole community has to be informed and sensitised (César Augusto Roldán, EPM).

This does not, however, mean that the whole community has to be mobilised by the company itself. Collective community action can also be fostered by a selected group of people who are integrated into the project. Holcim, for example, established so called 'project advisory panels' consisting of local people. Also, with Gas Natural, the 'mobilising events' to gain support and participation in the gasification projects are community-driven.

> Whilst the idea is to mobilise the entire neighbourhood, in our experience there are always community members who do not want to participate due to doubts or economic situations that do not allow them to. Our minimum 70% adhesion rate guarantees an already high level of community participation (Gabriel Lanfranchi, Fundación Pro Vivienda Social).

There is also another advantage when mobilising the whole community:

> The whole community consumes products and services. The people integrated in the project, convert automatically into consumers (Javier Contreras, Siconterra).

We can therefore conclude:

> *Proposition: If the project is in the industry of common pool goods such as infrastructure (e.g. electricity, communication) the whole community should be mobilised and collective community action fostered. If the company is entering the consumer goods market, a selection of individuals and groups can be integrated. Mobilising the whole community might still be useful in order to fill gaps within lacking or imperfect markets (e.g. knowledge, infrastructure).*

10.2.2 Power relations and elite capture

How important are power relations in the communities where companies have their BoP projects? What are the consequences of such relations?

Power relations play a role in BoP projects. When a company wants to enter a community, it is usually the leaders who are first detected. But it is often not the formal leaders (e.g. local government officials). Rather, it is the informal ones who have the community's trust and who the community consider to be their representative, protector or supporter (BAC COM/FINCA[12] and Sucromiles). Without the approval of the community leader there is, in most cases, no entry—especially in urban slums.[13] Particularly important are the motivations and goals of the community leader (political or authentic motivation), and these motivations should match both the communities' needs and the interests of the company.[14] Companies usually approach a community indirectly; not via the leader, but via an existing local organisation (e.g. company, NGO, foundation). Especially at the beginning of a project, it is important to be aware of the main structures of a community in order to prevent the creation of further inequality. But, depending on the project set-up, the company does not necessarily need to know the power structures of a community. In the case of Nestlé, it is enough if the micro-distributors and, especially, the *revendedoras* have the information needed. It is therefore easier if *revendedoras* work in the area in which they live, as they are familiar with the structures within these communities. In the case of BAC COM, the facilitator of FINCA needs to pay attention to the rule of 'zero exclusion' (and not BAC COM), as there can be powerful clans who distribute the credits and positions within their group.[15] By applying FINCA's methodology correctly, these problems can be avoided.

---

12 It was also mentioned that if the integrated people already have a lot of other tasks in the community they are often not as focused as they should be.

13 Every time the author entered a dangerous area the visit had to be first arranged with the informal community leader.

14 The opposite is also true, according to David Gomez, Community Leader Siloé, Cali, Colombia. If the interests of the company do not match the goals of the community leader then the chance of entering is non-existent.

15 For example in Talamanca, an indigenous region in Costa Rica, so-called 'women clans' exist who hinder non-indigenous people from participating in a CCE.

According to BAC COM and FINCA, the more informed people are, the better the education is and the more mature/empowered the people are, the less elite capture is possible. CCEs usually notice themselves if a small circle of people are favoured by credits and positions in a CCE because growth slows down. This risk of elite capture could not be detected in the other in-depth cases. In the project of Sucromiles and Nestlé, elite capture is, in any case, minimal, because the (informal) leaders usually want the best for their community. If they were to steal the earnings of the *revendedoras/TriCaldamas* they would be quickly replaced. Another issue is the existence of 'drug traffic leaders' and gangs. But for them, the earnings of the *revendedoras/TriCaldamas* are, at present, too small. In rural areas, local structures may be more important than in urban areas (more anonymous).

We can therefore conclude that the company, or its partners, needs to be aware of local structures of power. Working with leaders who are accepted and respected by the community is important in order to gain support and implement a project. However, elite capture could *not* be detected as a relevant problem. It can only be assumed that this is more of a problem when a more significant amount of capital is involved and distributed within a community.

The questionnaire respondents verified the importance of the local structure of power:

> The structures of power lead the decisions of the community (Javier Contreras, Siconterra).

> Our experience with local community 'promoters' who manage and organise the social capital in the areas we work has been highly successful. Without these community leaders the work would be almost impossible (Gabriel Lanfranchi, Fundación Pro Vivienda Social).

However, the risk of elite capture was not pointed out in these cases.
We can therefore state:

> **Proposition**: *For successful projects, the company or its partners must be well aware of the local structures of power.*

Power structures do not only exist within the communities, but also between the company and the targeted communities and involved people. The higher the level of power and responsibility that is shifted to the poor, the greater the extent to which they must be accountable. The experience of the participating companies in the in-depth case studies shows that—even though leaving all power to the poor sounds preferable—a certain level of control is necessary; the poor can be very opportunistic. Enforcement of agreements is not possible when no contracts exist.[16] Therefore, motivation and incentives are required, depending on the project.

> Teaching discipline and giving incentives is important. Many *TriCaldamas* do not have the necessary discipline (Astrid Villalobos Camacho, *TriCaldama*).

Sucromiles, Nestlé and FINCA have established (external) incentive schemes (e.g. concert ticket for highest sales volume, price for highest repayment rates).

> Without incentives, people do not react (María Marta Padilla, FINCA).

Nestlé and Sucromiles also monitor attendance at training workshops. According to Nestlé, incentives also have the advantage that the people who benefit from them talk about them to their friends who in turn may decide to take part. In most cases, though, the main incentives to do it well are the results of the project itself (e.g. if *revendedoras/TriCaldamas* sell more, they earn more). FINCA found that in small rural communities people are not, in general, very motivated to take risks.[17] For new CCEs to become established, pioneers are needed. Once the CCE is working smoothly, people are more easily motivated. If money is involved, financial accountability is essential. *Revendedoras* in the Nestlé system must pay their credits back on time. Also, EDESA monitors the financial state of the CCE in relation to risk before they get an external credit. This control/pressure/motivation does not necessarily have to come from the company. It can also come from within the communities themselves. In the BAC COM project, for example, peer pressure to manage the funds correctly comes from the community, as the members of the community are partners in every sense and invest their own economic resources as shareholders.

We can therefore conclude that accountability, transparency, a certain level of surveillance and incentives are important. The further the project is developed, and the higher the number of elements managed by the target group, the more the community itself takes up this function.

> Respondents of the questionnaire confirmed this assumption. An example:

> The control and transparency concerning the management of resources leads to trust in the community (Javier Contreras, Siconterra).

We can therefore state:

> **Proposition**: *The more responsibility companies shift to the BoP, the more they have to hold them accountable and the more transparent*

---

16 This was the case in all the in-depth case studies, except for people working in production facilities (Nestlé, Sucromiles) or people from the communities employed as facilitators (BAC COM/FINCA).

17 A member of the board of a CCE even said that people in her community are usually lazy and that it is important that a facilitator, somebody from FINCA or EDESA comes by from time to time to control what they are doing.

processes must be. Also, some level of surveillance and incentives (at the beginning external) are necessary.

10.2.3 Community and targeting

Who is the target market? What about the targeted communities?

All companies represented in the case study research target the BoP. Sometimes they serve the poor with a special product/service; sometimes their entire business is targeted at the BoP. But, within the BoP, it is usually not the people living in extreme poverty who are targeted. In most cases, there was no income level set[18] and companies focused more on strata defined by their countries.[19] Mostly, there was no assessment made in order to determine what income level the people that buy the products/services really have. Some, however, monitored the strata of the participants.[20] The clients usually consisted of the upper part of the BoP, or even slightly above it. This group is quite big in the LAC region as we have seen in Chapter 8. But even though companies define their target groups in terms of income or strata, they satisfy broader needs. Nestlé and Sucromiles encourage a healthy diet; BAC COM fosters economic development. Basic needs such as housing or electricity are satisfied within the projects of Tecnosol, Holcim, EPM, Gas Natural, MIA, Cemex and Siconterra. All these products and services are needed by the poor to allow further development. Other goals, apart from increasing income or purchasing power, are set. With the integration of the target group less tangible needs are also satisfied. They become empowered and their self-esteem is increased.

Depending on the project, companies know a lot about the communities in which their projects are located. However, many projects are not just in a single community (or slum), but tend to be more widely spread. Furthermore, it is often not the companies that approach every community they offer their products and services to; rather, intermediaries are used. In the case of Sucromiles and Nestlé, the *TriCaldamas* and *revendedoras* have this role. In the case of BAC COM, where the projects are really limited to specific communities, the issue is different and (via FINCA) they know a lot more about the communities. We can therefore *not* conclude that companies generally need detailed knowledge of the local communities where their products and services are sold. Intermediaries or the included people from the target group can take on that role.

Some communities are easier to work with than others. The level of the community's development, for example, is an issue. On one hand, the business models were developed for less developed regions and communities (for example, in the case

18 As, for example, the US$3,000 PPP by Hammond *et al.* 2007.
19 In Cali, Colombia, for example, strata are defined according to areas and not individual persons. In Costa Rica and Brazil, it is according to income.
20 Sucromiles has a detailed statistic on the strata, income and professions of its *TriCaldamas*.

of Nestlé, selling the products from door-to-door would not work in richer areas, as people there do not open their doors for strangers and poor people value the service, including credit, a lot more). Also, in the case of Sucromiles, richer people usually do not buy calcium powder as they have the financial resources to buy milk, cheese and other calcium-rich food, supplements or fortified food. In the case of BAC COM, people with enough resources would simply obtain credit from a bank rather than use a CCE. What's more, as the work in the CCEs is mostly not remunerated, richer people do not want to participate. People with low incomes are more motivated to participate in a CCE because they learn a lot for themselves.

On the other hand, a certain level of development is favourable—better streets, for example, make the distribution process for the micro-distributors of Nestlé easier. With more educated people, less training is necessary. Self-esteem is often low among the poor and it can take a lot for the poor to build up enough confidence to consider participation.[21] The *TriCaldamas* need a place to store TriCaltone safely and, if they live in the lowest strata (0), this is generally not possible.

> Underdevelopment means inconsistency (Gonzalo Gnecco, Sucromiles).

As the calcium powder needs to be taken every day, the *TriCaldamas* need be in daily contact with their clients. The leaders of the *TriCaldamas* often come from a higher stratum (strata 2 or 3), but the important point is that they identify themselves with the poor. Micro-credits in the BAC COM case work better in more productive areas as there are different possibilities for economic activity and better diversification. We can therefore conclude that a certain level of development is necessary.

The respondents of the questionnaire also confirmed this conclusion. In the case of Cemex, for example, logistics and infrastructure are important issues:

> Patrimonio Hoy, so far, is not able to work in rural areas due to logistics and infrastructure difficulties (Henning Alts, Cemex).

We can therefore state:

> **Proposition**: *Applying a bottom-up approach in BoP ventures is easier in regions and communities with a certain level of development.*

Besides the state of development, other factors in a community were considered important, depending on the projects. For a distribution system with 'selling ladies' it is important to have a certain population density as they have to be able to go on foot from door to door to sell the products. Bus tickets or the metro would make travel costs too high. In the BAC COM project it is the opposite. As it is very important that people know each other well to give credits, rural areas with a low density are more suitable.

---

21 More on this issue in Section 10.2.4.

> We know how much money you can make with a cow here, so we know how much credit people are able to pay back (Shareholder of CCE in La Fuente, Turrialba).

Also, low levels of 'machismo' can be an advantage, as some men in LAC are averse to successful women. A *TriCaldama* of Sucromiles, for example, could not attend some of the training because her husband would not let her leave their children at night. Many women participating in CCE were single. Husbands usually did not like their wives to participate at the beginning, but when they saw that additional money was being contributed to the household income, they mostly agreed. The women that were participating successfully in the projects were usually quite strong and determined.

Except with regard to the level of development, as mentioned earlier, no general conclusions can be drawn on how what a 'perfect' BoP community looks like as it is too dependent on the type of project.

Generally, giving more responsibility to the target group fosters preference targeting. In the case of Sucromiles the company developed the product without previously consulting the target group. But now, for new products, a high level of input is coming from the *TriCaldamas*. As they are a lot closer to their clients, they are more aware of what they want (ingredients, packaging, tastes). Nestlé had already integrated the target group in an earlier process and completed extensive market research. As the *revendedoras* have direct access to the end consumers, they receive more relevant and trustworthy information (market research is often second-hand). This market research is also cheaper and they can easily define what the kits they sell should contain, and what should not be included. If the target group is included in the distribution process, it makes a lot of sense to also include them for market research and idea generation. Separate workshops are less necessary where this is the case. Also, all those involved in the BAC COM project are convinced that the poor themselves are capable of lifting themselves out of poverty, because it is about their needs, of which they have a better knowledge. Facilitation is nevertheless needed. However, lack of knowledge and education means that the poor do not always know what they need. For this reason, Sucromiles supports so-called *brigades* (health campaigns) where the poor can measure their calcium levels and receive information about nutrition, calcium and the products. Some form of education is, depending on the project, often appropriate.

Preference targeting therefore is a reason to use a bottom-up development approach in BoP ventures. The questionnaire participants also agreed with this assumption. We can state:

> **Proposition**: *Giving more responsibility to certain individuals from a BoP community during the innovation process fosters the match between what the respective community wants and what it obtains.*

10.2.4 Local knowledge as the base for capacity building

> External people often underestimate the strengths a community has (David Gomez, Community Leader Siloé, Cali, Colombia).

How and where can existing local knowledge play a role in BoP projects? How can it be detected? How much capacity building is necessary?

Local knowledge of the poor has been used widely in the projects of this research. Sucromiles and Nestlé make use of the *TriCaldamas* and *revendedoras* as they know more about the behaviour of the people living in their respective communities. Nestlé is convinced that the experiences the *revendedoras* accumulate from surviving in difficult conditions help them to sell and to persevere. BAC COM trusts in the knowledge of the responsible persons in the CCE to reach low paying defaults. Including local knowledge may also lead to more innovative solutions. According to FINCA, the poor are very creative in finding solutions to their specific needs.

> From childhood on, they have to be more creative, as they do not receive everything they want (María Marta Padilla, FINCA).

The CCEs come up with various business ideas that no one would have imagined, and many offer other services aside from credits alone. As the poor themselves often lead the processes where local knowledge is important, it was not so important for the companies to analyse it in detail. More emphasis is placed on understanding the ways in which local knowledge is exchanged and disseminated. All cases rely on the assumption that the participating poor exchange and disseminate their experiences and know-how. Sucromiles, for example, train the *TriCaldamas* in the use of the internet, so that in a later phase they can exchange best practices and product ideas over the company intranet.

It is principally the specific local knowledge applied that companies value in the projects. Inputs about product/service ideas and features can be used well so that the company can develop a suitable product. But, often, this input must be combined with the companies' know-how to reach a solution. In all cases, a relatively high amount of training was necessary for implementing the more technical tasks, especially when the product is complex. Nestlé and Sucromiles offer, for example, training in selling and nutrition; BAC COM supports knowledge generation in financial and organisational tasks. Also, in the projects that were included with the questionnaire research, all projects rely on capacity building. Still, they see the advantages of integrating local knowledge into projects and are convinced that this leads to more innovative solutions. It is, however, the type of product that determines how much capacity building is necessary. TriCaltone, for example, is so much cheaper than competitors' products that consumers questioned its effectiveness, and the *TriCaldamas* had to learn the best arguments to overcome this perception. There was also a substantial lack of knowledge about nutrition, potentially hindering the sale of the product. Where those included are required to be entrepreneurial (e.g. in distribution), they need to be well organised with good administrative skills.

TriCaldamas with these skills and who attended all the training sessions were much more successful in selling than those who did not have these skills.

Including people who have different levels of knowledge is a challenge for capacity building. Training should neither be too difficult nor too easy (to prevent boredom). If a large number of people are integrated (as in the case of Nestlé or Sucromiles), it is too costly to evaluate the existing knowledge of every person. It is more important that capacity building is adapted to the way they prefer to learn and expand their knowledge. For this reason, it is important to know how knowledge is generated. Nestlé, for example, developed a training programme in the form of a '*telenovela*', as these programmes are popular among women in Brazil. However, people often learn more by doing than watching. Supervisors accompany the Nestlé *revendedoras* on the streets and support them according to their needs. The training Nestlé developed is based on the experiences and best practices of the *revendedoras*. Also the training FINCA offers through facilitators to the CCEs is very much adapted to their specific level and the way in which knowledge is transferred is considered to be very important:

It is not only local knowledge that can be used. Some cases also relied on local resources. Nestlé uses locally sourced ingredients for its popularly positioned products. The CCEs build on local financial resources. Siconterra uses a traditional Mexican clay paste for construction. Time, as a local resource, is also widely used. Many projects integrate the poor into labour-intensive processes. This is less costly but, equally, it means that the target group is better reached.

We come to the following conclusions based on these findings:

- Local knowledge can lead to innovative solutions; involving the BoP is a more viable strategy in non-technical activities than in technical activities

- Projects should build on knowledge and resources already available

- It is important to analyse local knowledge, and the ways in which it is generated, exchanged and disseminated

The respondents of the questionnaires also agreed with these assumptions:

> Including the BoP's local knowledge is crucial for success . . . not only in terms of innovation, but also in terms of acceptance within the community (Henning Alts, Cemex).

> Accompanied by training programmes and demonstration areas, the community has the responsibility to adapt the constructions to their needs (Javier Contreras, Siconterra).[22]

---

22 Construction of houses.

> Knowledge is power and having community members with the necessary skills is fundamental in the advancement of projects. Whilst we have always taken advantage of existing know-how and skills, we also promote training in new areas for the benefit of the project and the local residents (Gabriel Lanfranchi, Fundación Pro Vivienda Social).

We can therefore state:

> **Proposition**: *Including the BoP's local knowledge can lead to more innovative solutions.*

> **Proposition**: *Without capacity building, involving the BoP is a more viable strategy in non-technical activities than in technical activities. Ideas and opinions can also be generated and included for technical activities.*

> **Proposition**: *Where possible, BoP ventures have to build on the existing knowledge and other resources available.*

> **Proposition**: *Companies must analyse the ways in which local knowledge is generated (important for capacity building/training), exchanged (important for the exchange of best practices) and disseminated (important for distribution/marketing).*

In some projects, the involved poor are not only trained in what is immediately important to fulfil their tasks. An issue that came up several times is a lack of self-esteem. The poor are frequently stigmatised and do not feel capable of real participation.[23] In the BAC COM project, the women especially, but also the indigenous people, lacked self-esteem as they were constantly being told that they were worthless. Many were very used to being told what to do.[24] But to really play an important role, economic and personal autonomy are important. Self-esteem is very closely linked to independence. Gaining self-esteem is a process. Most of the time, self-esteem evolves naturally and is obtained indirectly once individuals are participating in a project. In addition, Sucromiles held a training programme which included self-esteem building and empowerment. Valuing what is available in the communities and supporting an established solution (as BAC COM is doing with existing CCEs) also leads to an increase in self-esteem. Self-esteem is an issue that does not arise that frequently in bottom-up literature.[25] The questionnaire participants also confirmed that increasing self-esteem within a project plays a crucial role and unveiled more details:

---

23 During observation in the field, it was found that many religious people had more self-esteem than non-churchgoers.
24 In the case of BAC COM, for example, people of the CCEs always asked the facilitator to solve a problem, even though they were able to do it just as well themselves.
25 'Empowerment' certainly contains self-esteem as an element, but is a much broader notion.

> Everything that contributes to an increased self-esteem leads to better participation of the community (Javier Contreras, Siconterra).

> Depending on the community, self-esteem has to be built up to a certain extent before a project can start (Stefanie Koch, Holcim).

Increasing the self-esteem of the participating poor can also affect others:

> Since the inception of the gasification projects, 120 'community workers' have benefited from training and employment. This has had a significant impact on the self-esteem of those directly involved as well as spin-off effects in their families and communities (Gabriel Lanfranchi, Fundación Pro Vivienda Social).

We can therefore state:

> **Proposition**: *Ventures have to help increase the self-esteem of the (mostly) stigmatised BoP so that they feel able to participate and play a more important role. Economic autonomy and emotional/ personal autonomy are important.*

Another advantage of products and services that are developed together with the BoP is that they are more readily accepted. In the case of Sucromiles, the *TriCaldamas* usually start selling calcium to their family, friends and neighbours. Buying is related to trust and emotions, and people quickly accept something that comes from someone with whom they have a close relationship. Also, Nestlé is convinced that it is an advantage to use local people for selling, even though the brand recognition is also important for acceptance. The poor cannot afford to make a mispurchase, which is why relying on trustworthy experience is important. In the case of BAC COM, people invest their money as shareholders over a longer term. This means that trust is even more important. The people who were directly involved in the establishment of the CCEs accepted the credit services quickly. But for many it was hard to find new shareholders before the CCEs had proven that the money was well managed and would not be spent on other things.[26] The slight discrepancy of the BAC COM/FINCA case with the experience of Sucromiles and Nestlé can be explained by the very high level of responsibility that the target group has in the former.

However, the experiences reported by the questionnaire case studies confirm the increased acceptance of products and services developed with the integration of the target group:

> Our methodology incorporates local community members directly into the communication and 'selling' of ideas process. Via this method the very

---

26 Many communities had bad experiences with state projects or with NGOs where money was given to a selected group of people to start a project. In the end, there was usually nothing left for those who had not been involved from the beginning and the locals no longer believed that 'their people' could do it.

community members who will benefit from the gas projects are those who convince their fellow neighbours to join up to the project (Gabriel Lanfranchi, Fundación Pro Vivienda Social).

Additionally, as shown by the experience of Holcim, products and services are not necessarily accepted at the start of projects. Later—when positive experiences have been accumulated and the knowledge of the participating poor has come to represent the knowledge of the community as a whole—products and services are much more readily accepted.

We can therefore state:

> **Proposition**: *Products and services that are developed with the inclusion of the BoP are more readily accepted by them as soon as a positive impact is visible.*

10.2.5 Ownership

The great majority of people involved in the projects observed were very proud of their roles. The *revendedoras* from Nestlé and *TriCaldamas* from Sucromiles are independent and represent micro-enterprises.[27] As Nestlé's *revendedoras* have a wide variety of products to choose from to sell, their level of ownership is higher and they become more entrepreneurial. The importance of an 'entrepreneurial spirit' has been previously mentioned on a number of occasions, as it is only when this is present that bottom-up solutions can really work. The success or failure of CCEs show that it is important to break the 'lazy–I can't attitude' and 'wake the people up', as FINCA states. When they see the positive changes of a market-based system, they usually become more motivated and active.

It is also very important that the integrated people have a high commitment to make longer-term investments. The *TriCaldamas* are very intrinsically motivated as they are helping to improve their community's health.[28] As TriCaltone is not advertised (to keep the price as low as possible), and Sucromiles is not a well-known consumer brand, the *TriCaldamas* have to put in a lot of effort and time to build up their market. So far, resources other than time have not yet been invested by the sales women of either Nestlé or Sucromiles. In the case of BAC COM, however, members of the CCEs must invest their own financial resources from the beginning. They also have to pay the lawyer and associated costs to register their CCEs as a corporation. New shareholders pay an 'affiliation fee' that can be as high as US$50 in order to buy shares.[29] Also, the board members invest a large amount of time

---

27 However, depending on the person, it can take some time until they really feel and act like entrepreneurs as they first have to feel secure and competent in their new role.

28 When asked why they became a *TriCaldama*, the first answer was always 'to help people' rather than to earn 'more income'.

29 The affiliation fee is determined by the CCE. 25,000 colones (approx. US$50) was the highest fee seen within a CCE that had been in existence for more than ten years. But even

which is usually not remunerated.[30] Still, the people participating in the board gain a lot of know-how from both the work and the training provided, which can also be used in their private businesses. There are, however, limitations. Investments are, for example, not made to exchange with other CCEs (renting a room, travel costs) and FINCA organises the events. Also, some CCEs have problems finding enough shareholders and board members before positive results can be seen.

We can therefore conclude that people are willing to invest resources in a project when they have control over the process. This assumption was confirmed by the questionnaire respondents. The experience of the Multiahorro Barrio stores of TIA confirms that time is invested. Gas Natural's experience shows that the more community members work together with people they know and trust, the more they are willing to commit the time, assets and funds required.

We can therefore state:

> **Proposition:** *The people at the BoP are more willing to invest their own resources (especially time, but also other assets) in a project, the more they have control over the process.*

Ownership is given from the beginning if companies make links with existing initiatives in the respective communities. But, in practice, this seems to be quite a difficult undertaking. All projects were initiated by an external agent, rather than by the poor themselves. However, companies screened existing initiatives (mostly initiated from outside). Sucromiles looked for existing selling networks in poor areas with similar objectives. But existing networks all sold non-healthcare consumer goods such as beauty products, make-up or clothes. These products are a lot easier to sell and the sales women would not have made the extra effort necessary to sell TriCaltone. So Sucromiles decided to build up its own network. Nestlé also preferred to build up its own selling network, as otherwise the focus of the project could be lost. BAC COM, on the other hand, did rely on an existing solution as building a micro-credit system single-handedly and from scratch would have been too expensive. FINCA was already well established with a proven methodology, and EDESA had well-established credit channels. With FINCA, BAC COM already had a long-term relationship built up from philanthropic projects. FINCA itself is convinced that existing innovations can be used as a base (e.g. existing saving groups); however, it considers that every CCE should begin at zero and apply the whole methodology in order to be successful.

So, building on existing local innovations can foster ownership within a BoP project—if innovations exist and are in line with the goals of the project. But one

---

though this amount is quite high for local people (it is about one-fifth of the minimum monthly salary), people were ready to pay it as the advantages they got as shareholders (lower interest fee, dividends, trainings, etc.) made it worthwhile. New CCEs usually start with an affiliation fee of around US$2–10.

30 In bigger CCEs, the treasurer sometimes gets paid a salary because the role demands a much higher workload than any other board member. Other members of the board are paid expenses. The aim is for all CCEs to cover these costs.

has to be careful with their selection. This assumption was also confirmed by the questionnaire respondents. In the case of EPM there was nothing available to link up to, but they were nevertheless still looking. Siconterra warns:

> Even if local innovations exist, one has to be careful. Not everything has been well done. You always have to study them well and take the best of them for other developments (Javier Contreras, Siconterra).

And the experience gained from the Gas Natural project supports FINCA's view:

> Whilst acting with other pre-existing local innovations is a great way to enter into a community and become involved in its activities, it is not enough to integrate into the neighbourhood. Our experience in hooking up with community groups, local businesses and labour in the target communities has been a rich one; however, the project initiation (if it's new) needs to be a separate process (Gabriel Lanfranchi, Fundación Pro Vivienda Social).

An additional issue detected in the case of the Multiahorro Barrio stores of TIA is that if well-established local innovations already exist, the communities will want to maintain ownership of it. Depending on the case, a company therefore needs to find a way of mutual partnership and cannot simply acquire such innovations.

In terms of increasing ownership, we can therefore state:

> **Proposition**: *When established and well-done innovations already exist in communities, companies can try to hook up to them.*

Ownership usually comes step by step during the process. During facilitation, capacity building and other support is necessary—especially at the beginning of a project— but it should be made clear from the beginning that support diminishes as the process evolves and the included poor will be expected to become independent. FINCA, for example, has integrated this goal into the methodology. All CCEs follow 22 steps until they are inaugurated. After that, they receive a limited amount of support until they are completely autonomous. If it is not made clear from the beginning, the integrated poor continue to be reliant and demand support. Total independence is, however, hard to reach in practice.

This issue did not emerge in bottom-up development literature. But the assumption was confirmed by the participants in the questionnaire.

> From day one of the projects, the neighbour's financial participation is clear (Gabriel Lanfranchi, Fundación Pro Vivienda Social).

We can therefore conclude:

> **Proposition**: *It has to be made clear from the beginning of a project that the participating poor must become increasingly independent and that external support will decrease over time.*

10.2.6 **Networks**

Acceptance of a company in the community is very important when choosing a bottom-up approach. In indigenous villages there is no entry without the support of the local (indigenous) organisation, as FINCA has experienced. People need to have had good experiences with the entrants and companies and their brands need to be respected and have a good image. The existing view of a company's ethical behaviour and CSR must also be favourable. Even though Sucromiles does not have a well-established brand image, community members valued their activities concerning social responsibility (e.g. how they treat their employees). Nestlé has a very good image within the target group of the popularly positioned products. The superiority of quality compared to other products is highly valued.

Again, the questionnaire case study respondents also confirmed this assumption. Acceptance can be gained by integrating the target group at an early stage, and by fulfilling promises during the project:

> If the community is integrated from the beginning of a project, it has more information and accepts the company more readily (Javier Contreras, Siconterra).

> The point is how you generate trust and how people start recommending you. It's important what the people involved in the BoP initiative really do at the local level, and if they are fulfilling promises or not (Henning Alts, Cemex).

It is not only important that the company is accepted by the communities; its partners must also be.

> The business partners and social networks we work with in the communities (gas providers, local know-how, technicians etc.) must also be recognised by the community as trustworthy institutions (Gabriel Lanfranchi, Fundación Pro Vivienda Social).

We can therefore conclude:

> **Proposition**: *A high acceptance of the company and its partners by the community is very important when choosing a bottom-up approach.*

Yet trust and acceptance of a company and its project do not depend solely on the company itself. Acceptance by community members also depends heavily on the previous experiences the community has had with other companies, governmental and NGOs. FINCA frequently experienced problems in finding enough people willing to participate on the board of a CCE; at first people were hesitant to become active stakeholders due to the fact that many communities had already had contact with several failed projects initiated by the state or by NGOs. They did not want to get their fingers burned again. On one hand, people did not believe in their own capacity because they had always received 'top-down' development aid.[31] On the other, they were very critical until they saw that it really worked—especially because they were required to invest their own money. Trust and previous experiences were also important in the other projects. And for community leaders it is essential that the company can demonstrate that the project has a positive long-term social impact on the community.

The finding that previous experiences with NGOs or state agencies can hinder a market-based approach did not emerge from bottom-up development literature but, especially in the case of BAC COM and FINCA, it was emphasised several times in the case study research. The questionnaire respondents also confirmed this assumption, and it became clear that previous unsatisfactory experiences with companies and other organisations can adversely impact on participation levels. In the case of Gas Natural, other companies had previously entered the target communities with promises that were never realised. Thus, trust had to be gained right from the start. Cemex also had a similar experience:

> We have to combat distrust in the local communities due to many other initiatives, which cheated on the people (Henning Alts, Cemex).

We can therefore state:

> **Proposition**: *It is easier to use a bottom-up approach within market-based solutions in communities that have had good experiences in previous projects with companies, NGOs, governmental and other organisations, and where the entrepreneurial spirit is alive and kicking.*

Most companies represented in the case studies relied on local networks and organisations, developing their projects in line with existing projects and development goals. Sucromiles started without local partners. But now, as the project reaches new neighbourhoods, it partners more frequently with other, locally active and embedded organisations (for example to recruit new *TriCaldamas*). This makes things a lot easier as the acceptance and goodwill of the community and, especially, its leader is achieved more quickly. Partners are chosen carefully. Similar elements in the vision, principles and motivation are important; partners have to strengthen the model with complementary capacities, and they need to have experience and be trusted by the communities. If individuals work in the same area of interest, this is also an advantage. The most important asset of a locally established organisation is that it knows the community better. BAC COM chose FINCA and EDESA as its partners—more or less outsourcing the implementation of the project to them—because of their extensive knowledge of the communities and market, many years'

---

31 Expressions used during the case study research that described this issue included: '*personas victimas*'; '*clientelismo*'; and '*clientes de la pobreza*'.

experience, their established methodology and the relationships they have built up over the years.

> Doing a project such as this alone would not be possible. Working with FINCA increases the effects. This project's strength and ability to be innovative lies precisely in this interrelation and the confidence attained between partners (Laura Porras Alfaro, BAC COM).

FINCA, in turn, can profit from the extensive financial knowledge of BAC COM. FINCA itself works with local organisations to enter communities and gain the necessary information. It also relies on other partners in the community who deliver solutions relating to, for example, agricultural production, commercialisation and technology.

But it is not only local partnerships that are essential. Strategic alliances on a national or global level can also foster success. The UN, WHO, IDB or governments were mentioned as important international partners with which to maintain dialogue. In the case of Nestlé, for example, acceptance by the government was very important in order to be able to sell on the streets.

Another possibility is to partner with other companies and form consortia. None of the in-depth case studies have used this approach so far. Sucromiles could generally imagine itself partnering with other companies, for example a company offering blood pressure tests could also carry out calcium screening. Other companies would need to bring different competencies to the project. BAC COM partnered with American Express to help establish a guarantee fund for the credits given out. However, partnering with a competitor would not usually be a possibility, for commercial reasons. BAC COM does not see the CCEs as competition as they operate on a very small scale. If they were able to give credits of a similar size to those given by BAC COM, then BAC COM would need to rethink its approach. Within big companies and with large-scale projects partnering with other companies is challenging and difficult to realise; the projects are complex enough even when managed by one company alone.

We can therefore conclude that carefully chosen partners foster success in BoP ventures. However, even though it might make sense in terms of development goals, entering into consortia with other companies is difficult. The latter assumption could therefore *not* be confirmed.

The questionnaire respondents agreed on the importance of partnerships.

> In the case of Antioquia Iluminada, EPM looked for participation of other governmental and non-governmental organisations for additional work that was not included in our project, as, for example, the internal network of the houses. This was essential for the success of the project (César Augusto Roldán, EPM).

Holcim distinguishes its partners in more detail:

> For implementation, partners should be local. But for financing, they can also be non-local (Stefanie Koch, Holcim).

We can therefore state:

> **Proposition**: *Partnering and entering with carefully chosen partners (other companies, NGOs, governmental or other organisations) increases the success of BoP ventures. For implementation, partners have to be local. For financing, they can be non-local.*

The base of working together with others is, as we have seen, trust. Established relationships and networks (social capital)[32] enhance the success of a project not only between the company and its partners, but also within the groups of participating poor and between the participating poor and their communities.

> The lower in the pyramid people are, the more important become relations (Sylvain Darnil, Nestlé).

Revendedoras who have an established personal network are usually more successful in selling. People from lower strata usually show significant solidarity towards each other and have close relationships with their neighbours. Therefore, bills are generally settled on time as pride becomes a factor. The contact between the participating poor is not only important for the exchange of best practice, but also to foster team spirit. For many *TriCaldamas* of Sucromiles, for example, getting to know more people, making new friends, interpersonal relations and having a good time with other *TriCaldamas* are reasons to participate. It is also common for *TriCaldamas* to exchange products if one of them has already sold their stock and the next delivery is some days away. Participating poor can come from different financial and social contexts, so group work fosters a mix of social classes. As, in general, no formal contracts are made with the participating poor, retention can be a problem if there is no close relationship established and the poor do not see the additional benefits that could result from their participation. But commitment can also come from the involved group itself. For example, as TriCaltone is not advertised, *TriCaldamas* depend on an active network to generate publicity. In the case of Nestlé, the relationship between the *revendedoras* and their supervisors is very important for retention purposes. Often, companies have to foster and support social capital building between the participating poor, even if they are from the same neighbourhood, offering events, meetings and training in their chosen meeting place. The social capital gained with the projects is also an advantage for other forms of development within the communities.

We can therefore see that social capital plays an important role in BoP ventures. However, a company cannot rely solely upon existing social capital. In many cases, it has to be built up with the project. This was also confirmed by the questionnaire respondents:

---

32 Social capital in the sense of relationships/networks; social capital within the participating poor, between participating poor and company (intermediaries/partners included), between participating poor and community, between community and company.

> Using existing social capital in our case helps, but is not the only and crucial key factor for success (Henning Alts, Cemex).

> In the communities where we work, like in any community, there is a sense of group identity and desire for a common goal. However, a major objective of the programmes is to strengthen these sentiments via mobilising events which require community involvement (Gabriel Lanfranchi, Fundación Pro Vivienda Social).

We can therefore state:

> **Proposition**: *To be successful in mostly informal markets companies have to build, make use of and knit together existing social capital.*

10.2.7 Scaling up the process

What kind of process should be chosen? Do the projects have to be small in scale and non-complex in order to choose a bottom-up perspective? How can the necessary scale be reached to make BoP projects profitable?

A long-term perspective is essential when serving the BoP. Within the first couple of years, ventures are usually not profitable but do provide other advantages, such as getting to know the market and establishing important partnerships. The strategies chosen by the participating companies were flexible in their outcome. Sucromiles mentioned the 'blue ocean' strategy.

> All innovation processes that include a social component do not have a very defined track (Gonzalo Gnecco, Sucromiles).

The strategy in particular must be very open when the company does not have experience in this type of project, as was the case with Sucromiles. However, a clear vision is indispensable. Some processes can be defined as well and a general framework is necessary. Nestlé also used a flexible strategy with a step-by-step model that worked well, and the managers were often surprised by the most popular products. For them, the learning process occurs through an experimentation process. Being able to make mistakes and thinking outside the box is important; but the first thing a company must know is where it wants to go. The experience accumulated in BAC COM's project shows that planning is, ultimately, not very successful because things will constantly change. FINCA's methodology, and the project's principles and values, are constant, but all details are flexible and depend on the community.

A flexible strategy with a clear long-term vision was also considered important by those who participated in the questionnaire. Gas Natural additionally sees clear objectives and targets as imperative.

We can therefore state:

> *Proposition: Successful strategies must be flexible in their outcome and adaptable throughout the process. A clear long-term vision is important, though.*

The size of the projects included in the case study research differed a lot. Some were still small in scale, while others were already very large. This signifies that it is not essential to stay small in scale when a bottom-up approach is chosen. However, many started small. For example, Nestlé started in São Paulo with a pilot project. The project was analysed and adjusted and the door-to-door distribution system is now being expanded all over Brazil. The pilot project was necessary in order to see whether the system could gain value for everyone involved. TriCaltone is, thus far, only sold in Cali and Palmira, but increasing numbers of *TriCaldamas* are joining the network in these cities. For Sucromiles, it was best to start where the company was located, as it knew the cities, organisations and issues. A pilot project does not, however, need to be perfect before it is scaled up. For BAC COM, a CCE always starts very small and then grows larger. It is only when they are bigger and prove that they are able to manage their funds that external credits are approved. The CCEs usually want to grow faster in order to receive external credits (which are higher) sooner, but it is important that they are stabilised first.

The questionnaire respondents also confirmed the importance of pilot projects before scaling-up can occur. In the project with Gas Natural, Fundación Pro Vivienda Social used a similar strategy to that used by Nestlé—a pilot project for evaluation, then systemisation and transfer of activities to new communities on a larger scale. In the view of Siconterra, communities are used to starting a project on a small scale and, therefore, it is more familiar to them. There were, however, also some projects from the questionnaire cases that did not start small. Antioquia Iluminada of EPM, for example, was born big. In this case, experiences from other projects could be used. Similarly, the MIA project started on a large scale.

> A small project does not have the same complications as large projects; therefore a success in a small project doesn't guarantee the same result after escalation. Projects should start at medium/normal scale (Guillermo Jaime Calderón, MIA).

Holcim favours a mixed approach. A project can start small, but the conditions for scaling up must be in place from the beginning. If the project works on a small scale it does not necessarily mean that it will also work on a large scale. Larger scales therefore have to be planned. With previous experience, projects can also start big.

We can therefore state:

> *Proposition: If little or no previous experience has been had by the company, projects should start with small- to medium-scale pilot projects, and only be scaled up after successful evaluation. The conditions for scaling up must be in place from the beginning.*

When local knowledge was used within the projects, how can these innovations be scaled up? Different ways of scaling up were observed in the case studies: expanding the project locally; and into other regions. Sucromiles is, at this point, strengthening the selling network for future scaling-up. Nestlé has already expanded its selling network to several other states in Brazil. In the case of BAC COM/FINCA, the CCEs themselves scale up by attaining more capital, and more and more CCEs are emerging in Costa Rica. The FINCA methodology is also being applied in other countries. When scaling up in the same region within a similar context, no, or at least only very small, changes were needed. But when scaling up to include other regions within different contexts, changes were necessary. It is necessary to adapt products to suit other tastes. Package size, form and prices can vary in different areas. Also, cultural factors and habits will vary. Sucromiles was convinced that if it were to sell TriCaltone in Bogotà or Medellín, for example, it would have a higher take-up rate, as users would be more diligent in observing regular dose patterns. Products must also be adapted to correspond to varying hygiene standards. In slums with extreme poverty, for example, Sucromiles would only sell the calcium in the single-serve sachets instead of the jar. Nestlé also adapts its products according to the region in which they will be sold. Average prices, the size of the kits, the composition of the kits and gadgets that come—depending on the micro-distributor—with the kits may vary.[33] The model does not, however, necessarily have to be adapted. In the case of FINCA, the methodology is constant in all regions, with some adjustments in its application.

We can therefore conclude that products and services have to be adapted to fit into other contexts. Processes and methodologies, however, stay the same where the context is not extremely different. The questionnaire respondents agreed with this assumption:

> Through our experience we have come to believe that the lessons learnt from a lived experience are invaluable. Through a process of systemisation the project should be able to be replicated in a variety of other urban situations. Some adaptation is required. However, the practices and methodology should not need to be amended fundamentally (Gabriel Lanfranchi, Fundación Pro Vivienda Social).

We can therefore conclude:

> **Proposition**: *If the project is scaled up in a new context, products and services must be adapted to fit this context. Processes and methodologies can stay the same if the context is not extremely different.*

In certain steps, integrating the poor into the innovation process leads to more efficiency. Linking the distribution system with ideas generation (as is done in the case of Nestlé and Sucromiles) produces a permanent flow of ideas from the

---

33 Consumers very much appreciate gadgets they can use for other purposes (e.g. a bag).

poor, avoiding the need for separate extensive market research. The main reason why FINCA can reduce transactional costs—which is essential when serving the poor—is that the CCEs have structures that work on their own. Also, the CCEs have very low operating costs and therefore can offer credits at a lower rate than other service providers. But, depending on the knowledge of the target group, especially at the beginning of a project, the integration of the target group can also lead to higher costs (e.g. for capacity building).

The respondents of the questionnaires reported corresponding experiences:

> The lack of experience and or know-how in the management, impacts levels of efficiency and costs (Gabriel Lanfranchi, Fundación Pro Vivienda Social).

Holcim experienced that, initially, a bottom-up approach is more expensive. Although this leads to a higher level of sustainability, it may also take longer.

We can therefore state:

> **Proposition**: *Once the project is established, shifting more responsibility to the BoP leads to higher efficiency and cuts down costs.*

Integration of the target group is also an important factor in the process of scaling up. It eases the adaptation to the local context, helps to cut down costs and fosters the exchange of best practices.

> Costs for scaling up can be cut down by including external partners (Jaime Dario Colmenares, Sucromiles).

In the case of Sucromiles, selected leaders of the *TriCaldamas* can be used for the scaling-up process locally.[34] Furthermore, the experience and best practice of existing collaborators can be utilised for new participants. Sucromiles started to distribute a publication, written by the *TriCaldamas*, within their networks, while CCEs exchange best practice tips at monthly sector meetings. However, this can sometimes be difficult as very advanced CCEs need different and new input as they cannot learn any more from smaller CCEs. Some CCEs are also in competition with each other and therefore do not want to exchange information. Nestlé uses ideas for best practice gleaned from their *revendedoras* to develop training programmes. So far, they are able to train all *revendedoras* by themselves but, as the network grows, existing micro-distributors and *revendedoras* can become more engaged.[35] Micro-distributors also exchange their experiences and best practices with each other, but it is important that they do not compete for the same market.[36] An internet platform also fosters this exchange.

---

34 Experience has shown that it works better when the involved poor themselves elect their leaders.

35 A local sales person of Nestlé and an external, local nutritionist hold the training sessions.

36 Every micro-distributor has its assigned area where it can be active.

> One of the key words is 'reciprocity', since they are used to help each other in order to survive. They really build a long-term relationship with institutions if they see their lives are improving (Fabio Megid, Nestlé).

FINCA has also made use of existing CCEs. The large majority of facilitators were recruited from other CCEs.[37] This is significantly cheaper than engaging external facilitators.[38] However, it is essential that they are selected carefully and are capable of using the methodology and manuals correctly.

> People from successful CCEs often apply a top-down approach and tell others to do it the way as they did. Not all persons that work good in a CCE are also good facilitators (María Marta Padilla, FINCA).

The questionnaire participants confirm the advantages of including the BoP in the process of scaling up. Siconterra reported positive experiences related to such an adaptation:

> The involvement of the community makes that new products and services are adapting more quickly to the life of the community. By using the experience of the integrated partners, costs can be decreased (Javier Contreras, Siconterra).

However, involving local people to too great an extent can also slow down the process of scaling up, as experienced by MIA:

> Participation of local communities should be in balance with operational efficiency (Guillermo Jaime Calderón, MIA).

We can therefore state:

> **Proposition**: *Involving local people in every community/region helps in reaching the adaptation to the local context in the process of scaling up (if an adaptation is required).*

---

37 In this case, as Costa Rica is a very small country, the distances are easily manageable.
38 External in the sense that they can be from other communities not involved with the project.

Part IV
Framing the bottom-up development perspective in the innovation process of BoP ventures

A closer look at the current state of BoP ventures in LAC under the perspective of bottom-up development approaches revealed new insights about the applicability of such a perspective in practice. Part IV first delivers a summary of the findings from the case study research, before arranging the resulting propositions in a framework. Finally, the framework and its implications will be discussed.

11
Summary of the results

The main difference between BoP projects and development projects is that companies work continuously together with the poor and the projects are never completed—as is often the case in development projects. Except in the case of BAC COM/FINCA, where the poor have a very high level of autonomy within the process, the projects can generally be seen under the view of partnership and mutual value creation rather than a shifting of all responsibility and control to the target group. Still, companies that serve the BoP with products and services apply many elements of bottom-up development approaches. All are convinced that the integration of the target group into the innovation process yields higher success rates—for both the companies' goals and for development goals.

The processes, products and services have to fit to the special needs and circumstances of the target group, which does not mean that Western accomplishments should be withheld from the poor. In general, it can be said that there are advantages for bottom-up approaches in more developed regions and with more developed people. But the specific projects were targeted at the opportunities and needs found at the BoP and this would not necessarily work in a more developed environment. A decentralised organisational structure of a company fosters the emergence of BoP ventures, although coordination and commitment from the top is still important in any case. Economies of scale set limits.

Only in some cases was the target group integrated throughout the whole process. Mostly, they were integrated, considered or consulted where needed. Depending on the project, they did not even want to be active in the whole process. Ideas and opinions can generally be integrated throughout the whole process, but how much they are involved in each step depends upon the project, products and services offered. That the integrated group of people represents the pluralism in the target group is especially important during the process of idea generation and, to a lesser extent, in the other steps of the innovation process. Here, it is more important that the people involved reflect what the BoP means and that they know it well. Depending on the task they fulfil, selection criteria become more demanding than 'representing' the target group. In all cases studied, the BoP had freedom of decision-making in the area under its responsibility and companies were building up systems to involve the poor in a greater number of decisions. Equality in every decision-making process has not been seen. The poor themselves do not even want to be involved in every decision that has to be made. It is important, however, that there is a steady flow of information between the company and the involved poor so that they can make informed decisions. In projects involving common goods or services (e.g. electricity supply), as many people from the community as possible were mobilized, not necessarily by the company itself, but sometimes by a selection of community members. In turn, projects involving consumer goods relied on a selection of individuals and groups. Collective community mobilisation can, however, be used to fill gaps in education and information. People who are integrated, mobilised or otherwise informed usually turn into clients.

Power relations play a role within BoP projects, especially if they are located in communities where social structures are rigid. The approval of informal leaders and the matching of community and project objectives are essential. But even though the company should have some knowledge of the community and be accepted locally, depending on the project, it is sufficient if an intermediary partner has an in-depth knowledge of the power structures.[1] If the workload for the participating poor is substantial, people who already have many other tasks in the community should not be selected. Elite capture is only an issue when a significant amount of responsibility is shifted to the participating poor and if there are large amounts of money involved. The more power and responsibility that is shifted to the BoP, the more the company must hold them accountable and a certain level of control is necessary. With specific reference to the beginnings of projects, motivation and incentives are required. External incentives become less important/necessary as the performance of the project improves and as positive results become visible to the target group. As there are mostly no formal contracts made, commitment and trust become important elements of the partnership. Motivation, control or pressure does not exclusively have to come from the company, but can also come from the included group itself.

With their BoP projects, companies target the needs of people with reference to achieving a 'decent life'. The target group is more broadly defined than in the BoP literature or in the official poverty lines defined by development actors, but it is in line with more extensive concepts such as the HDI or the UN MDGs. The goals of the projects are not limited to increasing income or purchasing power; less intangible needs are also envisaged. The target group has to be extensively studied and known before a product or service can be offered. This can also be achieved, however, through intermediaries and does not necessarily need to be

---

1 Intermediaries can be companies, NGOs or other organisations that work locally; they can also be the included part of the BoP.

done by the company directly. Giving more responsibility to the target group in the innovation process fosters the match between what the community wants and what it gets. As the involved poor are a lot closer to the clients, they have a better knowledge of what they want. Companies entered the communities and regions in which their products and services were needed. Other selection criteria varied a lot between projects and could not be generalised. The selection criteria mentioned in development literature (such as high mobility, egalitarian preferences, open and transparent systems of decision-making, clear rules to decide who is poor, no land inequality) could not be proven to make targeting easier.

Local knowledge—especially regarding habits, tastes and the application of products—of the poor was widely used in BoP projects and can lead to more innovative solutions. In no case was a 'disruptive' innovation developed though, due to the input of local knowledge. Local knowledge was never idealised nor instrumentalised. With the knowledge available, it was easier to include the poor in non-technical rather than in technical activities. Ideas, however, could be integrated for technical decision-making, and with capacity building the poor could also conduct technical activities. Analysing the way local knowledge is generated, exchanged and disseminated also proved necessary in many projects. However, delving too deeply into local knowledge and finding out how it is transformed, consolidated, stored, retrieved and utilised is unnecessary for the needs of most companies. As it is the poor themselves who will apply this knowledge during the projects, it is also not always necessary for the company to know everything. The input of the BoP is, however, always combined with the knowledge of the company, and capacity building was necessary as the knowledge of the poor alone was not sufficient. It is the type of project, product and service which determine the type of, and how much, capacity building is necessary. The existing knowledge has to be taken into account and capacity building must be adapted in accordance with it. Different levels of knowledge proved to be a challenge and meant that individual coaching was necessary. Training the involved poor, not only in what is immediately important in order to fulfil their tasks, is sensible in order to reach a higher level of development, but is also indirectly valuable for the project itself. Self-esteem, for example, is a very important asset when applying a bottom-up approach. When people do not feel capable of lifting themselves out of poverty, they are hardly motivated to participate. Project managers therefore always need to keep in mind that the process should empower the poor. Sometimes it is even the case that self-esteem must be built up prior to the project start—this is especially important in order to avoid excluding the most vulnerable. Not only local knowledge, but also local resources (e.g. time, natural resources, capital) are used in BoP projects. Products and services that are developed through local knowledge and with local resources are more accepted as soon as a positive impact is visible.

By involving the BoP in projects and giving them an important role, ownership is fostered and an 'entrepreneurial spirit' can be developed. With more commitment, the poor are also more willing to invest their own resources in the project. Chiefly, it is time they invest, but in some cases investment can also include financial capital or natural resources. The people who are more involved are more likely to invest. Linking up with solutions in a community where ownership already exists has proven difficult and there are often no suitable solutions. But, if there is a suitable and well thought out solution already available, and a company 'only' wants to leverage that project, it can be successful. Even though facilitating, support and capacity building is necessary—especially at the beginning—it should be clearly communicated to the participating poor that the goal is for them to become autonomous and responsible for themselves. Support from the company can be justified over a longer period of time, but it should never create dependency. On the one hand it is just too costly if they do not operate independently, but on the other it does not foster their development.

Companies have to be accepted and respected in the communities in which they hope to be active. Previous positive experiences will simplify familiarisation with the company. Companies rely heavily upon locally active and embedded organisations that know the community well in order to become closer to the communities. Trust must be first established and partners should be chosen carefully. Partners have to be respected community members. They also need to share the vision, principles and motivation of a company in order to reach goals together.[2] For financial support, non-local partners can also be of use. Entering in consortia with other companies—which would have greater effects on development—is also seen, but is mostly associated with the project and not with separate goods and services. Trust and acceptance can be difficult to achieve, especially when a community has had negative experiences with previous projects in the past. Communities that have been the focus of many top-down managed projects are used to receiving without actually doing anything, and it is hard to build up the 'entrepreneurial spirit' that is necessary for successful projects. Networks are also important among the participating poor, between the participating poor and the rest of the community, and also between the poor, the community and the company. Existing social capital can be an advantage in projects. But, as experience has shown, it is not enough to rely solely on available social capital; a company often has to help build it up.[3]

When a company does not have experience of BoP projects, the strategies must be flexible in their outcome. A clear long-term vision is essential so that objectives and targets can be set. Some processes can be defined in advance and a general framework or 'road-map' is necessary. Still, it should be possible to make mistakes, admit them and adjust the project accordingly. A bottom-up approach does not necessarily have to be small-scale, but the project could be tested on a smaller scale as a pilot project. However, the more experience a company has, the more successful it can be when starting on a bigger scale. Even when starting small, the conditions for scaling up must be in place from the beginning. If the context is different, products and services developed with local knowledge have to be adapted.[4]

---

2 This is in line with the research of Dahan *et al.* (2010: 326).
3 This is also in line with the research of Bruni Celli *et al.* (2010: 38, 42ff.).
4 This is also in line with the findings of Bruni Celli *et al.* (2010: 51ff.).

The models and principles can, for the most part, stay the same, with some adjustments in application. At the beginning of a project, integrating the poor often leads to higher costs, especially when more capacity building is necessary. As soon as the project is more advanced and the included target group acts in a more autonomous way, costs are in turn reduced. In the process of scaling up, a vivid exchange of experiences and best practices foster the efficiency of a project and cut down the costs. Too high a level of inclusion of the BoP in the scaling-up process can, however, slow the process down.

12
The framework

During the process of case study research, it became clear that theoretically developed assumptions made sense in practice. Some could be combined, some had to be adapted, some were dropped and new ones could be developed. The propositions symbolise informed assertions that were—based on theoretical research as guidance—concluded from, and validated in, case study research. However, to gain more certainty, they would have to be tested on a much larger scale.

In the following, from qualitative social science derived, framework the propositions are summarised and gathered around the innovation process of BoP ventures. In the cases studied, the innovation process was in a steady flow with feedback loops and the people engaged. Once a product/service is on the market, it can be continuously adapted if necessary. It is not possible to arrange the success factors precisely to the different process steps, because it depends on which step the BoP is to be integrated into. Some propositions make more sense in certain steps than in others, but this has been explained previously in detail. The framework does not intend to replace other frameworks or methodologies, it is seen as complementary.

The elements of a bottom-up development perspective applied in practice are grouped around the research questions: Drivers, circumstances and success factors. Drivers can be understood as motivation or reasons to choose a bottom-up development perspective in BoP ventures. They answer the questions relating to *why* companies use a bottom-up approach. Circumstances that help or hinder the application of a bottom-up development perspective in BoP ventures answer the questions that ask *when* a bottom-up approach is applied. Circumstances can be of company-external or company-internal nature. But in any case, a company is not able to change those over a reasonable period of time. Success factors when choosing a bottom-up development perspective in BoP ventures in turn can be changed by the company and are applied during the project implementation. Success in

Figure 12.1 **The bottom-up development in BoP ventures framework**

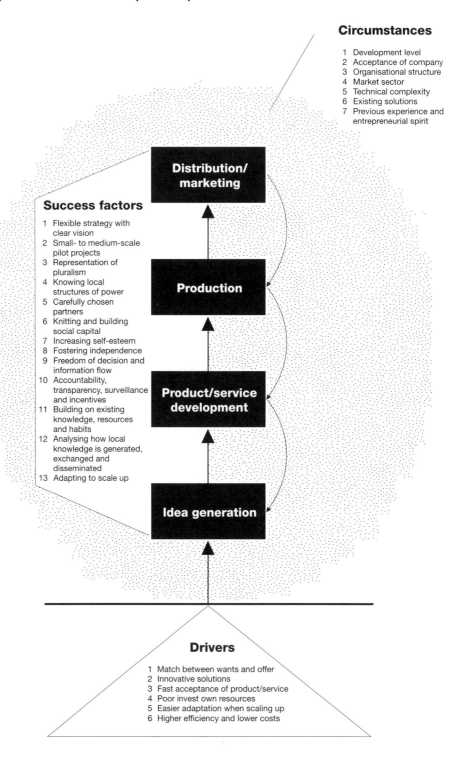

this sense means that the companies' goals and development goals are reached. These factors answer the questions of *how* companies should apply a bottom-up approach.

Drivers to apply a bottom-up development perspective in BoP ventures

1. Giving more responsibility to certain individuals from a BoP community during the innovation process fosters the match between what the respective community wants and what it obtains.

2. Including the BoP's local knowledge can lead to more innovative solutions.

3. Products and services that are developed with the inclusion of the BoP are more accepted by them as soon as a positive impact is visible.

4. The people at the BoP are more willing to invest their own resources (especially time, but also other assets) in a project the more they have control over the process.

5. Involving local people in every community/region helps in reaching the adaptation to the local context in the process of scaling up (if an adaptation is required).

6. Once the project is established, shifting more responsibility to the BoP leads to higher efficiency and cuts down costs.

Circumstances that help or hinder the application of a bottom-up development perspective in BoP ventures

1. Applying a bottom-up approach in BoP ventures is easier in regions and communities with a certain level of development.[1]

2. A high acceptance of the company and its partners by the community is very important when choosing a bottom-up approach.

---

1 A certain level of development means, for example, basic education, infrastructure, etc.

3. A decentralised organisational structure of the company makes it easier to use bottom-up strategies. Some central coordination is nevertheless important.

4. If the project is involved in common goods such as infrastructure (e.g. electricity supply, communication) the whole community should be mobilised and collective community action fostered. If the company is entering the consumer goods market, a selection of individuals and groups can be integrated. Mobilising the whole community might still be useful in order to fill gaps within lacking or imperfect markets (e.g. knowledge, infrastructure).

5. Without capacity building, involving the BoP is a more viable strategy in non-technical than in technical activities. Ideas and opinions can also be generated and included for technical activities.

6. When established and effective innovations already exist in communities, companies can try to hook up to them.

7. It is easier to use a bottom-up approach within market-based solutions in communities that have had good experiences in previous projects with companies, NGOs, governmental and other organisations, and where the entrepreneurial spirit is alive and kicking.

Success factors when choosing a bottom-up development perspective in BoP ventures

1. Successful strategies must be flexible in their outcome and adaptable throughout the process. A clear long-term vision is important, though.

2. If little or no previous experience has been had by the company, projects should start with small- to medium-scale pilot projects, and only be scaled up after successful evaluation. The conditions for scaling up must be in place from the beginning.

3. It is important that the people involved in the project represent the pluralism in the targeted community, especially in certain steps of the innovation process.

4. For successful projects, the company or its partners must be well aware of the local power structures.

5. Partnering and entering with carefully chosen partners (other companies, NGOs, governmental or other organisations) increases the success of BoP ventures. For implementation, partners have to be local. For financing, they can be non-local.

6. To be successful in mostly informal markets, companies have to build, make use of and knit together existing social capital.

7. Ventures have to help increase the self-esteem of the (mostly) stigmatised BoP so that they feel able to participate and play a more important role. Economic autonomy and emotional/personal autonomy are important.

8. It has to be made clear from the beginning of a project that the participating poor must become increasingly independent and that external support will decrease over time.

9. The involved poor need freedom of decision in defined areas and the company has to assure a steady information flow between all partners involved.

10. The more responsibility companies shift to the BoP, the more they have to hold them accountable and the more transparent processes must be. Also, some level of surveillance and incentives (external at the beginning) are necessary.

11. Where possible, BoP ventures have to build on the existing knowledge and other resources available.

12. Companies must analyse the ways in which local knowledge is generated (important for capacity building/training), exchanged (important for the exchange of best practices) and disseminated (important for distribution/ marketing).

13. If the project is scaled up in a new context, products and services must be adapted to fit this context. Processes and methodologies can stay the same if the context is not extremely different.

13
Comparison with literature and implications for theory and practice

When considering the resulting propositions compared to existing BoP and bottom-up development literature one can find the following differentiations:

1. Propositions derived from bottom-up development literature and the case study research, and are in line with BoP literature

2. Propositions derived only from bottom-up development literature and the case study research

3. Propositions derived only from the case study research

Table 13.1 shows the affiliation of the individual propositions.

BoP literature benefits in two ways from the research presented here:

- The BoP research agenda is enriched by additional know-how from bottom-up development literature and the case studies

- Existing BoP literature that touches upon bottom-up development approaches gains more detailed insight into the prevailing issues

As we can see, the majority of the propositions were derived from bottom-up development literature and the case studies; they were not previously mentioned in BoP literature. Also, the three propositions derived from the case study research alone can be considered as an additional contribution. Even though they are closely related to bottom-up development literature, these issues did not arise in the literature. Nine propositions are in line with, often very recent, BoP research. Neverthe-

Table 13.1 **Derivation of propositions**

1. Bottom-up development literature, case studies and BoP literature	2. Bottom-up development literature and case studies	3. Only case studies
Drivers		
• Innovative solutions[a]	• Fosters match between wants and receipt • Quicker acceptance of product/service • Poor invest own resources • Easier adaptation when scaling up • Higher efficiency and lower costs	
Circumstances		
• Acceptance of company[b] • Organisation structure[c] • Already existing solutions[e]	• Level of development • Type of market[d] • Technical level	• Previous experience and entrepreneurial spirit
Success factors		
• Representation of pluralism and knowing local structures of power[f] • Carefully chosen partners[g] • Knit and build social capital[h] • Building on existing knowledge, resources and habits[j] • Adapting to scale up[k]	• Flexible strategy with clear vision • Small- to medium-scale pilot projects • Freedom of decision[i] and information flow • Accountability, transparency, surveillance and incentives • Analysing how local knowledge is generated, exchanged and disseminated	• Increasing self-esteem • Fostering independence

a e.g. Hart 2007; Prahalad 2006.

b e.g. Simanis and Hart 2008.

c e.g. Hart 2007.

d Bruni Celli *et al.* (2010: 43) only mention that, in one of their studied cases, collective action was necessary because the project required building a large piece of common infrastructure.

e e.g. London and Hart 2004; Seelos and Mair 2006.

f Only Simanis and Hart (2008) touch on this issue in the BoP Protocol.

g e.g. Hart 2007. Gradl *et al.* (2010b) analysed partnerships in detail and Dahan *et al.* (2010) discovered that a common vision, principles and motivation are important.

h BoP literature generally mentions that ventures should build on existing social capital (e.g. Hart 2007), but only Bruni Celli *et al.* (2010) found that it also has to be built up.

i Bottom-up development literature (e.g. Oakley *et al.* 1991) even stipulates equality in decision-making over the whole process.

j e.g. London and Hart 2004

k Bruni Celli *et al.* 2010: 51ff.

less, this research also contributes additional knowledge and more details to these issues, as they are so far inadequately covered in BoP literature.

The framework and the additional knowledge gained surrounding the 26 propositions enrich current BoP literature. Researchers in the area of BoP 2.0 approaches can particularly profit from new insights gained by analysing BoP ventures under the perspective of bottom-up development literature. That products and services are more accepted when local knowledge has been integrated into the innovation process, for example, delivers additional know-how for the debate on 'acceptability'. A great deal of BoP 2.0 literature does not rely on empirical evidence. This research delivers (additional) empirical evidence on certain findings, as explained before. Certainly, additional research could be conducted on every proposition. This would help unveil further details and a specification of the propositions in terms of markets, sectors and geographical locations.

Exponents of bottom-up development literature and development practitioners can benefit from the results. As previously mentioned, the role of companies in poverty alleviation is marginalised in development literature. When related to literature about public–private partnerships, development scholars can consult this book in order to better understand the motivation of the corporate sector. They can further support the private sector in applying a bottom-up development approach, but also accept its limitations. Differences that appear between the corporate and development sectors in applying a bottom-up development perspective become comprehensible. Certain limitations that pose difficulties for the development sector can be overcome in partnership with companies. Problems for scaling up development projects are often related to resource scarcity or the lack of scaling-up logistics. By acknowledging and supporting the important role companies play in development, these limitations could partially be overcome. Additionally, the results can support the development sector when following market-based solutions to poverty alleviation.

Furthermore, business practitioners can consult the framework and its implications for their BoP ventures. They are motivated to choose a bottom-up approach as this delivers the potential to have a more positive impact on development goals, and also to make markets truly inclusive. The circumstances can be consulted when it is necessary to decide on a location for their projects and the success factors are a guide for planning and during implementation. However, in no case will this framework deliver sufficient knowledge to conduct a project successfully. It does, however, complement and enrich currently available know-how. Companies that rely on partnerships with public and private development organisations will understand their 'language' better with this book in mind.

Antagonisms also appear; once compared to bottom-up development literature, and once to BoP literature. 'Avoiding Westernisation' was no reason to choose a bottom-up approach for the companies observed. Accordingly, the notion of 'corporate imperialism' cannot be neglected—even in BoP ventures. The definitive bottom-up development perspective has not (yet) arrived in BoP ventures. The target group is always participating in an externally initiated process (as opposed to 'real participation'). Likewise, participation in the whole innovation process was seldom feasible, especially when the goal of the venture was not to have the poor manage the entire process (as was the case in the BAC COM/FINCA project). Managers are, however, willing to step back from certain elements of a project. They clearly acknowledge the superiority of the target group's knowledge in certain domains. A reason might be that efficient processes are key to cutting the costs of the products and services for the poor. In general, company representatives were not keen to know all the details about the targeted communities and their local knowledge. Elite capture was not a big issue. But because the involved poor managed the processes close to the target communities, this was also not necessary. The involved poor led the use of local knowledge. For the same reason, the results of this research show a divergent picture on 'total immersion' of managers or the 'embeddedness' of a company in local communities, as recommended in the BoP Protocol (Simanis and Hart 2008). If a bottom-up development approach is applied consequently and the poor control the processes, there is no need for managers to spend a lot of time in the target communities. Contrariwise, in practice, companies employ people from poor communities in order to acquire direct insight into those communities. It can be assumed that it is easier for companies to train slum dwellers in corporate practices than existing employees in the practices of poor communities.

Part V
Final conclusions and reflections on further research

Companies have proved that it is possible to make an important contribution to poverty alleviation with their core business activities. It is up to company managers to take advantage of the tremendous opportunities that accelerate the fulfilment of the UN MDGs for 2015. Serving the 4 billion people in the world who do not have the resources for a dignified life with products and services they need is one means of combining business and development goals. Integrating the poor as partners into the innovation process, rather than seeing them simply as potential customers (BoP 2.0 approaches), promises to make the ventures more successful—both for the companies and for development in general. This book is a contribution to the advancement of this issue in theory and practice. Analysing bottom-up development literature in terms of its application in BoP ventures in LAC has led to new insights and the development of a guiding framework.

In general, the results of this research demonstrate that a combination of 'bottom-up' and 'top-down' approaches will lead to the desired results. This confirms the notion of 'co-creation' (Gardetti 2009; Prahalad and Ramaswamy 2004) and one of the principles set out by London (2007)—that BoP ventures connect local to non-local. However, in certain parts of the projects, the BoP is able to manage the process alone after a phase of capacity building. While co-creation does not mean that processes are outsourced to the poor, a bottom-up development perspective in BoP ventures can imply this. The results also support the 'embedded innovation paradigm' (Simanis and Hart 2009) and the development of a 'native capability' (Hart 2007) to a certain extent. However, arm's-length project management with intermediaries and engaging the poor more is a valid alternative as well. Companies do not necessarily have to become 'embedded' and the level of closeness can also be too high.

> It is important that the owner of the company and managers who want to make a project with us are visiting the community. This doesn't mean that they have to become like us (David Gomez, Community Leader Siloé, Cali).

Even though it would be desirable to let the poor manage the entire processes by themselves—and therefore let them define their own development (as in the 'dialectical modernisation theory')—a certain amount of capacity building and introduction of 'Western knowledge' will probably be necessary for quite some time. External knowledge should, however, be used carefully and only to enable the poor to become the protagonists of their own development. It should not be imposed 'from above'. The more the process resembles a bottom-up development perspective, the less the charge of a 'new corporate imperialism' will resonate when companies engage with the BoP.

The distinction between the 'wants' and 'needs' of the poor has to be kept in mind. Generally speaking, the poor can and should decide which products and services they want to buy—even though their decisions might appear 'irrational' from the point of view of a Western perspective (e.g. to buy a skin-whitening cream). The more bottom-up the processes are arranged, the more BoP ventures will satisfy the 'wants' rather than the 'needs' of the poor. An exception should therefore be accepted when products and services serve real, objectively detected needs that the poor may not know about (e.g. nutrient deficiency). In general, though, companies should focus on the assets available within poor communities, not the needs.

We are still at the beginning of a long road to align profitable business solutions with the needs of society. Most of the cases studied still have the potential (and representatives expressed the will) to shift more responsibility to the participating poor within their projects. It can also be assumed that a great deal more of the knowledge provided by bottom-up development literature can be taken into consideration in BoP ventures. But the status of the companies observed in practice does not allow more conclusions without contradiction.

It could not be proved within this research that further integration of the poor into the innovation process would lead to greater success. Even though all participants are convinced that this is the case, it is still too early to tell. It can be assumed that there is a greater positive effect on poverty alleviation when the poor themselves create more value, but this was not measured within this research. Further research could follow this issue by comparing ventures that demonstrate varying levels of involvement of the poor (0 to 100%) with regard to their profitability and impact on poverty alleviation.

Additionally, the results are valid for ventures based in LAC. However, they can probably be applied, to a large extent, in other regions as well; more research in different national and regional contexts would be necessary in order to establish global applicability.

This research summarises the elements of bottom-up development literature and gives more insight. Behind all of these elements lie a huge amount of further literature and experiences from practice that go into much more detail. Further research could therefore also focus on specific elements in a much more in-depth way. In particular, more research in the areas of 'scaling up the process' or 'ownership' would be helpful for BoP ventures.

The environmental dimension of BoP ventures was only touched upon. In most cases, however, higher levels of consumption still mean further environmental degradation. Meeting the basic needs of a growing and increasingly urbanised population in developing countries—as well as the aspirations of their middle classes—will intensify the pressure on the world's ecosystems. In the case studies there was no evidence that the poor have a higher ecological awareness (except for the fact that they certainly consume less). Many products contained in the case studies were no more ecological than products developed for the top of the pyramid. Relying on local natural resources within BoP ventures can have a positive effect on environmental sustainability. Further research could extend this study by analysing the correlations of the ecological behaviour of the poor, their integration and the ecological sustainability of products and services developed.

For rural poverty alleviation, a pluriactive path and non-agricultural employment are very important. We are facing a global food crisis. The rate of climate change will accelerate. It is therefore essential that companies also focus on these areas, in order to avoid further rural exodus, and not only on the fast growing middle class (top of the BoP) in urban areas. To enable a pluriactive path, the poor cannot only be seen simply as (potential) consumers. Engaging them as suppliers, employees and as part of the innovation process is essential to generate the income they need in order to become customers. Many poor are—as is often the case with people not living in poverty—not necessarily 'creative entrepreneurs' and prefer a stable employment and income.

We can see that more and more often, companies are entering into the market at the BoP where development organisations are familiar. On the other hand, development organisations are also more frequently using market-based approaches and therefore moving in the direction of companies. Together, they can make a significant contribution to poverty alleviation. Governments need to set favourable conditions in order for BoP ventures to evolve. Development money can be used to accelerate corporate BoP ventures. NGOs and other organisations have to accept the new players in their market, partner with them and complement their activities.

What I have experienced in the case study research is that the poor really do benefit from bottom-up development initiatives. I met many strong people who want to lift themselves out of poverty, are ready to do it or who have already achieved it.

When they do it themselves, their future is much more sustainable as the means to change lies within them. However, they often lack opportunities and do not have the necessary resources or knowledge to escape the poverty trap. In some cases they are also affected by political conflicts. By facilitating the process of bottom-up development, and combining this with business goals, companies can move the world in the 'right' direction.

Questions remain: do companies need to internalise knowledge provided by bottom-up development literature or can they just engage partners such as NGOs who already possess it? And when NGOs consistently apply a bottom-up development approach, thus shifting far greater responsibility to the poor, what sorts of development will we face?

References

Agrawal, A. (1995) 'Indigenous and Scientific Knowledge: Some Critical Comments', *IK Monitor* 3.3: 1-9.

Ahlstrom, D. (2010) 'Innovation and Growth: How Business Contributes to Society', *Academy of Management Perspectives* 24.3: 10-23.

Albernathy, W.J., and J.M. Utterback (1978) 'Patterns of Innovation in Technology', *Technology Review* 80.7: 40-47.

Anderson, J., and C. Markides (2007) 'Strategic Innovation at the Base of the Pyramid', *MIT Sloan Management Review* 49.1: 83-88.

Ansoff, H.I. (1957) 'Strategies for Diversification', *Harvard Business Review* 35.5: 113-24.

Antweiler, C., and C. Mersmann (1996) 'Local Knowledge and Cultural Skills as Resources for Sustainable Forest Development', Conference Room Paper for the Third Session of the Intergovernmental Panel on Forests (IPF), September 1996 (Eschborn, Germany: on behalf of the Federal Ministry for Economic Cooperation and Development [BMZ], Germany, and Deutsche Gesellschaft für Technische Zusammenarbeit [GTZ]; www2.gtz.de/dokumente/bib/02-5024.pdf, accessed 12 August 2012).

Apparundai, A. (2004) 'The Capacity to Aspire: Culture and the Terms of Recognition', in V. Rao and M. Walton (eds.), *Culture and Public Action: A Cross-disciplinary Dialogue on Development Policy* (Palo Alto, CA: Stanford University Press).

Arora, S., and H. Romijn (2009) *Innovation for the Base of the Pyramid: Critical Perspectives from Development Studies on Heterogeneity and Participation* (Working Paper No. 2009-036; Maastricht, Netherlands: United Nations University).

Ashley, C., and S. Maxwell (2001) 'Rethinking Rural Development', *Development Policy Review* 19.4: 395-425.

Baland, J.-M., and J-P. Platteau (1999) 'The Ambiguous Impact of Inequality on Local Resource Management', *World Development* 27.5: 773-88.

Banerjee, A.V., and E. Duflo (2006) *The Economic Lives of the Poor* (Cambridge, MA: Massachusetts Institute of Technology).

Banerjee, S.B. (2003) 'Who Sustain Whose Development? Sustainable Development and the Reinvention of Nature', *Organization Studies* 24.1: 143-80.

Bansal, P. (2002) 'The Corporate Challenges of Sustainable Development', *Academy of Management Executive* 16.2: 122-31.

Barki, E., and J. Parente (2010) 'Consumer Behaviour of the Base of the Pyramid Market in Brazil', *Greener Management International* 56: 11-23.

Barney, J., M. Wright and D. Ketchen (2001) 'The Resource-Based View of the Firm: Ten Years after 1991', *Journal of Management* 27.6: 625-41.

Bartlett, C., and S. Ghoshal (1989) *Managing across Borders: The Transnational Solution* (Boston, MA: Harvard Business School Press).

Bebbington, A. (1999) 'Capitals and Capabilities: A Framework for Analysing Peasant Viability, Rural Livelihoods and Poverty', *World Development* 27.12: 2,021-44.

Beebe, J. (2001) *Rapid Assessment Process: An Introduction* (New York: Altamira Press).

Binswanger, H.P. (2004) 'Empowering Rural People for their Own Development', revised version of H.P. Binswanger's farewell lecture from the World Bank, 30 November 2004; repr. in *Agricultural Economics* 37, Issue Supplement s1 (December 2007; ed. John W. Longworth): 13-27.

—— and S. Aryar (2003) *Scaling Up Community-Driven Development: Theoretical Underpinnings and Program Design Implications* (Policy Research Working Paper No. 3039; Washington, DC: World Bank).

—— and T.-V. Nguyen (2005) 'A Step by Step Guide to Scale Up Community Driven Development', paper presented at the International Workshop *African Water Laws: Plural Legislative Frameworks for Rural Water Management in Africa*, Johannesburg, South Africa, 26–28 January 2005.

Black, N. (2006) *Sustainable Global Enterprise: The Shape of a New Capitalism?* (Working Paper for the Kevin Roberts Sustainable Enterprise Scholarship Report Series; Waikato, New Zealand: University of Waikato).

Blowfield, M. (2005) 'Corporate Social Responsibility: Reinventing the Meaning of Development?', *International Affairs* 81.3: 515-24.

Booth, D. (1994) *Rethinking Social Development: Theory, Research and Practice* (Harlow, UK: Longman).

Bruni Celli, J., R.A. González and G. Lozano (2010) 'Market Initiatives of Large Companies Serving Low-Income Sectors', in P. Marquez, E. Reficco and G. Berger (eds.), *Socially Inclusive Business: Engaging the Poor through Market Initiatives in Iberoamerica* (Cambridge, MA/London: Harvard University Press): 27-62.

Buckley, P.J., and M. Casson (1991) *The Future of the Multinational Enterprise* (London: Macmillan Press).

Busch, T., and V.H. Hoffmann (2009) 'Ecology-Driven Real Options: An Investment Framework for Incorporating Uncertainties in the Context of the Natural Environment', *Journal of Business Ethics* 90.2: 295-310.

CEPAL (Economic Commission for Latin America) (2008) *Panorama Social de América Latina 2008* (www.eclac.org/cgi-bin/getProd.asp?xml=/publicaciones/xml/3/34733/P34733.xml&xsl=/dds/tpl/p9f.xsl&base=/tpl/top-bottom.xslt, accessed 26 August 2010).

—— (2009a) *Balance Preliminar de las Economías de América Latina y el Caribe 2009* (www.eclac.org/cgi-bin/getProd.asp?xml=/de/agrupadores_xml/aes251.xml&xsl=/agrupadores_xml/agrupa_listado.xsl, accessed 26 August 2010).

—— (2009b) *Panorama Social de América Latina 2009* (www.eclac.org/cgi-bin/getProd.asp?xml=/publicaciones/xml/9/37839/P37839.xml&xsl=/dds/tpl/p9f.xsl&base=/tpl/top-bottom.xslt, accessed 26 August 2010).

Chambers, R. (1983) *Rural Development: Putting the Last First* (Harlow, UK: Longman).

—— (1994) 'The Origins and Practice of Participatory Rural Appraisal', *World Development* 22.7: 953-69.

—— (1997) *Whose Reality Counts? Putting the First Last* (London: Intermediate Technology Publications).

Chan Kim, W., and R. Mauborgne (2005) 'Value Innovation: A Leap into the Blue Ocean', *Journal of Business Strategy* 26.4: 22-28.

—— and R. Mauborgne (2007) 'Blue Ocean Strategy', *Leadership Excellence* 24.9: 20.

Chase, R.S. (2002) 'Supporting Communities in Transition: The Impact of the Armenian Social Investment Fund', *World Bank Economic Review* 16.2: 219-40.

Chen, S., and M. Ravallion (2004) *How Have the World's Poorest Fared Since the Early 1980s?* (World Bank Policy Research Paper No. 3341; Washington, DC: World Bank).

Chesbrough, H.W. (2003) *Open Innovation: The New Imperative for Creating and Profiting from Technology* (Boston, MA: Harvard Business School Press).

Choi, C.J., S.H. Lee and J.B. Kim (1999) 'A Note on Countertrade: Contractual Uncertainty and Transaction Governance in Emerging Economies', *Journal of International Business Studies* 30.1: 189-201.

Christensen, C.M. (1997) *The Innovator's Dilemma: When New Technologies Cause Great Firms to Fail* (Boston, MA: Harvard Business Publishing).

——, T. Craig and S. Hart (2001) 'The Great Disruption', *Foreign Affairs* 80.2: 80-95.

Clague, C. (1997) *Institutions and Economic Development: Growth and Governance in Less-developed and Post-socialist Countries* (Baltimore, MD: Johns Hopkins University Press).

Coase, R. (1998) 'The New Institutional Economics', *American Economic Review* 88.2: 72-74.

Conner, K.R., and C.K. Prahalad (1996) 'A Resource-Based Theory of the Firm: Knowledge versus Opportunism', *Organization Science* 7.5: 477-501.

Conning, J., and M. Kevane (2002) 'Community-Based Targeting Mechanisms for Social Safety Nets: A Critical Review', *World Development* 30.3: 375-94.

Cooke, B., and U. Kothari (2001) *Participation: The New Tyranny?* (London/New York: Zed Books).

Cooper, R.G. (2003) 'Profitable Product Innovation: The Critical Success Factor', in L.V. Shavinina (ed.), *The International Handbook of Innovation* (Amsterdam: Pergamon): 139-57.

Crane, A., D. Matten and J. Moon (2004) 'Stakeholders as Citizens? Rethinking Rights, Participation, and Democracy', *Journal of Business Ethics* 53.1–2: 107-22.

Crawley, H. (1999) 'Living Up to the Empowerment Claim? The Potential of PRA', in I. Guijt and M.K. Shah (eds.), *The Myth of Community: Gender Issues in Participatory Development* (London: Intermediate Technology Publications): 24-34.

Dahan, N.M., J.P. Doh, J. Oetzel and M. Yaziji (2010) 'Corporate–NGO Collaboration: Co-creating New Business Models for Developing Markets', *Long Range Planning* 43.2–3: 326-42.

D'Andrea, G., and G. Herrero (2007) 'Understanding Consumers and Retailers at the Base of the Pyramid in Latin America', in V.K. Rangan, J.A. Quelch, G. Herrero and B. Barton (eds.), *Business Solutions for the Global Poor: Creating Social and Economic Value* (San Francisco: Jossey-Bass).

Danneels, E. (2004) 'Disruptive Technology Reconsidered: A Critique and Research Agenda', *Journal of Product Innovation Management* 21.4: 246-58.

Dees, J.G. (1998) 'Enterprising Nonprofits', *Harvard Business Review* 76.1: 55-67.

De Janvry, A., and E. Sadoulet (2000) 'Rural Poverty in Latin America: Determinants and Exit Paths', *Food Policy* 25.4: 389-409.

Denzin, N.K. (1970) *The Research Act in Sociology: A Theoretical Introduction to Sociological Methods* (Chicago: Aldine).

De Soto, H. (2000) *The Mystery of Capital: Why Capitalism Triumphs in the West and Fails Everywhere Else* (New York: Basic Books).

Deza (2004) *Perspektiven Schaffen für ein Leben in Würde: Grundsätze der Deza im Engagement Gegen die Armut* (Berne, Switzerland: Swiss Agency for Development and Cooperation; www.deza.admin.ch).

DiMaggio, P.J., and W.W. Powell (1983) 'The Iron Cage Revisited: Institutional Isomorphism and Collective Rationality in Organizational Fields', *American Sociological Review* 48.2: 147-60.

Dongier, P., J. Van Domelen, E. Ostrom, A. Rizvi, W. Wakeman, A. Bebbington, S. Alkire, T. Esmail and M. Polski (2002) 'Community-Driven Development', in J. Klugman (ed.), *A Sourcebook for Poverty Reduction Strategies* (Washington, DC: World Bank): 301-31.

Doz, Y.L. (1980) 'Strategic Management in Multinational Companies', *Sloan Management Review* 21.2: 27-46.

Echeverría, R.G. (1998) *Strategic Elements for the Reduction of Rural Poverty in Latin America and the Caribbean* (Policy Research Paper; Washington, DC: Inter-American Development Bank).

Eisenhardt, K.M. (1989) 'Building Theories from Case Study Research', *Academy of Management Review* 14.4: 532-50.

Ellis, F., and S. Biggs (2001) 'Evolving Themes in Rural Development 1950s–2000s', *Development Policy Review* 19.4: 437-48.

Engel, M., and F. Veglio (2010) 'A Business View on Development', *European Business Review Online* (www.europeanbusinessreview.com/?p=2339, accessed 24 September 2010).

Escobar, A. (1995) *Encountering Development: The Making and Unmaking of the Third World* (Princeton, NJ: Princeton University Press).

Farrington, J., D. Carney, C. Ashley and C. Turton (1999) 'Sustainable Livelihoods in Practice: Early Applications of Concepts in Rural Areas', *Natural Resource Perspectives* Briefing Paper No. 42; www.odi.org.uk/resources/details.asp?id=2110&title=sustainable-livelihoods-practice-early-applications-concepts-rural-areas.

Freire, P. (1970) *Pedagogy of the Oppressed* (New York: Herder & Herder).

Friedmann, J. (1992) *Empowerment: The Politics of Alternative Development* (Oxford, UK: Blackwell Publishers).

Gandhi, M.K. (1962) *Village Swaraj* (Ahmedabad, India: Navjivan Press).

Gardetti, M.A. (2009) *Textos Sobre la Base de la Pirámide: Hacia la Co-creación de Valor y Desarrollo* (Buenos Aires, Argentina: IESC).

—— and G. D'Andrea (2010) 'Masisa Argentina and the Evolution of its Strategy at the Base of the Pyramid: An Alternative to the BoP Protocol Process?', *Greener Management International* 56: 75-91.

Garriga, E., and D. Melé (2004) 'Corporate Social Responsibility Theories: Mapping the Territory', *Journal of Business Ethics* 53.1–2: 51-71.

Gradl, C., A. Krämer and F. Amadigi (2010) 'Partner Selection for Inclusive Business Models: The Case of Casa Melhor', *Greener Management International* 56: 25-42.

——, S. Sivakumaran and S. Sobhani (2010) *The MDGs: Everyone's Business. How Inclusive Business Models Contribute to Development and Who Supports Them* (New York: UNDP).

Gran, G. (1983) *Development by People: Citizen Construction of a Just World* (New York: Praeger).

Gruner, K.E., and C. Homburg (2000) 'Does Customer Interaction Enhance New Product Success?', *Journal of Business Research* 49.1: 1-14.

Guijt, I., and M.K. Shah (1998) 'Waking Up to Power, Conflict and Process', in I. Guijt and M.K. Shah (eds.), *The Myth of Community: Gender Issues in Participatory Development* (London: Intermediate Technology Publications): 1-23.

Haan, H.C. (2005) *Knowledge and Pro-Poor Business Development* (Den Hague: Netherlands Development Assistance Research Council).

Haddad, L., M.T. Ruel and J.L. Garrett (1999) *Are Urban Poverty and Undernutrition Growing? Some Newly Assembled Evidence* (FCND Discussion Paper No. 63; Washington, DC: International Food Policy Research Institute).

Hall, A. (2006) *Public Private Sector Partnerships in an Agricultural System of Innovation: Concepts and Challenges* (Working Paper Series No. 2006-002; Maastricht, Netherlands: United Nations University).

Hammond, A.L., W.J. Kramer, J. Tran and R. Katz (2007) *The Next 4 Billion: Market Size and Business Strategy at the Base of the Pyramid* (Washington, DC: World Resources Institute and International Finance Corporation; www.wri.org/publication/the-next-4-billion).

Handwerker, W.P. (2001) *Quick Ethnography* (New York: Altamira Press).

Hardin, R. (1982) *Collective Action* (Baltimore, MD: Johns Hopkins University Press).

Harriss, J., J. Hunter and C.M. Lewis (1995) *The New Institutional Economics and Third World Development* (London: Routledge).

Hart, S.L. (2005) 'Innovation, Creative Destruction and Sustainability', *Research Technology Management* (September/October 2005): 21-27.

—— (2007) *Capitalism at the Crossroads: Aligning Business, Earth, and Humanity* (Upper Saddle River, NJ: Wharton School Publishing).

—— (2010) 'Preface', *Greener Management International* 56 (Special Issue on the Base of the Pyramid in Latin America): 3-5.

—— and C.M. Christensen (2002) 'The Great Leap: Driving Innovation From the Base of the Pyramid', *MIT Sloan Management Review* 44.1: 51-56.

—— and T. London (2005) 'Developing Native Capability: What Multinational Corporations Can Learn from the Base of the Pyramid', *Stanford Social Innovation Review* (Summer 2005): 28-33.

—— and M.B. Milstein (2003) 'Creating Sustainable Value', *Academy of Management Executive* 17.2: 56-69.

—— and S. Sharma (2004) 'Engaging Fringe Stakeholders for Competitive Imagination', *Academy of Management Executive* 18.1: 7-18.

Haugh, H. (2007) 'Community-led Social Venture Creation', *Entrepreneurship Theory and Practice, Baylor University*, March 2007: 161-82.

Heckathorn, D. (1993) 'Collective Action and Group Heterogeneity: Voluntary Provision versus Selective Incentives', *American Sociological Review* 58.3: 329-50.

Helmsing, A.H.J. (2001) *Partnerships, Meso-institutions and Learning: New Local and Regional Economic Development Initiatives in Latin America* (Working Paper; Den Hague, Netherlands: Institute of Social Studies).

Herzig, C., S. Schaltegger and T. Klinke (2005) 'Tools for Corporate Sustainability Management', *ASEP Newsletter* 22.4: 1-3.

Hoskisson, R.E., L. Eden, C.M. Lau and M. Wright (2000) 'Strategy in Emerging Economies', *Academy of Management Journal* 43.3: 249-67.

IDB (Inter-American Development Bank) (2006) *The Market of the Majority: The BOP Opportunity Map of Latin America and the Caribbean* (Development Through Enterprise Project, World Resources Institute; www.iadb.org/news/docs/wri.pdf, accessed 15 September 2010).

IFAD (International Fund for Agricultural Development) (2001) *Rural Poverty Report 2001: The Challenge of Ending Rural Poverty* (Oxford, UK: Oxford University Press).

ILO (International Labour Organisation) (2002) *Key Indicators of the Labour Market* (Geneva: ILO, 2nd edn).

Immelt, J.R., V. Govindarajan and C. Trimble (2009) 'How GE Is Disrupting Itself', *Harvard Business Review*, October 2009: 1-12.

Jagtap, S., and P. Kandachar (2009) 'Towards Linking Disruptive Innovations and BoP Markets', paper presented at the *17th International Conference on Engineering Design* (ICED '09), Stanford University, CA.

Jalan, J., and M. Ravallion (2003) 'Estimating the Benefit Incidence of an Anti-poverty Program by Propensity-Score Matching', *Journal of Business and Economic Statistics* 21.1: 19-30.

Jazairy, I., M. Alamgir and T. Panuccio (1992) *The State of World Rural Poverty: An Inquiry into its Causes and Consequences* (New York: New York University Press).

Jenkins, B., and E. Ishikawa (2010) *Scaling Up Inclusive Business: Advancing the Knowledge and Action Agenda* (Washington, DC: IFC and the CSR Initiative at the Harvard Kennedy School).

Jensen, M., and W. Meckling (1976) 'The Theory of the Firm: Managerial Behavior, Agency Costs and Ownership Structure', *Journal of Financial Economics* 3.4: 305-60.

Jonker, J., and M. De Witte (2006) *Management Models for Corporate Social Responsibility* (Berlin: Springer).

Kandachar, P., and M. Halme (2005) 'Introduction', *Greener Management International* 51 (Special Issue, 'An Exploratory Journey towards the Research and Practice of the Base of the Pyramid'): 3-17.

—— (2009) 'Romanticizing the Poor', *Stanford Social Innovation Review*, Winter 2009: 38-43.

Katz, T., and J. Sara (1997) *Making Rural Water Supply Sustainable: Recommendations from a Global Study* (Washington, DC: World Bank).

Keating, C., and T. Schmidt (2008) 'Opportunities and Challenges for Multinational Corporations at the Base of the Pyramid', in P. Kandachar and M. Halme (eds.), *Sustainability Challenges and Solutions at the Base of the Pyramid* (Sheffield, UK: Greenleaf Publishing): 387-409.

Khan, M.H. (1986) 'Landlessness and Rural Poverty in Underdeveloped Countries', *Pakistan Development Review* 25: 374-94.

—— (2000) 'Rural Poverty in Developing Countries', *Finance & Development* 37.4: 26-29.

—— (2001) 'Rural Poverty in Developing Countries: Implications for Public Policy', *International Monetary Fund, Economic Issues Series* 21: 1-13.

Khwaja, A.I. (2001) *Can Good Projects Succeed in Bad Communities? Collective Action in the Himalayas* (Working Paper No. 01-043; Cambridge, MA: Department of Economics, Harvard University).

Kirchgeorg, M., and M.I. Winn (2006) 'Sustainability Marketing for the Poorest of the Poor', *Business Strategy and the Environment* 15.3: 171-84.

Korten, D. (1980) 'Community Organization and Rural Development: A Learning Process Approach', *Public Administration Review* 40.5: 480-511.

Kotler, P., and G. Armstrong (2004) *Principles of Marketing* (Upper Saddle River, NJ: Prentice Hall).

Krämer, A., and F-M. Belz (2008) 'Consumer Integration into Innovation Processes: A New Approach for Creating and Enhancing Innovations for the Base of the Pyramid?', in P. Kandachar and M. Halme (eds.), *Sustainability Challenges and Solutions at the Base of the Pyramid: Business, Technology and the Poor* (Sheffield, UK: Greenleaf Publishing): 214-41.

Kretzmann, J., and J. McKnight (1993) *Building Communities from the Inside Out: A Path toward Finding and Mobilizing a Community's Assets* (Chicago: ACTA Publications).

—— and J. McKnight (1999) *Leading by Stepping Back: A Guide for City Officials on Building Neighborhood Capacity* (Chicago: ACTA Publications).

Kuhn, K., and M. Rieckmann (2006) *Wi(e)der die Armut? Positionen zu den Millenniumszielen der Vereinten Nationen* (Bad Homberg, Germany: VAS [Verlag für Akademische Schriften]).

Lal, S. (2002) 'Social Capital and Industrial Transformation', in S. Fukuda-Parr, C. Lopes and K. Malik (eds.), *Capacity for Development: New Solutions to Old Problems* (New York: UNDP/London: Earthscan).

Landrun, N.E. (2007) 'Advancing the "Base of the Pyramid" Debate', *Strategic Management Review* 1.1: 1-12.

Leal, P.A. (1997) 'Obscuring the Politics of Participatory Action', contribution to email discussion with I. Guijt and M.K. Shah on PRA, August 1997.

Lewis, O. (1958) *Five Families* (New York: Random House).

Lipton, M., and M. Ravallion (1995) 'Poverty and Policy', in J.R. Behrman and T.N. Srinivasan (eds.), *Handbook of Development Economics* (Amsterdam: Elsevier).

London, T. (2007) *A Base-of-the-Pyramid Perspective on Poverty Alleviation* (Working Paper; Ann Arbor, MI: The William Davidson Institute/Stephen M. Ross School of Business, University of Michigan).

—— (2009) 'Making Better Investments at the Base of the Pyramid', *Harvard Business Review* 87.5: 106-13.

—— and S.L. Hart (2004) 'Reinventing Strategies for Emerging Markets: Beyond the Transnational Model', *Journal of International Business Studies* 35.5: 350-70.

—— and S.L. Hart (2010) ,Creating a Fortune with the Base of the Pyramid', in T. London and S.L. Hart (eds.), *Next Generation Business Strategies for the Base of the Pyramid: New Approaches for Building Mutual Value* (Upper Saddle River, NJ: FT Press): 1-16.

——, R. Anupindi and S. Sheth (2010) 'Creating Mutual Value: Lessons Learned from Ventures Serving Base of the Pyramid Producers', *Journal of Business Research* 63.6: 582-94.

Long, N., and M. Villareal (1994) 'The Interweaving of Knowledge and Power in Development Interfaces', in I. Scoones and J. Thompson (eds.), *Beyond Farmers First: Rural People's Knowledge, Agricultural Research and Extension in Practice* (London: Intermediate Technology Publications): 41-52.

López, R., and A. Valdés (2000) 'Fighting Rural Poverty in Latin America: New Evidence of the Effects of Education, Demographics, and Access to Land', *Economic Development and Cultural Change* 49.1: 197-211.

Lowe, P., J. Murdoch and N. Ward (1995) 'Networks in Rural Development: Beyond Endogenous and Exogenous Approaches', in J.D. Van der Ploeg and G. Dijk (eds.), *Beyond Modernization: The Impact of Endogenous Rural Development* (Assen, Netherlands: Van Gorcum): 87-106.

Lustig, N., and O. Arias (2000) 'Poverty Reduction', *Finance & Development* 37.1: 30-33.

—— and R. Deutsch (1998) *The Inter-American Development Bank and Poverty Reduction: An Overview* (Washington, DC: IDB).

—— and N. Stern (2000) 'Broadening the Agenda for Poverty Reduction: Opportunity, Empowerment, Security', *Finance & Development* 37.4 (www.imf.org/external/pubs/ft/fandd/2000/12/lustig.htm, accessed 24 September 2010).

Madavo, C. (2000) *Community-Driven Development: A Vision of Poverty Reduction through Empowerment* (Washington, DC: World Bank).

Maloney, W.F. (2004) 'Informality Revisited', *World Development* 32.7: 1,159-78.

Mansuri, G., and V. Rao (2003) *Evaluating Community-based and Community-driven Development: A Critical Review of the Evidence* (Washington, DC: Development Research Group, World Bank).

—— and V. Rao (2004) 'Community-Based and -Driven Development: A Critical Review', *World Bank Research Observer* 19.1: 1-39 (www.cultureandpublicaction.org/bijupdf/mansurirao.pdf).

Marquez, P., E. Reficco and G. Berger (2010) 'Introduction: A Fresh Look at Markets and the Poor', in P. Marquez, E. Reficco and G. Berger (eds.), *Socially Inclusive Business: Engaging the Poor through Market Initiatives in Iberoamerica* (Cambridge, MA/London: Harvard University Press): 1-25.

Marsden, D. (1994a) 'Indigenous Management and the Management of Indigenous Knowledge', in I. Scoones and J. Thompson (eds.), *Beyond Farmers First: Rural People's Knowledge, Agricultural Research and Extension in Practice* (London: Intermediate Technology Publications): 52-57.

—— (1994b) 'Indigenous Management and the Management of Indigenous Knowledge', in S. Wright (ed.), *Anthropology of Organizations* (London/New York: Routledge): 41-55.

Martinussen, J. (1997) *Society, State and Market: A Guide to Competing Theories of Development* (London/New Jersey: Zed Books).

Mason, J. (1996) *Qualitative Researching* (Thousand Oaks, CA: Sage).

Mathie, A., and G. Cunningham (2002) *From Clients to Citizens: Asset-Based Community Development as a Strategy for Community-Driven Development* (Occasional Paper Series No. 4; Antigonish, Canada: Coady International Institute, St Francis Xavier University).

—— and G. Cunningham (2003a) *Who is Driving Development? Reflections on the Transformative Potential of Asset-Based Community Development* (Occasional Paper Series No. 5; Antigonish, Canada: Coady International Institute, St Francis Xavier University).

—— and G. Cunningham (2003b) 'From Clients to Citizens: Asset-Based Community Development as a Strategy for Community-Driven Development', *Development in Practice* 13.5: 474-86.

Matsuyama, K. (2002) 'The Rise of Mass Consumption Societies', *Journal of Political Economy* 110.5: 1,035-70.

Matten, D., and A. Crane (2005) 'Corporate Citizenship: Toward an Extended Theoretical Conceptualization', *Academy of Management Review* 30.1: 166-79.

Meier, G.M. (1989) *Leading Issues in Economic Development* (New York: Oxford University Press).

Mendoza, R.U. (2008) 'Why Do the Poor Pay More? Exploring the Poverty Penalty Concept', *Journal of International Development*, 6 October 2008 (Wiley InterScience online); also in *Journal of International Development* 23.1: 1-28 (onlinelibrary.wiley.com/doi/10.1002/jid.1504/abstract?deniedAccessCustomisedMessage=&userIsAuthenticated=false).

—— and N. Thelen (2008) 'Innovations to Make Market More Inclusive for the Poor', *Development Policy Review* 26.4: 427-58.

Meyer, K.E. (2004) 'Perspectives on Multinational Enterprises in Emerging Economies', *Journal of International Business Studies* 35.4: 259-76.

Mikkelsen, B. (1995) *Methods for Development Work and Research: A Guide for Practitioners* (New Delhi: Sage).

Minh, Q.D. (2004) 'Rural Poverty in Developing Countries: An Empirical Analysis', *Journal of Economic Studies* 31.6: 500-508.

Moran-Ellis, J., A. Cronin, M. Dickinson, J. Fielding, J. Sleney and H. Thomas (2006) 'Triangulation and Integration: Processes, Claims and Implications', *Qualitative Research* 6.1: 45-59.

Munnecke, M., and R. Van der Lugt (2006) 'Bottom Up Strategies in Consumer-Led Markets', paper for the *Second International Seville Seminar on Future-Oriented Technology Analysis*, Seville Spain, 28–29 September 2006.

Münzing, T. (2001) 'Unternehmen im Zeitalter der Nachhaltigkeit: Werte und Wertschöpfung verbinden', *Zeitschrift für Wirtschaftsethik* 2.3: 410-19.

Narayan, D., K. Schafft, A. Rademacher, R. Patel and S. Koch-Schulte (2000) *Voices of the Poor: Can Anyone Hear Us?* (Washington, DC: World Bank/Oxford University Press).

—— (2002) *Empowerment and Poverty Reduction: A Sourcebook* (Washington, DC: World Bank)

Natcher, D., and C. Hickey (2002) 'Putting the Community Back into Community-Based Resource Management: A Criteria and Indicators Approach to Sustainability', *Human Organization* 61.4: 350-63.

Neath, G. (2006) 'Business as a Partner in Reaching the Millennium Development Goals', speech by Gavin Neath, Senior Vice President Global Corporate Responsibility at Unilever, given at the World Bank's Business and NGO Conference in Washington, DC, 10 April 2006 (www.wbcsd.ch/Plugins/DocSearch/details.asp?DocTypeId=35&ObjectId=MjA4MTk&URLBack=%2Ftemplates%2FTemplateWBCSD2%2Flayout.asp%3Ftype%3Dp%26MenuId%3DMTY4%26doOpen%3D1%26ClickMenu%3DLeftMenu%26CurPage%3D4%26SortOrder%3DPubDate%2520ASC, accessed 12 August 2009).

Nelson, J., and D. Prescott (2003) *Business and the Millennium Development Goals: A Framework for Action* (New York: UNDP).

Nelson, N., and S. Wright (1995) 'Participation and Power', in N. Nelson and S. Wright (eds.), *Power and Participatory Development: Theory and Practice* (London: Intermediate Technology Publications): 1-18.

Nemes, G. (2005) *Integrated Rural Development: The Concept and its Operation* (Discussion Paper; Budapest: Hungarian Academy of Science, Institute of Economics).

Norgaard, R. (1994) *Development Betrayed: The End of Progress and a Coevolutionary Revisioning of the Future* (London/New York: Routledge).

North, D.C. (1990) *Institutions, Institutional Change, and Economic Performance* (Cambridge, UK/New York: Cambridge University Press).

Oakley, P., *et al.* (1991) *Projects with People: The Practice of Participation in Rural Development* (Geneva: ILO).

Obrovsky, M., and C. Six (2005) 'Die Neue Agenda zur Wirksamkeit der Entwicklungszusammenarbeit', in Österreichische Forschungsstiftung für Entwicklungshilfe (ed.), *Österreichische Entwicklungspolitik: Analysen, Informationen* (Vienna: Südwind):7-11.

OECD (Organisation for Economic Cooperation and Development) (2007) *Business for Development: Fostering the Private Sector* (Paris: OECD).

Oliver, C. (1991) 'Strategic Responses to Institutional Processes', *Academy of Management Review* 16.1: 145-79.

—— (1997) 'Sustainable Competitive Advantage: Combining Institutional and Resource-Based Views', *Strategic Management Journal* 18.9: 697-713.

Oliver, P., G. Marwell and R. Teixeira (1985) 'A Theory of the Critical Mass. I. Interdependence, Group Heterogeneity, and the Production of Collective Action', *American Journal of Sociology* 91.3: 522-56.

Olson, M. (1973) *The Logic of Collective Action: Public Goods and the Theory of Groups* (Cambridge, MA: Harvard University Press).

Palazzo, G., and A.G. Scherer (2008) 'Corporate Social Responsibility, Democracy, and the Politicization of the Corporation', *Academy of Management Review* 33.3: 773-75.

Patton, M.Q. (1990) *Qualitative Evaluation and Research Methods* (Newbury Park, CA: Sage).

—— (2002) *Qualitative Research and Evaluation Methods* (Thousand Oaks, CA: Sage).

Pearce, R. (2006) 'Globalization and Development: An International Business Strategy Approach', *Transnational Corporations* 15.1: 39-74.

Peng, M.W. (2001) 'The Resource-Based View and International Business', *Journal of Management* 27.6: 803-29.

—— and P.S. Heath (1996) 'The Growth of the Firm in Planned Economies in Transition: Institutions, Organizations, and Strategic Choice', *Academy of Management Review* 21.2: 492-528.

Pettigrew, A.M. (1990) 'Longitudinal Field Research on Change: Theory and Practice', *Organizational Science* 1.3: 267-92.

Philip, D., and I. Rayhan (2004) *Vulnerability and Poverty: What are the causes and how are they related?* (Bonn, Germany: Centre for Development Research).

Platteau, J.-P. (2003) 'Community-Based Development in the Context of Within Group Heterogeneity', paper prepared for the *Annual Bank Conference on Development Economics*, Bangalore, May 2003.

—— and F. Gaspart (2003) 'The Risk of Resource Misappropriation in Community-Driven Development', *World Development* 31.10: 1,687-703.

Poole, N.D. (2004) 'Perennialism and Poverty Reduction', *Development Policy Review* 22.1: 49-74.

—— (2005) 'Poverty, Inequality and Ethnicity: A Note to Policy Makers on Latin America', *EuroChoices* 4.3: 45-49.

Post, J.E., L.E. Preston and S. Sachs (2002) *Redefining the Corporation: Stakeholder Management and Organizational Wealth* (Palo Alto, CA: Stanford University Press).

Pradhan, M., and L.B. Rawlings (2002) 'The Impact and Targeting of Social Infrastructure Investments: Lessons from the Nicaraguan Social Fund', *World Bank Economic Review* 16.2: 275-95.

Prahalad, C.K. (2006) *The Fortune at the Bottom of the Pyramid: Eradicating Poverty through Profits* (Upper Saddle River, NJ: Wharton School Publishing).

—— and A.L. Hammond (2002) 'Serving the World's Poor, Profitably', *Harvard Business Review* 80.9: 48-57.

—— and S.L. Hart (2002) 'The Fortune at the Bottom of the Pyramid', *Strategy & Business* 26 (1Q 2002): 1-14.

—— and K. Lieberthal (2003) 'The End of Corporate Imperialism', *Harvard Business Review* (Special Issue: Best of HBR) 81.8: 109-17. [Revised version of original article: C.K. Prahalad and K. Lieberthal (1998) 'The End of Corporate Imperialism', *Harvard Business Review* 76.4: 68-79.]

—— and V. Ramaswamy (2004) 'Co-creating Unique Value with Customers', *Strategy & Leadership* 32.3: 4-9.

Quang Dao, M. (2004) 'Rural Poverty in Developing Countries: An Empirical Analysis', *Journal of Economic Studies* 31.6: 500-508.

Rao, V., and A.M. Ibanez (2005) 'The Social Impact of Social Funds in Jamaica: A "Participatory Econometric" Analysis of Targeting, Collective Action, and Participation in Community-Driven Development', *Journal of Development Studies* 41.5: 788-838.

Ravallion, M., and G. Datt (1999) *When is Growth Pro-poor? Evidence from the Diverse Experiences of India's States* (World Bank Policy Research Working Paper No. 2263; Washington, DC: World Bank).

Reficco, E. (2009) 'Menos Voluntarismo, Más Innovación', *INCAE Business Review* 1.9: 1-10.

Roselli, M. (2006) 'Entwicklungspartnerschaften: Im Idealfall von gleich zu gleich', *Eine Welt* (Journal of Deza) 3 (September 2006): 6-11.

Rowntree, S. (1901) *Poverty: The Study of Town Life* (London: Macmillan).

Sánchez, P., J.E. Ricart and M.A. Rodríguez (2007) 'Influential Factors in Becoming Socially Embedded in Low-Income Markets', *Greener Management International* 51: 19-38.

Schaltegger, S., and M. Wagner (2006) *Managing the Business Case for Sustainability: The Integration of Social, Environmental and Economic Performance* (Sheffield, UK: Greenleaf Publishing).

Scherer, A.G. (2003) *Multinationale Unternehmen und Globalisierung: Zur Neuorientierung der Theorie der Multinationalen Unternehmung* (Heidelberg, Germany: Physica-Verlag).

Schneider, F. (2005) 'Shadow Economies around the World: What Do We Really Know?', *European Journal of Political Economy* 21.3: 598-642.

Schumpeter, J.A. (1934) *The Theory of Economic Development* (Cambridge, MA: Harvard University Press).

Scoones, I. (1998) *Sustainable Rural Livelihoods: A Framework for Analysis* (IDS Working Paper 72; Brighton, UK: Institute of Development Studies).

—— and J. Thompson (1994) 'Knowledge, Power and Agriculture: Towards a Theoretical Understanding', in I. Scoones and J. Thompson (eds.), *Beyond Farmers First: Rural People's Knowledge, Agricultural Research and Extension in Practice* (London: Intermediate Technology Publications): 16-32.

Scott, J. (1998) *Seeing Like a State: How Certain Schemes to Improve the Human Condition Have Failed* (New Haven, CT: Yale University Press).

Scott, W.R. (1995) *Institutions and Organizations* (Thousand Oaks, CA: Sage)

Seelos, C., and J. Mair (2006) *Profitable Business Models and Market Creation in the Context of Deep Poverty: A Strategy View* (IESE Occasional Paper No. 07/6; Barcelona, Spain: IESE Business School).

Sen, A.K. (1985) *Commodities and Capabilities* (Amsterdam: Elsevier)

—— (1999) *Development as Freedom* (New York: Knopf).

Sharma, S., and S. Hart (2006) 'Base of the Pyramid: Predicting MNC Entry and Success', presented at the *Academy of Management Annual Meeting*, Atlanta, GA, 13 August 2006.

Sillitoe, P. (2004) 'Interdisciplinary Experiences: Working with Indigenous Knowledge in Development', *Interdisciplinary Science Reviews* 29.1: 6-23.

Silverman, D. (2006) *Interpreting Qualitative Data. Methods for Analyzing Talk, Text and Interaction* (London: Sage).

Simanis, E. (2009) 'At the Base of the Pyramid', *Wall Street Journal*, 26 October 2009; sloanreview. mit.edu/business-insight/articles/2009/4/5144/at-the-base-of-the-pyramid, accessed 9 November 2009.

—— (2010) 'Needs, Needs, Everywhere, But Not a BoP Market to Tap', in T. London and S.L. Hart (eds.), *Next Generation Business Strategies for the Base of the Pyramid* (Upper Saddle River, NJ: Pearson Education Inc): 103-28.

—— and S.L. Hart (2006) 'Expanding Possibilities at the Base of the Pyramid', *Innovations* 1.1: 43-51.

—— and S.L. Hart (2008) *The Base of the Pyramid Protocol: Toward Next Generation BoP Strategy* (Ithaca, NY: Cornell University)

—— and S.L. Hart (2009) 'Innovation From the Inside Out', *MIT Sloan Management Review* 50.4: 77-86.

Simanowitz, A. (1997) 'Community Participation/Community-Driven', paper presented at the *23rd WEDC Conference*, Durban, South Africa, 1–5 September 1997.

Simon, D. (1997) 'Development Reconsidered: New Directions in Development Thinking', *Geografiska Annaler, Series B* 79.4: 183-201.

Srinivas, S., and J. Sutz (2008) 'Developing Countries and Innovation: Searching for a New Analytical Approach', *Technology in Society* 30.2: 129-40.

Start, D. (2001) 'The Rise and Fall of the Rural Non-farm Economy: Poverty Impacts and Policy Options', *Development Policy Review* 19.4: 491-505.

Subrahmanyan, S., and J.T. Gomez-Arias (2008) 'Integrated Approach to Understanding Consumer Behavior at Bottom of Pyramid', *Journal of Consumer Marketing* 25.7: 402-12.

Sull, D.N., A. Ruelas-Gossi and M. Escobari (2003) 'Innovating around Obstacles: How Three Developing-World Companies Approach Creativity Has a Lot to Teach Any Company Anywhere', *Strategy & Innovation*, November/December 2003: 3-6.

Tembo, F. (2003) *Participation, Negotiation, and Poverty: Encountering the Power of Images: Designing Pro-poor Development Programmes* (Aldershot, UK: Ashgate Publishing).

Tidd, J., J. Bessant and K. Pavitt (2005) *Managing Innovation: Integrating Technological, Market and Organisational Change* (Chichester, UK: John Wiley)

Tripathi, S.S., and S.K. De (2007) 'Innovation as a Tool of Building Competitive Advantage at the Bottom of the Pyramid', *Reader of International Marketing Conference on Marketing & Society*, 8–10 April 2007: 171-79.

UNDP (United Nations Development Programme) (2004) *Unleashing Entrepreneurship: Making Business Work for the Poor. Commission on the Private Sector and Development* (New York: UNDP).

—— (2008) *Creating Value for All: Strategies for Doing Business with the Poor* (New York: UNDP).

UNFPA (United Nations Population Fund) Information and External Relations Division (2011) *The State of World Population 2011* (foweb.unfpa.org/SWP2011/reports/EN-SWOP2011-FINAL.pdf, accessed 8 August 2012).

UN (United Nations) (2010a) *The Millennium Development Goals Report 2010* (New York: UN).

—— (2010b) *Achieving the Millennium Development Goals with Equality in Latin America and the Caribbean: Progress and Challenges* (www.eclac.cl/cgi-bin/getProd.asp?xml=/publicaciones/xml/5/39995/P39995.xml&xsl=/tpl-i/p9f.xsl&base=/tpl/top-bottom.xslt, accessed 30 August 2010).

Unmüssig, B. (2006) *The Millennium Development Goals: Are they Contributing to Sustainable Development?* (Washington, DC: Heinrich Böll Foundation North America).

Von Hippel, E. (1986) 'Lead Users: A Source of Novel Product Concepts', *Management Science* 32.7: 791-805.

Waddock, S. (2004) 'Parallel Universes: Companies, Academics, and the Progress of Corporate Citizenship', *Business & Society Review* 109.1: 5-42.

Warnholz, J.-L. (2007) *Poverty Reduction for Profit? A Critical Examination of Business Opportunities at the Bottom of the Pyramid* (Working Paper Series 160; Oxford, UK: University of Oxford).

WBCSD (World Business Council for Sustainable Development) (2004) *Doing Business with the Poor: A Field Guide* (Geneva: WBCSD).

—— (2006) *From Challenge to Opportunity: The Role of Business in Tomorrow's Society* (Geneva: WBCSD).

—— (2007) *Doing Business with the World: The New Role of Corporate Leadership in Global Development* (Geneva: WBCSD).

WCED (World Commission on Environment and Development) (1987) *Our Common Future* (Oxford, UK: Oxford University Press).

Weick, K.E. (1996) 'Drop Your Tools: Allegory for Organizational Studies', *Administrative Science Quarterly* 41.2: 301-13.

Weiser, J. (2007) 'Untapped: Strategies for Success in Underserved Markets', *Journal of Business Strategy* 28.2: 30-37.

WFP and ICBF (2005) *La ENSIN: Encuesta Nacional de la Situación Nutricional en Colombia.*

Wiggins, S., and S. Proctor (2001) 'How Special Are Rural Areas? The Economic Implications of Location for Rural Development', *Development Policy Review* 19.4: 427-36.

Williamson, O.E. (1975) *Markets and Hierarchies: Analysis and Anti-trust Implications* (New York: Free Press).

Woolcock, M., and D. Narayan (2000) 'Social Capital: Implications for Development Theory, Research, and Policy', *World Bank Research Observer* 15.2: 225-49.

World Bank (n.d.) *Latin America and the Caribbean* (devdata.worldbank.org/gmis/mdg/Latin_America_and_the_Caribbean.htm, accessed 27 March 2009).

—— (1975) *Rural Development Sector Policy Paper* (Washington, DC: World Bank).

—— (1998) *Indigenous Knowledge for Development: A Framework for Action* (Washington, DC: World Bank).

—— (2003) *Strengthening Implementation of Corporate Social Responsibility in Global Supply Chains* (Washington, DC: World Bank).

Wratten, E. (1995) 'Conceptualizing Urban Poverty', *Environment and Urbanization* 7.1: 11-33.

Wright, M., I. Filatotchev, R.E. Hoskisson and M.W. Peng (2005) 'Strategy Research in Emerging Economies: Challenging the Conventional Wisdom', *Journal of Management Studies* 42.1: 1-33.

Yin, R. (1984) *Case Study Research: Design and Methods* (Beverly Hills, CA: Sage).

Annex

1. Questions: first-round in-depth case studies

1. What is your field of responsibility in the BoP venture?

2. What are the reasons why the company started to focus on the BoP?

3. Where in the innovation process is the target group usually integrated?

4. What are the reasons to integrate the target group into the innovation process?

5. What are internal success factors when integrating the target group? Success factors for the company's development, success factors for poverty alleviation?

6. Which external circumstances favour success with the integration of the target group? How does the community/product/service have to be?

7. How does a company have to proceed when integrating the target group into the innovation process? Important points?

8. Do you see possibilities to integrate the target group even more? How? Where? Which tasks can they do, which not?

2. **Questions: second-round in-depth case studies**

The respondents had to say if they agree/disagree with the statements, drawn out of the assumptions developed in the theoretical part of the book, and explain why. This questionnaire changed for every in-depth case study as the assumptions were further elaborated continuously. This is the version for the first company (Sucromiles).

I. Reasons for choosing a bottom-up development perspective in BoP ventures

1. A bottom-up approach has to be chosen to avoid 'Westernisation'.

2. Giving more power to the poor during the innovation process fosters the match between what the community needs and what it obtains.

3. Including the experimental nature of poor people's local knowledge leads to innovative solutions.

4. Products and services that are not only adapted to the needs of the poor but are developed through local knowledge are more readily accepted by them.

5. The poor are willing to invest more resources (time, assets, and funds) in a project when they have more control over the process.

6. Involving local people as much as possible in every community/region helps to reach the required adaptation to the local context and simultaneously cuts down costs in the process of scaling up.

II. Circumstances that favour or hinder applying a bottom-up development perspective in BoP ventures

1. Bottom-up strategies are more successful in more developed economies with small, non-complex projects.

2. If the company is in the industry of common pool goods such as infrastructure (e.g. electricity, communication) it should mobilise collective community action.

3. If the company is trying to enter into the consumer goods market then individuals and groups can be integrated. Collective community action might, however, be useful to fill gaps within missing or imperfect markets (e.g. distribution/marketing).

4. Targeting the BoP is more easier for companies when they enter communities complying with certain criteria (communities have a high mobility [no rigid power relations], egalitarian preferences, open and transparent systems of decision-making, clear rules to decide who is poor, if the villages are not too isolated and no land inequality exists). Or, their solutions should help communities to reach them.

5. Involving the poor's knowledge is a more viable strategy in non-technical decisions than in technical decisions.

6. When innovations already exist in local communities, companies do not have to initiate the process, they can hook up to them.

III. Success factors when choosing a bottom-up development perspective in BoP ventures

1. BoP strategies are more successful when a decentralised organisation structure is chosen.

2. When companies choose a bottom-up approach, they have to integrate the poor into the whole innovation process and not only see them as target group.

3. Success depends not so much about the grade of participation but more on the form and representativeness of the community within the process.

4. Real participation requires equality in decision-making. Therefore, projects should be done under conditions of full information and full representation of all interests.

5. For successful projects, a deep sense of local structures of power is needed and the poor involved have to represent the pluralism in the targeted community.

6. The more power companies shift to the poor, the more they have to hold them accountable and transparent.

7. The risk of the elite capturing the benefits of a BoP venture is minimised in communities that are strong, empowered, self-conscious and organised, and when a strong local private sector exists prior to new programmes.

8. BoP ventures have to build on the existing knowledge, assets and resources. This leads to a better impact on poverty alleviation and environmental sustainability.

9. If capacity building is necessary, it should build on existing local knowledge and not be imposed from the 'Western knowledge'.

10. Companies have not only to discover knowledge available, but also analyse the ways in which knowledge is generated, exchanged, transformed, consolidated, stored, retrieved, disseminated and utilised.

11. Successful strategies have to be open to the outcome and adaptable on the way. With short steps, experience can be gained on the way.

12. Companies should start with small-scale pilot projects when entering the BoP.

13. Innovations based on local knowledge have to be adapted to fit into new contexts before they can be scaled up.

14. Partnering with carefully chosen (representing the companies and the poor's interests) locally embedded organisations increases the success of BoP initiatives.

15. To build trust, prerequisite for success in informal markets, companies have to knit social capital and embed themselves locally.

16. Entering in consortia is essential for responding better to the priority demands of a community and has an enhanced impact on poverty alleviation.

3. Questionnaire: second step of case study research

University of Zurich
Institute of Organization and Administrative Science
Chair of Foundations of Business Administration and Theories of the Firm

The Bottom Up Development Perspective in the Innovation Process
of Base of the Pyramid Ventures
Evidence from Corporations in Latin America and the Caribbean

Questionnaire
August 2010

Thank you very much for your participation!

Deadline: Please return the completed questionnaire to pwaibel@sunrise.ch by Friday, September 3, 2010.

Contact

If you need support, have questions or need further comments and more information please feel free to contact me anytime via email (pwaibel@sunrise.ch) or Skype (pierawaibel)!

Confidentiality

I ensure absolute confidentiality on all information gained from participating companies. Participating companies can also review the thesis before it is published and offer feedback. Company names will only be disclosed if the company agrees to it.

Part 1: General Questions

Company/respondent*

Company name: _____
Name(s) and position(s) of responding person(s): _____
Email: _____
Phone: _____

The project/venture*

Location of project/venture: _____
Start of project/venture: _____
Product(s)/service(s) offered: _____
Description of project/venture: _____

(Additional documents/info that help me understand the case better are very welcome and can be
sent to pwaibel@sunrise.ch)

Integration of the target group

In which parts of the innovation process is (part of) the target group integrated?
How? (Please feel free to change the innovation process steps if you use another scheme)

_____

Idea generation: _____
Product development: _____
Production: _____
Distribution/Marketing: _____

* This information will be handled strictly confidential if requested

Part 2: Propositions

This part contains several propositions (statements) that have been developed
theoretically and further elaborated with the in-depth case studies. There are three
categories: Reasons (A), circumstances (B) and success factors (C). The purpose
of this questionnaire is to gain a more quantitative validation of the propositions.
Please read them carefully and answer for as many propositions as you can. First,
tick the boxes how much you agree or disagree in general. The propositions depend
a lot on the context, product/service offered or innovation process step. Therefore,
in the comment section please elaborate why you come to this conclusion based
on your experience and point of view, under which circumstances, with what kind
of products or services and in which innovation process step you agree or disagree.
If you can back up your answers with an example from your project/venture, this
would be even better. Also, any comments that help rephrase the propositions to
capture the issue as you experience it more concisely are very welcome!

A) Reasons to choose a bottom up development perspective in BoP ventures

1) A bottom up approach has to be chosen to avoid "westernization"[1].

Strongly agree ❑   Somewhat agree ❑   Somewhat disagree ❑   Strongly disagree ❑

Comment: _____

2) Giving more responsibility to certain individuals from a BoP community during the innovation process fosters the match between what the respective community needs and what it obtains.

Strongly agree ❑   Somewhat agree ❑   Somewhat disagree ❑   Strongly disagree ❑

Comment: _____

3) Including the BoP's local knowledge leads to more innovative solutions.

Strongly agree ❑   Somewhat agree ❑   Somewhat disagree ❑   Strongly disagree ❑

Comment: _____

4) Products and services that are not only adapted to the needs of the BoP but are developed with their inclusion are more readily accepted by them.

Strongly agree ❑   Somewhat agree ❑   Somewhat disagree ❑   Strongly disagree ❑

Comment: _____

5) The people at the BoP are more willing to invest their resources (time, assets, and funds) in a project, the more they have control over the process.

Strongly agree ❑   Somewhat agree ❑   Somewhat disagree ❑   Strongly disagree ❑

Comment: _____

6) Involving local people of the BoP as much as possible in every community/region helps reaching the adaptation to the local context in the process of scaling up (if an adaptation is required).

Strongly agree ❑   Somewhat agree ❑   Somewhat disagree ❑   Strongly disagree ❑

Comment: _____

7) Shifting more responsibility to the BoP leads to higher efficiency in certain steps of the innovation process and cuts down costs.

Strongly agree ❑   Somewhat agree ❑   Somewhat disagree ❑   Strongly disagree ❑

Comment: _____

---

1   Westernization: Meaning that the "poor" (South/East) should develop as the "rich" (West/North) are.

B) Circumstances that favor or hinder applying a bottom up development perspective in BoP ventures

8) Choosing a bottom up approach is easier in more developed[2] economies, regions and communities.

Strongly agree ❑   Somewhat agree ❑   Somewhat disagree ❑   Strongly disagree ❑

Comment: _____

9) A high acceptance of the company in the community is very important when choosing a bottom up approach.

Strongly agree ❑   Somewhat agree ❑   Somewhat disagree ❑   Strongly disagree ❑

Comment: _____

10) A decentralized organization structure of the company makes it easier to use bottom up strategies.

Strongly agree ❑   Somewhat agree ❑   Somewhat disagree ❑   Strongly disagree ❑

Comment: _____

11) If the project/venture is in the industry of common pool goods as infrastructure (e.g. electricity, communication) it should mobilize the whole community and foster collective community action.

Strongly agree ❑   Somewhat agree ❑   Somewhat disagree ❑   Strongly disagree ❑

Comment: _____

12) If the company is trying to enter into the consumer goods market, a selection of individuals and groups can be integrated. Mobilizing the whole community might however still be useful to fill gaps within missing or imperfect markets (e.g. knowledge, infrastructure).

Strongly agree ❑   Somewhat agree ❑   Somewhat disagree ❑   Strongly disagree ❑

Comment: _____

13) Involving the BoP's knowledge is a more viable strategy in non-technical decisions (e.g. idea generation, distribution) than in technical decisions (e.g. product development).

Strongly agree ❑   Somewhat agree ❑   Somewhat disagree ❑   Strongly disagree ❑

Comment: _____

---

2 More developed meaning: better education, better infrastructure, better governance etc.

14) When local innovations already exist in communities, companies do not have to initiate the process, they can hook up to them.

Strongly agree ❏ Somewhat agree ❏ Somewhat disagree ❏ Strongly disagree ❏

Comment: _____

15) It is easier to use a bottom up approach within market-based solutions in communities that haven't been beneficiaries of many projects of development organizations/government and where the entrepreneurial spirit is awake.

Strongly agree ❏ Somewhat agree ❏ Somewhat disagree ❏ Strongly disagree ❏

Comment: _____

C) Success factors[3] when choosing a bottom up development perspective in BoP ventures

16) Successful strategies have to be flexible in their outcome and adaptable on the way. A clear long-term vision is important though.

Strongly agree ❏ Somewhat agree ❏ Somewhat disagree ❏ Strongly disagree ❏

Comment: _____

17) Projects should start on a small scale, and only be scaled up after successful evaluation.

Strongly agree ❏ Somewhat agree ❏ Somewhat disagree ❏ Strongly disagree ❏

Comment: _____

18) It is important that the people involved represent the pluralism in the targeted community.

Strongly agree ❏ Somewhat agree ❏ Somewhat disagree ❏ Strongly disagree ❏

Comment: _____

19) For successful projects, a deep sense of local structures of power is needed to avoid elite[4] capture.

Strongly agree ❏ Somewhat agree ❏ Somewhat disagree ❏ Strongly disagree ❏

Comment: _____

---

3 A successful BoP venture is one that fosters success on the company side (financial goals as well as market reach etc.), and success for development goals (poverty alleviation in broader sense; not necessarily only income, but also health, education, self esteem etc.)

4 "Elite" symbolizes the leaders, richer and more powerful people in a community.

20) Partnering and entering with carefully chosen partners (other companies, NGO, governmental organizations; local or non-local) increases the success of BoP ventures

Strongly agree ❑   Somewhat agree ❑   Somewhat disagree ❑   Strongly disagree ❑

Comment: _____

21) To be successful in mostly informal markets, companies have to help build new as well as knit existing social capital[5].

Strongly agree ❑   Somewhat agree ❑   Somewhat disagree ❑   Strongly disagree ❑

Comment: _____

22) Ventures have to help increase the self-esteem of the (mostly) stigmatized BoP so that they feel able to participate and play a more important role. Economic autonomy and emotional/personal autonomy are important.

Strongly agree ❑   Somewhat agree ❑   Somewhat disagree ❑   Strongly disagree ❑

Comment: _____

23) It has to be made clear from the beginning of a project/venture that the participating people living in poverty have to become increasingly independent and that external support will decrease over time.

Strongly agree ❑   Somewhat agree ❑   Somewhat disagree ❑   Strongly disagree ❑

Comment: _____

24) Real participation requires equality in decision-making. Therefore, projects should be done as much as possible under conditions of full information, and full representation of all interests.

Strongly agree ❑   Somewhat agree ❑   Somewhat disagree ❑   Strongly disagree ❑

Comment: _____

25) The more responsibility companies shift to the BoP, the more they have to hold them accountable and processes transparent. Also, some level of control and incentives are necessary.

Strongly agree ❑   Somewhat agree ❑   Somewhat disagree ❑   Strongly disagree ❑

Comment: _____

---

5 Social capital in the sense of relationships/networks; social capital within the participating poor, between participating poor and company, between participating poor and community.

26) BoP ventures have to build on the existing knowledge, assets, resources, and habits. If capacity building/training is necessary, it should build on what is already available.

Strongly agree ❑   Somewhat agree ❑   Somewhat disagree ❑   Strongly disagree ❑

Comment: _____

27) Companies have not only to discover the existing knowledge, but also analyze the ways in which this knowledge is generated, exchanged, transformed, consolidated, stored, retrieved, disseminated and utilized.

Strongly agree ❑   Somewhat agree ❑   Somewhat disagree ❑   Strongly disagree ❑

Comment: _____

28) Innovations based on a bottom up approach have to be adapted to fit into new contexts before they can be scaled up.

Strongly agree ❑   Somewhat agree ❑   Somewhat disagree ❑   Strongly disagree ❑

Comment: _____

Index